HALLIE's Story

profile of a battered woman

Linda DeWeese

MA.Ed., LPC
Psychotherapist

*To Barb —
Friendship & Peace —
Linda*

Alexander Books

Alexander, North Carolina

Publisher: Ralph Roberts

Cover Design: Ralph Roberts
Interior Design & Electronic Page Assembly: **WorldComm**®

10 9 8 7 6 5 4 3 2 1

Trade paper ISBN 1-57090-203-8

Contents

How vast is the number of men, in any great country, who are a little higher than brutes…

This never prevents them from being able, through the laws of marriage, to obtain a victim… The vilest male-factor has some wretched woman tied to him against whom he can commit any atrocity except killing her–and even that he can do without too much danger of legal penalty.

–John Stuart Mill
On the Subjection of Woman (1869)

The core of sadism, common to all its manifestation, is the passion to have absolute and unrestricted control over a living being–It is transformation of impotence into omnipotence.

–E. Fromm
The Anatomy of Human Destructiveness (1973)

To my husband, Art, and my sons, Michael and David,
and their families

To Nina Bell, wherever she may be

Acknowledgments

This book has been my burning desire for years. Many individuals have helped me at various stages, from the formation of the idea to the actual publication. I would like to express my deepest gratitude to all who have been with me during this dream.

First, my husband, Art, is the most gentle and kindest man I have ever known. He has always been by my side with unselfish love and support. He has often been my touchstone, encouraging me to go on with my dreams and he has always believed in my need to help battered women and their children.

Next, I would like to thank my sons, David and Michael. Throughout their lives they have often been my reasons for moving forward. They have taught me much about life and I could always count on their love. With their births I experienced a new revelation about the meaning of love.

Added thanks go to my son Michael, my computer guru. I am grateful for his patient coaching and answering my questions about the computer, which began with, "How do you turn this thing on?"

I would like to thank Tricia for her never ending interest and encouragement in this project. She realized how important it was to me and all women who have been or will be abused by someone they love and trust.

My sister, Kim, and her partner, Diana, have always been there for me no matter what time of day or how difficult the situation. I thank them for their never ending love and support.

Virginia McCullough is to be credited in a large way for the completion of this book. Without her expertise, advice, encouragement, insights, and her belief in this cause, this book may not ever have come to fruition. I feel blessed to have her in my life and it was no accident that she came along just when I needed her.

Many thanks go to Thea Schulze, LCSW, who has shared my enthusiasm and excitement about this project. She has unselfishly been interested in its progress and has given freely of her time and expertise in evaluating the book's content.

My appreciation and thanks go to Greg Narron, MD, who willingly gave of his time to hear my ideas and evaluate this work. His sincere interest and encouragement have always spurred me on and his insightful suggestions and expertise have been invaluable.

I am very grateful to Ralph Roberts of Alexander Books for his willingness to take a chance on a novice. His expertise and professionalism in the publishing field have made this dream come true.

Last but not least, I am grateful to so many women who trusted me with their stories and showed great courage in sharing them and allowing me to grow along with them.

Linda DeWeese
September 2002

Note: This book and its characters are composites drawn from many sources, including women and men I have worked with. Of course, I have disguised the details and any resemblance to an actual person or event is accidental. If a particular scene or situation seems familiar that can be attributed to the sad fact that abusive behavior involves patterns and abuse tends to play out in similar ways. Names of individuals and sources of material have been omitted and certain facts have been altered to protect the privacy of victims and their families. The therapist's notes, conclusions, and advice expressed in the book are solely those of the author.

Introduction

Although the story I tell in this book is presented as fiction, that doesn't mean it isn't true—at least in the broadest sense. In simple terms, Hallie is a battered woman, a victim of severe abuse. She fits the profile that mental health professionals, sociologists, and law enforcement professionals have created over the last several decades. While Hallie could be considered "typical," we may not truly know her because she is far more than a profile based on statistics.

I wrote this book in an attempt to bring more light to what is by its nature a dark topic. Most people have stereotypical images of battered women, some of which are based on objective statistical information and profiles of battered women and batterers. While most people know that domestic violence crosses all socio-economic lines, it is still widely believed that most battered women are uneducated and poor.

Given this image, it may seem that Hallie is an unusual woman. However, statistically, Hallie's situation is common. Many experts maintain that women with typical middle-class lives are less likely to seek help than their less educated and economically disadvantaged counterparts. This contention is born out in my experience of working with battered women and, on occasion, the batterer as well. In fact, wealthier women may be even more afraid of the batterer because he is well connected in the community. In other words, his power is firmly entrenched and extends beyond his ability to inflict physical harm. By outward appearances, Hallie has a privileged life, and Roger never fails to point out her material advantages; in a distorted way, Hallie begins to see herself as a "whiner" who doesn't appreciate her "hardworking" husband who gives her so much.

The Obvious Questions

More than ever before, the "Hallies" in our society are challenged to answer the key question, always asked in a perplexed tone: "Why do you stay with him?" Or, put another way, "Why don't you leave?" The unasked question, the one that often remains hidden, is: "What's wrong with you?"

It is not surprising that this question comes up at this particular time in our society. Women have more opportunities available to them than in any other time in our history; consequently, most people see no excuse for a woman to stay with a man who is abusing her. It seems like a logical conclusion. However, domestic violence cannot be viewed entirely through the prism of logic. For example, economic status is only *one* factor in determining a woman's decision to stay with an abusive man.

Domestic violence is our "official" word for violence between spouses and other intimate partners, and most of us know it represents a global problem. Ironically, violence between men and women, or same sex couples who are lovers or life partners, is assigned a separate term and viewed as a special type of conflict. It's sad but true that many cultures do not consider violence against women by husbands and lovers–and other male relatives–particularly serious. While many cultures do not overtly condone it, neither do they actively discourage this kind of violent behavior.

Our society's shifting attitude is still a work in progress. One need only read the newspapers, watch television magazine and talk shows, and simply talk to neighbors and friends to understand that we still have much work to do. Perhaps the most distressing recent trend is the violence perpetrated against teenage girls by their controlling and rage-prone boyfriends.

Regardless of the age of the battered woman or the violent man, most people are perplexed that the victim doesn't walk away at the first sign of abusive behavior. Frankly, the fact that we even ask the question amazes me. It shows how little we as a society understand the subtleties and nuances of abuse. Asking why the victim doesn't walk away is much like asking prisoners why they don't walk out of the prison. Consider prison guards; by definition they represent power and the ability to control behavior by any means necessary, but these guards also play the role of "savior," a person who can provide rewards and punishments, thereby fostering dependence.

As we see early in Hallie's story, abuse–battering–is often subtle, and the victim is undermined slowly and steadily. Like many women, Hallie begins to plan her life around pleasing the abuser in order to avoid the violent verbal or physical outbursts. Because the batterer almost always blames his victim, many women begin to believe that they are crazy, stupid, or deficient in some fundamental way.

My clients who have been victims of domestic violence did not *plan* to be in a violent relationship. Rather, they often say they didn't see the handwriting on the wall. Contrary to popular belief, most of these women start out physically and emotionally healthy, but they have chosen their mates based on old childhood messages.

Because we remain a patriarchal society, young girls are still given the message that a woman's greatest accomplishment is "winning" and "keeping" a man. This has resulted in great social pressure to please a man and stand by him, even when he turns out to be far less than the "prince" little girls read about in fairy tales. In some families, additional pressure exists that reinforces the message to stay married in order to preserve the family name and to make sure that the children have two parents, no matter how destructive the atmosphere in their home.

Through therapy, many battered women come to realize that they indeed have other options. By developing compassion for themselves, these women can begin to make healthy choices. It may take many months or years of therapy, but in more cases than not, women who remove themselves from violence find the strength to take charge of themselves and their lives. Almost always, these women eventually learn they no longer have to choose the victim role.

It is important to understand that abuse comes in many forms. Emotional and verbal abuse may be difficult to spot and the abuser may get away with a significant amount of this type of behavior before a woman realizes how destructive it is to her self-image. Some men control their partners by using their perceived power to issue threats. A woman who tells a man that she is leaving may hear him say, "You'll never see a penny from me. You'll end up in the street if you step out that door." Or, he may say, "You'll never see the kids again—I swear I'll get full custody and have you declared unfit." If the man is respected in the community and perhaps makes a very good living, this is not an empty threat. A man's ability to provide well for his children may make him appear to be the better parent. In addition, emotional and verbal abuse may be difficult to prove in court.

Who is Hallie?

Hallie is a composite character drawn from many sources, including women I have worked with. Of course, I have disguised the details and any resemblance to an actual person or event is accidental. If a particular scene or situation seems familiar that can be attributed to the sad fact that abusive behavior involves patterns and abuse tends to play out in similar ways.

By telling Hallie's story, I have tried to show that just as women do not become battered women overnight, they usually need more than one day to free themselves from the chains that keep them captive. This is Hallie's story, and more than that, it is the story of millions of women. I hope her story gives them a much-needed voice.

Who is Roger?

Roger is a compilation of many men. The fact that he is a neuroradiologist does not, by any means, suggest that neuroradiologists are prone to abuse. No profession is immune from "infestation" by abusers, even one whose purpose is to help people. Regardless of their job or career, all abusers behave in an authoritarian manner, and have both the power and the ability to brainwash their victims.

I designed the book in chapters, each of which consists of scenes from Hallie's life with Roger and their son Eric. These scenes illustrate the issues that battered women deal with on a daily basis. In addition, these chapters provide examples of the progressive nature of both the violence and the conscious and unconscious strategies women devise to deal with it.

Understanding Hallie

Following the "fictional" scenes, I include a section called "Getting to Work: What Can We Learn About the Cycle of Abuse?" This section gives the reader an opportunity to analyze what has been presented. It is my hope that women who are in a relationship like the one I portray will gain insight into how this situation happened, and of course, what they can do to break down the prison walls that surround them. Equally important, I expect that therapists and others in healthcare and the mental health field will deepen their understanding of family abuse and more readily recognize the signs in clients and patients.

After the epilogue, you will find a section that explains The Lifetime Messages Blueprint Inventory (LMBI), which is one of the most effective tools I've used with my clients. Working together, the client and I use this inventory to facilitate her understanding of the introjected, often unconscious, messages that motivate her choices and behavior throughout her life. Once these messages are brought to light and organized into an LMB (Lifetime Messages Blueprint), she gains insight into the driving forces that push her to make decisions, especially important ones such as the choice of a partner and how she reacts to that partner. This information provides tools she can use to take her desire for change and form it into a strong belief in herself and her ability to trust her own perceptions.

Many battered women have lost a sense of their own power and life skills, but when they finally sense their inner strength, they are able to implement desired changes and are well on their way to creating a life they truly want. No longer will they allow anyone else to control them through fear, guilt, intimidation, or any type of abuse.

Patience and Persistence

Many battered women relive their attacks and bondage for years after they have left the abusive environment. Tragically, some never seek help because they do not trust that anyone will be there to help them. They think, act, and feel like prisoners of war. Our society understands when victims of war, such as Vietnam veterans, display these symptoms. But society tends to label these women, who have also been victims of torture, "neurotic," "hysterical," or even "psychotic."

Hallie's story is by necessity compressed in time, but the treatment process is not as simple and quick as the previous brief description may sound. For example, most of the time victims of abuse are suffering from Post Traumatic Stress Disorder (PTSD). Many of these women suffer physical symptoms, such as gastrointestinal disorders, and these conditions must be treated. Depression and anxiety need to be addressed and alleviated, along with nightmares, fears, and phobias. Many battered women have become hypervigilant and filled with self-doubt. It takes time to restore the ability to trust. In my experience, trust in others must be delicately nurtured in order to bloom in a healthy way, and deep anger and resentment must be replaced with a healthy sense of strength.

A Final Note

As you will see, I expect that many of my readers are professionals who are in a position to work with battered women. However, I also am making great efforts to put the book into the hands of women who are living in the hell of domestic abuse. In order to help them the best way possible, much of the text is addressed to them. If you are among these readers, I urge you to stick with the book, even if Hallie's story seems much worse than yours or the violence that is perpetrated on her frightens you. While every woman's story is unique, if you are uncomfortable with what is happening in your home and you feel compelled to hide certain behavior from your children or others, then you may be at risk. Please read the entire book. Domestic abuse often is progressive, and the occasional shoving and grabbing that may not seem so critical now may soon escalate and over time become the terrorizing violence–and threat of violence–that is sadly a part of far too many relationships. As gruesome and even scary as some of this book may be, it ultimately provides a message of hope: no situation is too serious to escape and no woman's life needs to be any longer at risk.

1

Roger pressed her face into the wall and in one swift motion bent her right arm behind her back. Struggling to breathe through the pain ripping at her shoulder, Hallie was sure that this time her arm would break from the pressure.

"You just never learn, do you?"

At one time, Hallie would have tried to think of an answer that might satisfy her husband, perhaps a promise to do better or a contrite apology. But now, with tears flowing down her face, her cheekbone scraping against the woodwork, Hallie knew no such thing as a right answer existed. Trying to come up with one would only prolong the pain. If she learned nothing else, she'd learned that.

As usual, Roger eventually eased his grip, and with his hands firmly on her shoulders he turned her around and held her face in his hands with a tight grip, forcing her to look into his eyes. "I wish you would stop doing this to me," he said "You do it on purpose and then this happens." His voice, with its mixture of sarcasm and regret, was as familiar as the words he spoke. She'd heard them many times before.

Roger had managed to ruin another day. He had been irritable when he scrutinized her grocery list, checking it up and down the page to be sure they actually needed everything she'd listed. She hadn't argued with him or even tried to tease him out of his mood. She'd given up on that long ago, and her goal was always to have a peaceful day and protect Eric from the ugliness of his father's rages.

After she'd dressed Eric, she settled him in the car and Roger drove them to the supermarket. He gave her two twenty-dollar bills to pay for the groceries and said, "Eric and I will wait for you in the car–don't be long."

Fifteen minutes later he smiled pleasantly at Hallie as she pushed the cart towards the car. "Hey, you're getting faster," he said. "Good for you."

They drove home in silence, but Roger carried the bags of groceries into the house, and Eric happily helped Hallie put his favorite strawberry frozen yogurt into the freezer. For the first time that day, Hallie felt relaxed and happy.

"Hey, babe, what's this?" Roger asked, his voice suddenly sharp. He was holding two bags of chips in his hand.

"Oh, there was this great deal so I...." She tried to get the words out as quickly as possible.

"The list said 'one bag' of chips. We agreed on *one bag*."

Hallie felt her heart beat faster and her stomach started fluttering. It was too late. She hadn't explained fast enough.

"So, you think we're made of money, do you?" Calmly at first, Roger turned and opened a cabinet door, and with careful deliberation took a box of oatmeal off the shelf and dumped it on the floor. "So, I guess we can waste food, can't we?" One by one, he cleared one cabinet. Methodically at first, he opened each box of cereal and then moved on to the full bag of flour and then to the box of rice. Ripping each box open and lifting his arm high he spilled each onto the tile floor. His rage built, and he tore through the foods faster and faster, his breathing heavier. He opened the refrigerator and shook and tossed the bottles and jars of ketchup and mustard and salad dressing around the kitchen. Hallie watched the sticky liquids splatter on the curtains. One by one, eggs cracked and ran down the yellow and white walls and milk spewed from the carton like projectile vomit. And when there was no more food to dump or pour, Roger had grabbed her arm and banged her against the wall next to the doorway.

After Roger finally let her go, Hallie went to her screaming little boy and picked him up and carried him to his room, locking the door behind them. Like a mantra, she said again and again,

"It's okay, darlin', it's okay." She rocked back and forth on the bed until she felt his little body relax and her own breathing become even and steady. She laid Eric back, the tears still drying on his face. She covered him with a blanket as he fell into a deep, exhausted sleep.

When she had dried her own tears, Hallie went down the hall to the bedroom she shared with Roger. He was sitting at the desk thumbing through medical journals. She usually stayed out of his way, but now that the rage was over, she felt compelled to say something to break the silence. She walked hesitantly—carefully—into the room and sat on the bed and waited patiently for him to look up from his papers.

Roger finally turned and looked at her with an expectant expression. "Well? What do you want?" he asked in a calm but impatient tone.

"I-I-I need to explain about the chips," she said, angry that she couldn't keep herself from stuttering out the words. "There was a sale, you know the kind, 'buy one, get one free.' So I took advantage of it. You see, I didn't actually *buy* two bags. It was the same amount of money..."

"Oh this is great, just great," he said. "So, why didn't you just tell me? Oh wait, I know. You deliberately misled me. You know how concerned I am about money, but you didn't care enough to tell me. Now you've caused this terrible mess and you scared poor little Eric half to death. Because of you, we lost all this food—what a waste. And you don't even care."

"Roger, I tried to tell you, to explain...." She felt humiliated by the desperate, pleading tone she heard in her voice.

Before she realized what was happening, Roger had jumped from his chair, yanked her off the bed and pushed her out of the room and slammed the door. Afraid of starting a new scene, she went into the kitchen to begin the cleanup. It wasn't the first time she found herself scraping hideous streaks of butter and milk and eggs off the walls. Two weeks before, she cleaned pot roast, gravy, and potatoes off the floor and they'd eaten peanut butter sandwiches for dinner. She couldn't remember why dinner had been a few minutes late, the incident that had set off Roger's rage that particular day. It didn't matter anymore.

As Hallie swept and mopped, she thought about all the things she wanted to say to Roger—if only he'd listen to her. Despite the cruel things he did and said, Hallie was sure that he loved her. And without question he adored Eric. During one of Roger's scenes last year, she had blurted out that she was going to walk out on him and leave him alone with his rage. Without hesitating for a second, he slapped her and told her that not only would he take Eric, he'd make sure she never saw their little boy again. "Don't get any ideas about running away from me, you spoiled, foolish woman. I'll hunt you down—you'll never hide from me. You don't know how good you have it."

Roger came into the kitchen just as she was pulling the checkered curtains off the rod, getting ready to throw them in the washer again. "Hey babe, what's for dinner? Why don't you make that pasta dish I told you about—the one Joe's wife made last week for the department meeting?"

"I'll be happy to make whatever you want, Roger, but we don't have any pasta." Hallie kept her voice even and she didn't turn to look at him leaning against the doorway. She knew he'd look pleasant, even happy, as if nothing had happened. But she could barely listen, and only did so because she knew she had to.

The blinding pain of her headache made it almost impossible to concentrate on anything other than the task in front of her. The doctor said they weren't migraines but tension headaches, and the colitis she suffered from periodically was brought on by stress, too.

"No problem, babe. Just make out a list—I'll go to the store for you. Hey, are you paying attention here?"

"Yes, I just have a headache, that's all. I'll make the list."

Roger playfully rubbed her back as she bent over the counter and jotted items down on the fresh pad of paper she took out of the drawer. His hand slid down her back and began caressing her buttocks. "Nobody will ever love you like I do," he said. "You know that don't you? Please tell me you know that."

"I do, Roger, I do know that."

He took the list and quietly left. Hallie thought how odd it was that later, when they were in bed together, Roger would probably be more loving and gentle with her than he'd been in weeks. He'd croon about how much he loved her, and he would hold her close as they went to sleep.

Just that week, Hallie had seen a program on television about a woman whose husband was always so sweet right after he'd hit her or caused some destructive scene in the house. Hallie usually clicked the remote to avoid that kind of program, but this time something made her stay with it and she forced herself to listen. The woman on the talk show looked professional and was dressed in a smart suit set off with gold jewelry. Hallie marveled at how chic the woman looked. For days, the woman's words haunted her and were coming back to her now. "When I look back," the woman said, "I can see that the warning signs were there even *before* the wedding. There was that time when he..." Hallie didn't need to listen to anymore. She only had to look back a few years to understand.

* * * *

"Watch where you're going," he said, his voice irritated and impatient.

"I'm so sorry," Hallie said. Deep in thought as she walked through the medical school cafeteria, she'd accidentally hit the back of a man's head with her tray. He stood up and faced her with a glare on his face, and she recognized the tall, broad-shouldered man as the guest lecturer in her earlier class that morning.

"Oh," he said, his voice changing to pleasant curiosity. "weren't you in the class I just taught?"

"I sure was. I enjoyed your lecture—you know so much about the brain."

"Nah," he said, "it was just a bunch of stuff I threw together. I like the entire neurology field though. It's a special interest of mine. And you are...?"

Hallie told him her name, and he continued looking at her

intensely. She felt her face grow hot as she became more self-conscious. Small and thin, with a pixie-like face, she wasn't used to attention from men. No matter what kind of makeup she used or clothes she wore, she ended up feeling like a teenager in her mother's clothes.

Roger invited Hallie to join him and over lunch, Hallie learned that Roger was twenty-seven and an intern at a nearby teaching hospital. He had grown up in Manhattan and he'd whiled away many hours during his childhood lost in fantasies about becoming a famous doctor and a sought after professor delivering lectures to eager students.

Before he left her that day, she had agreed to go out with him the next weekend. To Hallie, this was the best thing that had happened since she'd come to Atlanta from North Carolina to attend nursing school.

Over the next months, as she listened to Roger talk about his dreams, Hallie couldn't help but think about her own life—her long-held dream of becoming a psychologist. Her father, however, had other plans, and in fact, he had threatened to cut off her college money unless she studied nursing. "It's a practical career for a woman," he'd said. "No matter what happens, you'll always have job security." He had then told Hallie about the college in Atlanta he'd picked out for her. Of course, Hallie found herself more interested in psychiatric nursing than any other specialty within the field.

Roger had lectured about this new field of imaging the brain to her nursing class, and when she looked back on the way her attraction for him started, it was the confident, powerful way he spoke that held her attention and led to her fascination with him. To her, he looked like a king directing his subjects. Although still an intern, Roger walked and talked with an air of authority. Periodically, he backed away from the podium and strode back and forth across the front of the room as he spoke. By the end of the lecture he'd made eye contact with each student.

Hallie felt a tingle of fear mixed with profound awe as she sat with him and listened to him describe his work, his mission. More than anything else, she was flattered that this charismatic teacher showed interest in her. He actually wanted to see her again. Nothing like this had ever happened to her before.

As the years passed, scenes from her early days with Roger would flash through Hallie's mind. The evening of their third or fourth date, Roger's rude attitude toward her classmates, Amanda and Carol, had startled her. The two young women had seen them in a small bistro near the campus and had come to their table to say hello. Naturally, they wanted to meet the man Hallie had described as brilliant and fascinating, not to mention handsome. But he'd been barely civil to Amanda and Carol, and later, when she asked him about it, he brushed her off by saying, "I was out with you—I had no interest in talking to a couple of kids."

Another night Roger told her exactly what to wear to a dinner with the chief resident and his wife. When he drove her to the beauty shop and told the hairdresser precisely how he wanted her shoulder length hair fixed, his tone was light and playful. After they'd left the shop, she tucked her arm in his and strolled proudly down the street, flattered with the attention he was showering on her. He must care so much, she'd thought, if he had such strong opinions about her hairstyles. Looking back, though, she recalled the troubled look on the hairdresser's face as she'd fixed Hallie's hair but avoided looking straight into Roger's eyes.

One evening stood out above the others. Roger showed up in an expensive suede jacket. He told her that Rhonda, a nurse he had once dated, gave it to him for his birthday. When she asked him why a former girlfriend would give him such an expensive gift, he dismissed her with a laugh. "She just won't accept that I dumped her. She'll figure it out eventually." In her heart, Hallie was sure he was still seeing this nurse, but when he changed the subject, she decided not to bring it up again.

When Hallie met Roger's mother, Anna had pulled her aside and said, "My son has some great qualities, but as you no doubt know, he's, well, different. He's moody and unpredictable. Just be patient with him and love him a lot. He'll be okay." Hallie wanted nothing more than to do just that. Yes, she thought many times,

Roger is difficult, but he loves me and I love him. Eventually, love will heal the hard, rough places in him.

They were married in a small chapel in the Blue Ridge Mountains, with only close family and friends invited. The rich reds and golds of the autumn leaves shimmered in the late afternoon sun and to Hallie, the vibrant beauty of the day was a symbol of the bright days she hoped were ahead of her. But just as dominant in her mind was the sour memory of wearing a wedding dress she didn't like. Roger, however, not only liked it, he had practically designed it himself.

The saga of the wedding dress started when Hallie picked out a pattern she liked and made an appointment with a seamstress. She was thrilled at the off the shoulder, scoop neck design, and the train added a hint of sophistication that was a new look for her. She was surprised when Roger wanted to go to the seamstress with her for the first fitting. At first she said no, and told him that bad luck would surely follow if they broke with tradition and let him see the dress. She teased and cajoled, but she might as well as given up before she started. He needled her until she gave in.

While they were with the seamstress, Roger was polite, even charming. He nodded with approval when Hallie asked him what he thought. But as soon as they got in the car, he kissed her gently and said, "Hallie, you know I'm only telling you this because I love you so much and because you asked me for my opinion. That low cut neckline you chose just isn't you, babe."

"What do you mean? I thought you liked it."

"Well, on another woman—say, Marilyn Monroe—it might be fine, if you know what I mean. But, well, let's face it, you are not exactly well-endowed, and I think a high neckline would flatter you more."

Hallie tried not to show how hurt she was, especially since she was self-conscious about her small breasts and felt like a stick figure anyway. Now she knew that her lack of womanly curves really did make a difference to him. "Well, the dress is cut," she told him, "and I can't afford more material. I'm afraid we're stuck with it - and anyway, *I really like it.*"

Roger flashed her a boyish frown as he said, "I know what we can do, and it isn't too late. Look, I only want you to be the most beautiful bride in the world, so you're going to tell the seamstress to take material from the train and the bottom of the dress and make a high neckline. I like that old fashioned, pioneer look. That's how I like my women," he'd teased.

The next time she saw Roger he asked about her next appointment with the seamstress and he arranged his schedule to be with her. The dress was pronounced finished only after he approved it and paid the seamstress himself.

When Hallie recalled the times she'd had second thoughts about Roger and the wisdom of pledging her life to him, the minutes just before her wedding always stood out. Standing in front of the mirror in a plain, street length gown with a high, Victorian neckline, she wasn't sure she knew the woman looking back at her any better than she knew the man waiting for her in the chapel.

Hallie heard the wedding march and she left the small room off the sanctuary, determined to forget about the dress. The minute she saw Roger, her doubts went away. He looked incredibly handsome in his tuxedo, and his eyes were so filled with love that her heart leapt with joy. How silly, she thought, to worry about anything. Of course she would become Roger's wife.

Getting to Work

What Can We Learn About the Cycle of Abuse?

When we first see Hallie, she is deeply immersed in the "dance" of violence with Roger. She has tried—in vain—to anticipate his moods and without realizing it, the way she feels is dependent on his demeanor. She is happy and relaxed when their outing to the grocery store seemed to go well; an element of relief emerges, and maybe, just maybe, they will have a pleasant day.

We can see that Hallie has altered her behavior in numerous ways. For example, Hallie does not even question Roger's scrutiny of the grocery list, nor apparently, does she think it's odd that he has kept track of how much time she spent in the supermarket. He controls the money, the list, and the time.

Roger also uses emotional manipulation to control her. He tries to make her feel guilty because she broke her "agreement" to buy one bag of chips. He behaves as if she has victimized him. Hallie attempts to use logic in response to Roger. After all, the chips were on sale. This is much like the reasoning she used over her wedding dress. She likes her dress and it is already cut, so, therefore, she expects him to back off. She assumes a logical explanation exists for his rude behavior to her friends. These are powerful "red flags" for a woman who is aware of patterns in abusive relationships. However, they represent only troublesome "quirks" to a woman who is unknowingly being seduced into the web of abuse.

Power and Control

Hallie was vulnerable to the power that Roger projected when she first met him. Remember that his very first words to her were spoken in a rude tone and her first words to him were an apology. He turned charming only when he realized that he had seen her earlier in the day. He recognized that Hallie had responded to his self-generated "importance."

Roger's controlling behavior began the minute Hallie saw herself as fortunate to be noticed by such an important and accomplished person. The balance of power was uneven from the beginning. This is one important way an abuser can begin the seductive dance.

Fluctuating between aggressive and loving behavior is an extremely effective way to control another person. When we first see Hallie, she already has very little life outside of fearing Roger, placating him to avoid scenes, second guessing his needs, and recovering from the episodes of violence. Over time, she begins to anticipate and even yearn for the times when he will treat her with tenderness.

Roger effectively keeps Hallie wondering about her own perceptions. After all, if Roger can be so loving, is it not possible that it truly is her fault when his rage is triggered? The logic is twisted, but she has begun to believe that he couldn't be as bad or as dangerous as her intuitive voice keeps telling her. His tenderness has her fooled. This fluctuating behavior is a form of brainwashing that is *consciously* used on prisoners of war and kidnap victims to keep them under control. In abusive relationships, the brainwashing is a typical pattern used by the abuser.

Much of what happens to reinforce Hallie's learned helplessness and acceptance of abuse is covert. On the surface, Roger is reacting to money and groceries, but of course, the issue is about power and control.

Understanding the Familiar

When we first see Hallie and get a glimpse of the horrific evidence of escalating abuse, she is finally beginning to pay attention to the messages around her that prompt her to listen to her inner voice. For some women, hearing another abused woman's story may be the first nudge they need to begin to confront the reality of their situation. In addition, Hallie finally may be linking her headaches and the bouts with colitis to the stress in her household. However, she may believe the stress is, in large part, her own fault.

We learn early that Hallie was not allowed to question her father's decisions for her, and in fact, she was grateful for the opportunity to be educated at all. Roger's control is not so far outside the realm of her father's controlling behavior. Unconsciously, his behavior feels familiar, and ironically, she feels secure at some deep level. It is puzzling that human beings will tend to choose partners who make them feel secure, even if the habitual behavior is destructive. Many people mistake security for love. Hallie still has a long way to go before she understands this on the most rudimentary level.

Ignoring the Signs

Roger used a boyish, benign charm to lure her—and keep her—in his circle of control. She overlooked or explained away so many warning signs. Like many women, she preferred to see his behavior as flattering and a sign of the intensity of his love. Even when he made disparaging remarks about her figure, she pushed aside her natural tendency to feel hurt. Because he is accomplished and bright, she consistently believes that he must know better.

What would happen if Hallie began to see her own perceptions as correct? What would have happened if she had called him on his behavior toward her friends? What if she had insisted that she choose her own wedding dress? Frankly, it is likely that Roger would have broken off the relationship with Hallie and searched for a more willing victim. Until Hallie understands this, she will continue to attempt to change her behavior to appease him, all the while hoping that he will change.

Hallie will make progress only when she understands that she learned her behavior from the day she was born, and it is possible that the cycle started even before. Within her family tree there are many men and women who perpetuated the cycle of abuse with their own behavior. Likewise, Roger comes from a line of men who exerted control over women.

Deeply embedded within her, Hallie carries the belief that it is her destiny to be with a man more powerful than she is. Until she uncovers this belief, quite literally, allows it to be seen in the light of consciousness; she will continue to be a victim. Hallie's willingness to listen to the story of a woman whose life resembles her own may be the first glimmer of the hidden truths Hallie allows to the surface. It could be the first step in a long process that will move her toward wholeness.

2

"I wish I could have taken my girl on a real honeymoon," Roger said. With his hands planted on his hips and shaking his head, he said, "This little cottage isn't good enough for my new bride."

"Don't say such things," Hallie said. She reached up and put her hands gently on his face. "This cottage is wonderful."

"They call it rustic when they really mean crude and primitive."

"No they don't Roger. It *is* rustic and I love it."

Nestled deep in the woods of the Blue Ridge Mountains, the honeymoon cabin was half a mile away from the main lodge. They could walk down the mountain path for their meals in the main dining room. But for their wedding night Roger arranged to have champagne and dinner brought to the cabin. When they first drove up, Hallie couldn't contain her joy at seeing the private little cottage with a porch swing and inside, a fireplace they would probably need during the chilly fall evenings.

"This is what I dreamed about," Hallie said as they carried their bags inside.

"Then you must have small dreams," Roger quickly replied.

"I didn't mean..."

"Oh never mind. Just unpack and let's go for a walk." Roger unzipped his bag and began tossing shirts and jeans on the bed.

Hallie felt a tightening in her stomach and the nervous flutter started again. It crossed her mind that the flutter was becoming familiar, but she immediately dismissed the feeling as normal wedding jitters. "Yes, a walk," she said, "that sounds wonderful."

For the next couple of hours they chased each other through the woods and waded across the stream and walked on a path to a waterfall Hallie read about in a guidebook. Hallie had never felt happier. Roger put his arm around her shoulder and held her close as they walked back to the cabin. A few minutes later, a jeep pulled up and two waiters delivered their dinner. First they laid the white linen tablecloth on the oak table in front of the low windows that looked out to the valley and the mountains beyond. One waiter opened the first bottle of champagne while the other spread out platters of food and arranged the china and crystal.

Roger was charming as he thanked the waiters for their kindness and pulled several bills out of his wallet and handed them to the young men. He closed the door behind them and poured two glasses of champagne.

Hallie felt the fullness of pride and happiness over her husband's generosity to the young men. This kind of mood made her heart sing, and Hallie quietly resolved to do whatever she could to make his life as pleasant as possible. She wanted to see him happy and relaxed.

"To us," she said as she clinked her glass to his.

"Yes, my darling," he said, "to us."

Over plates of broiled salmon and asparagus, Hallie talked about their new apartment and told Roger again and again how pleased she was that they'd found a place near the hospital. "So convenient for both of us."

"What do you mean 'us'?"

"Oh, I just mean that I'm sure I can get a job at the hospital now that I'm finished with school." In all the excitement of the wedding plans, at times Hallie almost forgot that she'd actually graduated from nursing school herself and was ready to start her own career. She hadn't wanted to bother Roger with talk of her own dreams because he was so preoccupied with the grind of his internship. But still, she took pride in having an accomplishment of her own.

"Are you trying to show me up?" Roger's fork clattered as it hit the plate with such force that it bounced off and landed with a thud on the tablecloth.

"Show you up? What do you mean?" Hallie's heart started to beat. She recognized the cold darkness in Roger's eyes, all trace of his earlier charm gone.

"You never said anything about wanting a job."

"Well, I suppose I assumed you knew I'd want to work. I worked hard for my degree, and now that all the wedding plans are behind me, I thought I'd see about working at the hospital."

"For God's sake Hallie, it's just a nursing degree. Believe me, the hospital will get along just fine without your skills."

The sarcasm in his voice shocked her, and she wondered if he was joking with her. "Are you teasing me again?" she said in a light tone. "Of course I know I'm not the big shot you are." She stretched the last words out in a light mocking tone, hoping that she was right, that he'd been teasing her.

"Mocking me now? How dare you mock me?" In an instant he was up from his chair and grabbed her arm and dragged her across the room.

"Roger, let go, let go," she said. "You're hurting me."

"You…don't…know…what…hurting…is," he said, enunciating each word carefully and slowly.

"Well you're hurting me now. Let go of my arm."

Roger yanked her harder and in long strides led her to the bathroom door. He pushed her inside and quickly closed the door.

"Roger, what are you doing? I'm not staying in here."

"Yes you are. You'll stay in the bathroom and think about the way you mocked me. I'm your husband now. I'll decide if you will have a job."

Hallie felt dazed and her stomach churned. She wasn't sure if it was from the champagne or the shock of Roger's hostility, but she was nauseous and dizzy. She rested against the cool porcelain of the tub and pulled a towel off the rack to wrap around her legs. She was shaking and her feet were freezing cold.

Soon, she thought, soon he'll open the door and apologize. He hadn't hit her, she reasoned. If he had wanted to he could have, but he didn't. He didn't mean to hurt her, Hallie thought as she rubbed the red marks on her upper arm.

She waited and heard shuffling noise outside the door before the sound of the screen door slamming shut. She exhaled and realized she'd been holding her breath. In the quiet of the small bathroom Hallie could feel her body gradually relax as tears brought release. A few minutes later, Hallie leaned over the toilet bowl and vomited up her dinner and the champagne that had tasted so good when she sipped it from the elegant crystal glasses and proposed the toast to their marriage. Hallie wasn't sure how many hours passed, but eventually she grabbed more towels and lined the bathtub with them and crawled inside the tub. Within minutes she was asleep.

* * * *

"So sleepy," Roger said as he lifted Hallie from the tub. His arms felt strong but gentle and before she was fully awake, Hallie rested her head against his chest. "I can't believe you would sleep in the tub. Why did you do that?"

More alert now, Hallie was surprised by the question. "You told me..."

"You believed me? You, my love, are not always so bright." Now his tone was teasing and Hallie had the urge to snap back at him and tell him how hurt she was by what he'd done. "You'll learn, Hallie, you'll learn what I need. I just hope you understand what you did. I don't want to have a fight like that ever again."

Hallie had no idea what she had done that led to the ugly scene. She waited for him to apologize and searched his face for a sign that he was sorry.

"Tell me you're sorry now, baby, and we'll finally start our honeymoon."

Hallie felt as if she didn't get the punch line of a joke. Although she thought it was crazy, she whispered, "I'm sorry," in Roger's ear.

He kissed her and gently placed her on the bed and then stretched out along side her. He filled their champagne glasses and coaxed her to take a sip, although she didn't want it. He was both gentle and passionate as he stroked her body and told her she was the most beautiful woman he'd ever seen. And later, after Hallie felt a warm contentment and the earlier nightmare felt like a distant memory, she sighed deeply when Roger said, "I love you more than anyone else in world could ever love you. I'll teach you what you need to know about me, my darling. We'll be happier than you ever believed possible."

Feeling safe in Roger's arms for the first time, Hallie held the thought that Roger loved her more than anyone else. From the time she was a little girl, she'd dreamed about a man saying those words to her.

The sun broke through the windows and cast shadows of tree branches across the floor. Roger was up and dressed and setting mugs and plates out on the table. Hallie loved the rugged handsome look of Roger in jeans and a tee shirt. She sighed from happiness, but scenes from the previous night brought on a lurching sensation in her stomach. A little voice that seemed to come from miles away told Hallie to get dressed and walk out the door and never look back. The voice lasted long enough for Hallie to quickly jump out of bed and run to her husband and put her arms around his waist. He turned and kissed her and she knew everything was okay again. Their sweet lovemaking hadn't been a dream. She had her Roger back.

* * * *

"You just don't understand the pressure, Hallie. You just don't get it."

"I try, Roger. That's why I'm sitting here listening. I want to understand."

"Those bastards don't pay me enough to make me jump through all these hoops. First the lectures, then the rounds, then the long shifts. And I get almost no respect even though I'm smarter than any of them. They treat me like I'm no better than a damned nurse!"

Hallie felt a stab of pain at his insult to her profession, but no matter, she thought. She started to offer–again–to get a job and help ease the financial burden he felt. But she quickly changed her mind. When Roger was in this particular mood, the victim mood, or that's how she saw it, he didn't want to hear about her working. Besides, if she did, then she'd have to hear another disparaging remark about her career. She hoped, for her sake as well as his that the situation would change soon.

In the months since they'd been back from their four-day honeymoon she'd worked on numerous applications for residency positions. She was excited by the prospect of moving to a place she'd never been. San Francisco, Houston, Seattle, Boston, Chicago. They all sounded like wonderful new cities to explore. Secretly, though, she had doubts if Roger would be satisfied with any level of respect short of running his own department. She kept her feelings to herself and hoped that maybe a colleague would point out that his attitude was contributing to his problems. She certainly couldn't take that on.

"Maybe a new position will come through soon, and then we'll have a new adventure." Hallie kept her voice low, but inside she was desperate to keep the atmosphere calm.

Roger flashed her a disgusted look. "Adventure, huh. Easy for you to say. You can have an adventure. You don't have anything else to do."

Without thinking, she snapped back, "That's because you don't want me to get a job."

"So now you're saying you're bored being my wife? You need a job because being my wife isn't enough?"

When Roger started this line of talk, she knew she was defeated. "No, of course not. Anyway, I didn't say I don't have enough to do. I keep busy trying all those recipes your mother gave me." Hallie attempted to keep her voice light, even playful. Sometimes she could shift the mood. In truth, she was tired of making sure the apartment was neat and clean and these recipes were becoming tiresome, too.

Sometimes Hallie thought she would never find a way to win. Most nights she cooked a nice dinner, but he often stayed late at the hospital and the food grew cold in the pans. The next night he turned up his nose at the leftovers. At month's end he complained that she spent too much money on groceries, so she decided to stop cooking ahead. But the first night he came home and dinner wasn't ready he pounded his fist in the wall and told her she was a lousy wife.

That night he'd stayed up until 4:00 o'clock in the morning working on a paper he was writing with the head of the department. "You don't know how important this is to my future," he'd said. "Be patient with me. I don't mean to be in such a bad mood all the time. I know you try." Roger even agreed to call her by mid-afternoon and let her know if he was coming home for dinner. "Just be here to take the call, though, honey. I don't want to talk to the answering machine."

Hallie was frustrated by not having an outside job or friends of her own. She especially didn't like planning her days around Roger's call, which sometimes didn't come at all. But at least on a few days she didn't have to spend hours making homemade stews and breads that Roger's mother insisted he loved. Except when he was being especially sweet, he barely commented on dinner, so Hallie wasn't sure what he liked.

One evening over dinner Roger told her they were going to the department head's home for dinner on Saturday night. "He's invited all the interns and their spouses, if they're lucky enough to have them," he said. "But no one has a wife as pretty as you."

After dinner Roger went to the closet and started looking through her clothes. He pushed the hangers back and with each piece that he brought out to examine he became angrier and angrier. "Garbage," he said, "pure garbage."

"Why Roger, you helped me pick out that red pantsuit yourself. It's silk and lovely for a dinner party."

"You little idiot," he said. "Do you really think a red pantsuit is what you should show up in? I don't want my wife looking like a whore."

Hallie was taken aback by the cold hatred in his voice. "I-I-I just thought that since you picked it out..."

"To wear with me, when I want you to look sexy—for me, not

for other men. The guys I work with will be at the party. Do you want to look sexy for them?"

"No, of course not. I only meant."

"You only meant, you only meant. Don't you ever think before you talk?"

Her heart pounding and stomach rolling and turning, Hallie turned and walked out of the room. She began to clear the table and wipe the counters in the kitchen, even though she'd wiped them clean earlier in the day.

She went into the living room and picked up a magazine off the coffee table and tried to pretend that she was living a normal life with a normal husband. Hallie had read that the first year of marriage was the hardest. *This is just the adjustment period* she told herself, as she rubbed her temples and tried to stop the headache that was building. He'll be coming around the corner and apologizing any minute now. She was right.

Roger came and sat down next to her. "Wow, I don't know what got into me. You are so beautiful that I go crazy when I think of other guys looking at you. I should have known you were kidding about that suit."

Hallie hadn't been kidding, but she didn't say as much. "Did you find something you liked?" she asked. "I know this will be an important night for you so I'll wear whatever will please you."

"I know you will babe, but nothing you have will do."

"I could shop tomorrow and find something."

"Alone? No way. We'll go tomorrow after I get off work. I'll help you find something."

Hallie felt the comfort of his arm as he put it around her shoulders and pulled her close. "My sexy wife, my sexy, sexy wife. And it's all for me," he whispered. No one else?"

"No Roger, no one else." Hallie hoped that soon Roger would stop needing the reassurance that he was the only man for her.

Getting to Work

What Can We Learn About the Cycle of Abuse?

Hallie is right to believe that the first year of marriage can be difficult. This is what she tells herself as life with Roger becomes increasingly tension-filled. These are not normal adjustments, but because of Hallie's background, she does not understand that. Beginning on their honeymoon, we notice that Hallie's life revolves almost totally around Roger, and she is losing a sense of herself and her own value.

Roger insults Hallie in numerous ways, and in fact, on their honeymoon, he belittles her profession in casual conversation. He emphasizes the point that she could never be as important as he is, which reinforces the position of women in her birth family. Light-hearted teasing is misinterpreted as mocking him, and his ego is so fragile that mocking is a serious insult. Although she cannot do this perfectly, Hallie is trying to learn to carefully consider her choice of words and is deeply involved in an ongoing struggle to both understand Roger and predict his wants and needs, much as many female relatives have done in their marriages. Beyond that, Hallie is attempting to predict his reaction to common situations in order to modulate her response. She represses her anger and irritation with him, as well as her sense of fun and play. Roger continues his pattern of behaving as if it's his job—indeed his duty—to teach her what she needs to know about being a good wife to him.

The Struggle is Underway

Hallie has made it through the honeymoon, although she rationalizes Roger's behavior and is deeply hurt that he has used his physical and emotional power to control her actions. She is clearly afraid to leave the bathroom and is unduly relieved that he has not hit her. Hallie and Roger are engaged in a struggle she will not reveal or discuss with anyone else. She is already engaged in secrecy, and no matter how Hallie rationalizes, she knows this isn't normal honeymoon behavior. A great sense of shame accompanies her hurt feelings.

Clearly, Hallie ignores the clear voice of her intuition that warns her that this relationship is not going to match her dreams. Like many women in her situation, she represses the internal voice that tries to protect her and direct her, literally, to walk out the door. This is a dramatic moment and defines the quality of her life for years to come.

Roger knows how to be charming and offers large tips to the waiters in order to impress Hallie and ensure that he will be treated with respect in the dining room of the lodge. Roger's ability to turn on the charm is part of what drew Hallie to him in the first place. However, he needs constant reassurance and probably feels genuinely sorry that the honeymoon he can afford is not more lavish. This concern is self-centered; he's preoccupied with his own image, not about Hallie's pleasure.

Roger Defines Hallie's Life

Hallie spends her days alone, and Roger controls how she spends her time by expecting dinner when he comes home, yet he sabotages her efforts by not showing up on time or calling ahead to let her know. His idea of accommodation is to promise to call Hallie if he won't be home for dinner, but he adds the condition that she must be home to take his call. This further controls the way she spends her time. Typical of women caught in the cycle of emotional abuse and control, Hallie does not have friends, nor does she feel free to make connections outside her marriage. She doesn't have a job or a social life of her own, so Roger is becoming even more central to Hallie's life.

Roger has adopted a victim stance, typical of certain types of narcissistic abusers. No one respects him enough, no one understands him and realizes how talented he is. He depends on Hallie to reinforce his own sense of importance and she does not defend her desire for a job because she knows this will set off a fit of temper. Roger has not hit her yet, but he has controlled her behavior with the underlying threat of violence and force.

Roger doesn't want anyone else to find Hallie attractive. Again this is a self-centered, narcissistic concern. He sees her as his property, and he believes it is his right to dress her to fit an image he wants to project to his colleagues. Hallie is understandably confused that he rejects an outfit he bought for her and calls her an "idiot" because she believes it is appropriate. In a matter of minutes, Roger has determined that he will choose her clothes, and in doing so she continues to be the object of his narcissism and he molds her to suit and reflect himself. He feels completely free to tell her that the outfit he labels "whorish" is fine if it suits the momentary image he chooses for her.

What Does Hallie Know and Feel?

At this point, Hallie knows something is amiss in Roger's behavior and she persists in trying to "figure him out." Hallie has not abandoned the hope that Roger will settle down, that her acquiescence to him will smooth out what she continues to refer to as the "rough edges" of his personality. She puts aside her reservations and tries to believe his behavior is entwined with his loving feelings toward her.

Hallie is also beginning to show *physical* symptoms common to women in the cycle of abuse. Prior to her marriage, Hallie did not suffer from headaches or digestive complaints. We can expect that even without physical battering, Hallie's headaches and colitis will continue and her health will deteriorate.

3

Hallie was so filled with joy and happiness she almost skipped down the street. She felt like shouting her glee to passersby. After months of trying, she was finally pregnant. Roger would be so pleased, she thought, as she hurried home, stopping only at the market where she splurged on two thick steaks and the ingredients for Roger's favorite white chocolate cheesecake. She considered buying a bunch of flowers, but decided against it. She was already spending beyond their budget and besides, she'd let Roger bring her flowers. After all, she was making Roger's dream come true.

For the last few months, Roger had talked about almost nothing except having a child. And as each month passed without a pregnancy, she felt his disappointed, and noted his accusatory, looks. Apparently, once Roger determined that the time was right to have a baby, he expected her to become pregnant immediately. Hallie suspected that Roger thought something must be wrong with her or surely it would have happened by now. Mixed in with all the happiness and joy, Hallie felt a sense of relief that finally, she was giving Roger what he wanted.

Some days Hallie desperately wanted to have a baby, but other times, she wondered how ready she was. For days on end, or so it seemed, her thoughts were filled with Roger. Figuring him out, pleasing him, and avoiding the angry outbursts that went on and on felt like a full-time job. Still, she was restless at home and needed something to occupy her time. Starting a family had been her dream, too.

For the last two years Roger had remained adamant that she would not, could not, work. It would humiliate him. What would his colleagues think? Hallie couldn't figure out what Roger meant.

Time and time again she'd talked to the wives of Roger's male colleagues, only to learn that these women had careers of their own. In fact, the wife of the head of the radiology department at the large teaching hospital where Roger now worked was a respected obstetrician. Respected by everyone, that is, except Roger. Or so it seemed. He constantly referred to her as a "loser."

When she came home, she called Roger's pager and when he returned the call she heard the irritation in his voice. He hated being bothered at work, and she'd expected that tone, but all would be forgiven once he learned the reason for her call. Hallie had debated whether to surprise him or give him the news over the phone. The phone was safer, she thought. If he came home and saw steaks grilling, he might hit the roof before she had a chance to explain her surprise

"I'm sorry to bother you at the hospital," she said quickly, "but I have wonderful news."

"It better be, Hallie. You know how I feel about you paging me."

"It's the best possible news, Roger. I'm pregnant. We're having a *baby*. A summer baby. The baby is due in June."

"Oh Hallie," Roger said, his voice softening. "That's the best news I've ever had. I can't wait to get home. I'm taking my best girl out to dinner for a big celebration."

Hallie told him about the steaks and the cheesecake she was planning to make, but Roger insisted that they were going out. "Nah, just put all that stuff in the freezer. You deserve a real celebration. I'll be home in two hours. Be ready for a good time."

When Hallie hung up the phone, she was happier than she'd been in the three years of her marriage. She hummed to herself as she went through her closet and picked out something to wear. She longed to put on the red silk pantsuit, but pushed it back. Roger only liked her to wear that at home. The navy suit was too prim. Even though he'd picked it out, he'd told her it made her look like a mousy schoolteacher, so she pushed that aside, too. She settled on a paisley print dress and for the next two hours she fixed her hair and carefully applied her makeup. When Roger came through the door with a bunch of roses in his hand Hallie was certain it was going to be a perfect evening. And so it was.

Years later, Hallie wished she could go back to the days of her pregnancy. For the first time, Roger showered her with attention, but more than that, Hallie felt respected. At times she wondered how having a child could have brought about such a drastic change. But when these questions weighed too heavy for too long, she brushed them aside and berated herself for not just enjoying Roger's contentment and the changes in his behavior. "Don't look a gift horse in the mouth," she told herself. "Just be grateful for what you have."

In the early months of her pregnancy Hallie felt better than she had in years. The morning sickness was a small price to pay for the absence of tension headaches. Even her bouts with colitis had disappeared. Roger brought her flowers at least once a week, and he helped her pick out attractive maternity clothes. Well, Roger thought they were attractive. Hallie thought she looked much older than her 25 years in these dowdy clothes, but he had taken such pleasure in shopping with her she kept quiet about what she'd have chosen if she'd been picking them out. The pleasure of spending that time with him was more important than arguing over their different taste in her clothes.

Hallie also was pleased that Roger seemed to be coming out of his shell. He even talked about joining a country club in the spring. "It's just about expected of me," he said. "As if I don't have enough to do," he added. The new Roger also took her to more parties at the hospital and encouraged her to invite some of his colleagues' wives to their apartment for lunch. Two had accepted, and Hallie had prepared a quiche and a salad and made a crusty French bread from scratch. The women praised her cooking and complimented the attractive table, but they didn't stay long. One woman had to get back to work, and the other had three children to pick up from school.

Hallie had enjoyed chatting with the women, but once, when she had laughingly mentioned all the attention Roger heaped on her now that they were expecting a baby, the two women had exchanged glances but then quickly looked away. When Hallie mentioned her nursing degree, both women exchanged that look again, and one asked her why she didn't work. She'd said something about how she and Roger had wanted to start a family and that early in their marriage they'd expected to be moving. "I didn't want to become attached to a job only to leave it when we moved or had a baby," she'd said. Neither woman looked convinced. *Why should they*, she thought. It was a lie.

Later, when she was alone and washing up the dishes, Hallie thought about the way the two women had looked at each other across the table, as if they knew something she didn't. She *had* sounded nervous when she'd tried to explain why she didn't work and while the two women hadn't said anything, they'd appeared nervous, even uneasy. Hallie couldn't help but wonder if they knew something about Roger that she didn't. What kind of reputation did he have around the hospital anyway?

As the pregnancy progressed, Hallie felt secure in the knowledge that she and Roger had finally found a rhythm together. She filled her days preparing for the baby and taking good care of herself and in the evenings while Roger wrote papers for medical journals, she tried to stay out of his way and read novels or watched television. At times she felt lonely, but the baby would change all that.

* * * *

Roger wrapped his arms around her as his eyes filled with tears, which like hers, were tears of relief as much as joy. Eric had made it safely into the world, an event that hadn't been a certainty. Early in her seventh month, premature labor had threatened the pregnancy and Hallie was ordered to spend the last three months in bed. Roger had gone from attentive to doting. Both their mothers had offered to help, but he had been insistent about taking care of her himself. Hallie wondered how Roger managed to take so much time away from the hospital, but he told her not to worry. "I have it covered," he'd said. "I always have these things covered. My job is to take care of you."

As they shared tender moments in the hospital, Hallie felt all her worries fade away. "You're a real woman now, Hallie, and you've made me so proud of you," he said. That wasn't exactly what she wanted to hear, but she told herself not to be so silly all the time, always wishing for particular kinds of recognition, as if she could control Roger's words. Before her pregnancy, Roger used to regularly berate her for not being grateful enough for the life he'd provided for her. "He's right," she said to herself, "I'm not grateful enough for the wonderful husband Roger has become over the last months."

Hallie was thrilled by how much Roger enjoyed Eric. He helped feed and bathe him and the minute he came home from work, he picked Eric up and danced around the house with him cradled in his arms. A few weeks after Eric's birth Roger came home with the news that he'd found a new apartment for them. "It's closer to the hospital, but the best part is that it has two bedrooms so Eric doesn't have to sleep in our room. And the bedroom is big enough for my desk. That way I can work on my papers at night while you tend to Eric. I love him, but I can't concentrate when he cries. Besides, I have to catch up on my work. It isn't your fault, but I'm behind in my publishing schedule."

Over the next months, Roger spent more and more time in the bedroom by himself while Hallie tended to Eric's needs. Roger had begun a book manuscript and in addition to teaching, the head of the department wanted him to write two papers based on some research Roger had pioneered in the emerging field of brain imaging. Roger had always wanted to make a name for himself, and it appeared that his efforts to publish were paying off. Still, his success came at a price. "You can't believe the pressure I'm under babe. It's getting worse every day."

"Do you want to look for another job?" Hallie asked. Roger had been particularly tense that evening at dinner and Hallie had held Eric all through dinner to keep him from fussing.

"You are such a *stupid* woman," he responded, shaking his head and stabbing at his food with his fork.

"Roger, don't call me stupid," Hallie said. "You have talked about nothing but the pressure you're under so I thought that perhaps you'd be happier somewhere else."

Roger picked up his plate and flung it, baked chicken and peas and all, against the wall behind Hallie's chair. She clung to Eric and dashed into the kitchen, hoping Roger would leave her alone. She hadn't seen *this* Roger in almost a year and she'd hoped the rage-filled, quick-to-anger Roger had disappeared forever.

"Put Eric in his crib," Roger said. He was standing in the doorway. "Don't argue, just do it." He moved aside to make way for her to pass.

"I'll just stay in Eric's room with him," she said. "That way you can do your work. I'll clean up later."

"You'll clean up when I tell you to clean up," Roger said, his voice icy and distant. "Put him down and come back out. You and I have some talking to do."

Hallie's heart beat hard in her chest as she put Eric in his crib. She hoped he would be quiet. She hadn't been this afraid of Roger in a long time and she didn't want Eric to hear what she knew would be an ugly scene.

She found Roger in the kitchen and when she went toward him and started to speak, she was stopped by the full impact of his hand across her face. She felt like her right eye would explode out of its socket and blood started dripping from the corner of her mouth. She bent over double in pain and Roger grabbed her by the hair and dragged her into the living room. Too stunned to say anything, she broke away from him and ran toward Eric's room. Roger caught her by the neck of her blouse and dragged her back to the living room and shoved her down on the couch.

"You are one ungrateful bitch," he said. "*You* want *me* to get another job. I guess all I do for you just isn't good enough. Of course, you come from such class yourself, you little hick."

"No Roger, that's not what I meant…"

"Shut up. You hear me? Shut up or I'll break your stupid little neck."

For the next half-hour, Hallie listened to Eric's crying and to Roger's ugly bitter words about how helpless she was, how stupid, how insensitive to his needs. When Hallie tried to get up to tend to Eric, Roger shoved her back down and said he wasn't finished setting her straight. Finally, when Eric's crying turned to helpless screams he ordered her to go to him. "Maybe you can do that right," he said.

Hallie ran to Eric and took him into the kitchen where she fixed a bottle and tried to soothe him. Right behind her, Roger took ice from the freezer and filled an icepack and handed it to Hallie. "Put ice on your face. It's starting to bruise and swell. You'll have to stay inside for the next few days. And don't forget to clean up that mess you made in the dining room." With that he walked away.

* * * *

When Eric was about four months old, Roger told her that he'd been invited to deliver the luncheon speech at a pharmaceutical convention in Chicago. It was quite an honor and the company insisted that Hallie join him. They'd have four days in Chicago and Roger was thrilled. Hallie didn't like the idea of flying with Eric, even though the prospect of a few days away pleased her, and she'd never been to Chicago. She also hoped that getting this professional recognition would soften Roger's attitude toward her. He alternated between being attentive and sweet and cold and nasty. Some evenings he seemed to enjoy having dinner with her, while other evenings, he ate in silence and left the table and went directly to his desk.

Roger was relaxed and happy on the plane. He carried Eric through the airport and called for a skycap to handle their luggage. Confident and self-assured, Hallie wondered if this was the face he showed to everyone except her. His presence, the image he projected, she thought, could easily look like arrogance. When they checked into the hotel the desk clerk told them their babysitter had been arranged.

Hallie was puzzled. "What is she talking about?" she asked as they followed the bellman to the elevator.

"I assumed you'd want to hear my talk tomorrow, so I asked them to arrange a sitter. She'll be here the whole day, so we can get away and see some of the city."

"But who is she?"

"I don't know. Just someone the hotel uses. I'm sure they do it all the time."

"Roger, we can't leave Eric with a stranger. I'll bring him with me to the talk. He'll be fine."

Roger waited until the luggage was in the room and the bellman left before he started in. "No you will not bring him to my talk. What if he misbehaves? Don't be stupid."

"Please understand," Hallie said, "I want to hear your presentation. I really do. But I would be worried sick about leaving Eric with a stranger in a city we know nothing about."

"Ah, the little hick comes through again. You are the most selfish woman, Hallie. I can't imagine what I *ever* saw in you. But, have it your way. Cling to the baby and I'll give my speech without you." He turned away from her and walked out the door.

All evening Hallie sat upright in bed and flipped through the television channels, wondering where Roger had gone and afraid to imagine what he'd be like when he came back. She was hungry and tired. What had Roger thought she was supposed to do for dinner? It was almost midnight when she heard the door open. Without acknowledging her he turned on all the lights and went to the closet where she'd hung their clothes. With slow deliberation, he took one of her blouses off its hanger and ripped it apart. Then he shredded the lining in her suit jacket; next he started on her slacks and sweaters and even her underwear.

Hallie ran for the closet and tried to grab her things before he managed to get everything. He pushed her away but she managed to grab one dress, which she hid under her pillow. The whole terrifying event was carried out in silence. She was afraid to say anything or even plead for him to stop. When he was done, Roger sat on the edge of bed and took off his shoes.

From a safe distance across the room, Hallie said softly, "Why, Roger, why? This makes no sense. You've ruined everything I have for this trip."

"I'm just making sure you don't hear my talk tomorrow babe. See? I made it easy for you to do exactly what you wanted to do.

You can't leave the room because you have nothing to wear. So, it all worked out just as you wanted it."

Hallie spent the next three days in a red and white pinstriped dress and all the while, she felt guilty. It had been her irrational fear of a strange babysitter that had started everything. On their last evening in Chicago they attended a reception and she looked at all the other women in their sophisticated cocktail dresses and she knew the kind of woman Roger had wanted her to be on their trip. And she had ruined it. Roger was charming and the women were polite to her, but Hallie felt just like the dowdy little country girl Roger accused her of being. By the time their flight left the next morning, Hallie was almost sick with the throbbing pain in her head. She wasn't sure which was worse, the physical pain or the ache in her heart.

Getting to Work

What Can We Learn About the Cycle of Abuse?

We see that Hallie is mired in a situation in which she tries constantly to guess Roger's moods and then, either head off the conflict by placating him or figuring out a way to keep his anger to a "manageable" level. This is part of co-dependency in relationships. You can see that Hallie has "bought into" the belief that she has some control over his moods, and even worse, that she even *causes* much of his anguish and abusive behavior. As a result, Roger needs only "threaten" abuse through his words or body language to keep her in his control.

Trying to Manage—Or, "Coping" Can Make Hallie Ill

Most of Hallie's mental energy goes into "managing" Roger and anticipating the next event. Although she doesn't understand that this isn't normal, she does appreciate that the situation produces great stress and anxiety. In Hallie's case, the constant stress and anxiety lead to the physical symptoms of colitis, along with frequent tension headaches. The potential symptoms fall into a range of health complaints and may change over time. For example, some women may develop depression, which they try to alleviate by self-medicating with alcohol, drugs, heavy cigarette smoking, or overeating. (They may gravitate toward these substances unconsciously.) Until Hallie realizes that she has no control over Roger and his moods and behavior, she will continue her attempts to please him. And her physical and emotional stress will increase, maybe to the point of danger for her. We have already seen Hallie literally sick from stress.

Hallie's relief over her pregnancy is an important clue. It is all about Roger. Maybe he will be proud of her. Maybe if he gets what he wants, then he will be good to her. Although Hallie is not completely convinced that this is the right time for a pregnancy, she pushes aside her doubts, one more time, to please him. And pleased he is. Roger hears about the pregnancy and makes her feel special through his doting and loving behavior. These changes most certainly reinforce the idea that indeed, she has the power to change his moods. Unfortunately, Hallie does not realize that while Roger is happy about the baby, he knows she really does need him. She is in an extremely vulnerable position in relation to him. This is exactly what a man like Roger wants.

Roger's Attitudes Come Through

We can see other of Roger's personality traits, which do not necessarily directly affect Hallie. Look at the way in which Roger refers to a woman who is his professional equal. He doesn't like her so, therefore, she's a "loser." (We can see that Hallie winces at that kind of talk, but he doesn't care.) Men like Roger do not respect women with personal and professional power and self-assurance. They show overt disrespect because these women intimidate them. Roger knows that he cannot control or intimidate this woman so he puts her down the only way he can, and that's through calling her degrading names behind her back.

Roger easily dismisses a powerful woman and will include in his circle of attention only those women he can control through overt or covert behavior. By degrading this woman to Hallie, he is covertly sending Hallie the message that she had better stay submissive to him if she wants to keep him—and for now, he is sure she wants him.

Moving Forward

If women in abusive relationships would remove themselves as "victims" of their husbands and boyfriends they would find that the men lose their power. The question is how women can accomplish this. Fortunately, several ways exist to begin the process. Even though Hallie has not become alert and energized to her situation, some women do see the reality early on. If women sense abusive patterns in their partners are emerging and strengthening, they can:

- start keeping a secret journal of the abuse;
- secretly plan ahead and find a safe hiding place;
- pack up enough money and clothes for themselves and their children and keep these things hidden;
- begin confiding in a trustworthy person about the abusive relationship;
- ask that person to help with an escape plan;
- gather information about legal rights and the legal issues involved once they have left.

Leaving Before Things Get Worse

If you are in this situation, you must be certain you are willing to leave and not go back, no matter how much he begs. And many men will plead and cajole and make promises to change. When you are ready and you are sure you will go through with your plan, you will have some basic preparation in place, including your escape route and time. Then, at the appropriate time you will:

- let your trusted friend know what she/he can do to help;

- leave when your husband/mate is not home;

- know that he will try to get you to return either through playing the wounded, bewildered, helpless "little boy" or by threatening you with further harm to you and/or your children, getting custody of the children by proving that you're an unfit mother, and so forth.

These threats are just that, threats, and you must be ready to believe that you have as much power as he does. Remember that these threats to gain custody or declare you unfit and so forth, can wither away to nothing if you keep your journal–and pictures–that document the abuse. By confiding in another person you are laying groundwork for future legal action, including protecting your own position. Hallie is not ready for these steps yet, but perhaps one day she will be.

Roger Leaves More Clues

During Hallie's pregnancy someone had to take care of her. Roger decided to do it himself, which on the surface could be seen as a sign of his devotion. However, Roger is motivated by his need to keep her isolated and have her all to himself. What would happen if other family gathered around Hallie to support her? Roger could not risk having family around because that might divert Hallie's attention from him. In addition, he could not take the chance that other family members would detect his abusive ways.

Hallie and Roger grow closer after Eric's birth, at least this is how Hallie sees it. And when the perception of a strengthened bond is real, that is how it should be. However, with a controlling man like Roger, there's more than meets the eye behind his joy. Now, he has a family who truly needs him and having a baby certainly makes Hallie more dependent on him.

Roger makes the decision to move to another apartment without consulting Hallie–another example of the lack of respect he has for her and how much he believes he has the right to control her.

Hallie still fails to see—or at least truly face—that Roger controls her in every way, even through his supposed "kindness." Oh, he puts on a show all right. He takes her shopping and picks out her clothes and makes her feel that he's motivated by love. He would say he encourages her to invite women friends to the house, but the fact is, he is giving her permission. Hallie sees this as a change in Roger, when in reality it is still control, but with a different twist. He likes to appear kinder and more appreciative, but this is a distortion.

If Roger truly respected and loved Hallie in a healthy way and viewed her as an independent person, he would be content to leave Hallie alone to choose her own clothes, for example. He would not be involved in decisions about whom she invited to lunch and when she scheduled such social events. Equally important, Roger would make sure that Hallie wanted his help instead of forcing it on her. However, she has become so fearful of his unpredictable abuse that she is happy to have the change, even if it is controlling.

Those Nagging Thoughts

When she has the two women over for lunch, Hallie notices the looks they exchange when she talks about Roger, explains her decision to not work outside the home, and even laughs about Roger's attentiveness during her pregnancy. We can see that even after they leave she continues to question what they were thinking.

It is possible this was Hallie's way of *projecting* her own questions and fears outside herself and onto these women. This is a common response. By projecting her fears onto their concerned looks, she could see things more clearly. If you have been in a situation like Hallie's, you may have noticed that you are conscious of the way others react to you. During an encounter with someone we may sense that their words or behavior give us a message, one that is congruent with a fear about ourselves, especially if we feel uncomfortable in their presence.

It is also possible that most people know about Roger's moodiness, but they have not retreated into denial about it as Hallie has chosen to do. Most of the time people know more than we think they do, especially when abusive behavior is going on. Most of the time these individuals do wonder why the woman is choosing to stay in it.

The Storm Returns

It has been almost a year since Roger has shown full-blown rage. Hallie thought these outbursts might be over, but this is never a likely development. Roger experiences tension at work, and we can't say if this is tension he creates or if he truly is under pressure to perform at higher levels. It doesn't matter because men like Roger will begin to cycle through the stages of aggressive behavior and use their partners and perhaps even children as an outlet for their anxiety and tension. As the cycle progresses, Roger becomes paranoid again and hears anything Hallie says as criticism.

The cycle of violence can have long interludes between the various stages. In Roger's case, he first controls through kindness, then takes on the helpless little boy stage persona, and then cycles into an aggressive stage. Unless the man is willing to get therapeutic help and perhaps go on medication to control his outbursts, we can be certain that the aggressive outbursts will come again. It may be months or years, but the cycle will be complete.

Roger's Projections

When Roger is at a breaking point in the cycle, when his little boy behavior has run its course, he begins lecturing Hallie, berating her and calling her names. In Hallie's case, Roger is able to push the buttons where Hallie has insecurities. He calls her a little "hick," which is one of Hallie's fears. Maybe, she thinks, she *is* unsophisticated and needs his counsel to fit into the "important" world to which he has introduced her. Further, she believes he is rising in this world and if she doesn't fit she could hold him back. All this is ridiculous, of course, but remember that Hallie has been isolated for several years now.

Roger finally lashes out physically and leaves bruises that will show, so he orders her to cover up for him by staying inside until the bruises are gone. Once again he blames her for his behavior. Look at the words he uses to describe Hallie and degrade her–stupid, insensitive, ungrateful, helpless, hick, and so forth. Those words could apply to him; in all likelihood, a part of Roger fears he is all of these and more, so he obsessively works to prove that part wrong. Once again we may be seeing projection–Roger is projecting onto Hallie what he fears and knows *he* may be. Perhaps that is why he is a workaholic. It is his way of trying to prove that part of himself wrong.

The next time someone verbally abuses you, listen closely to the words they use, and then see how closely those words apply to them. Just because Hallie herself may have self-doubts and vulnerabilities that Roger's words stir up, this does not mean that Roger himself isn't walking around with similar insecurities, despite his great show of self-importance.

Caught Off Guard

Hallie is not completely aware that she has schemed and planned in order to keep Roger on an even keel. But the disastrous Chicago trip shows us that she can't plan everything and she will be caught off guard. We once again see that Roger does not respect Hallie enough to ask her opinion about having a babysitter for Eric, especially a sitter they do not know. When Hallie refuses to go along with his plan, he feels threatened. Because he is emotionally immature, he is unable to empathize with her and understand why she will not leave Eric alone with a stranger. Roger can think only of his immediate desires.

Roger has set up Hallie for a fall. She cannot win. If she goes with Roger and leaves Eric alone, she will constantly worry about Eric. And Roger sees her refusal to do this as a slap against him.

Again he thinks only of himself, and in a perverted way, he rips all her clothes as a way to make sure that she will go against him. Unable to change her mind, she "proves" she is his enemy. Once she becomes an identified enemy, he must control her through abuse. It's a sick way of thinking but it has worked so long that he has no reason to think otherwise.

When Roger tears up her clothes he sends a message that he can do the same to her and Eric. Destroying objects is a powerful way of keeping someone under control through fear. Hallie is so completely brainwashed and afraid by now that she focuses solely on survival for Eric and herself.

Hallie is deep in this "dance" with Roger. For years, she has placated him by down playing her own and Eric's needs, so when she finally stands up to him, even for Eric's sake, she places herself and Eric in a dangerous position.

What is it that Hallie has not yet learned? She doesn't yet grasp the whole picture. If she did, she'd see that Roger is too narcissistic to empathize and understand her view of any situation. It is all about him. It's too difficult for Hallie to see the dynamics because she is too close to the situation. Add to this the fact that she is a product of lifelong brainwashing that gives her the idea that she has no rights in this marriage and it is her duty to "stand by her man" no matter the price. Hallie is enmeshed in the victim role, too frightened to see that Roger is totally responsible for his own behavior. Hallie is still controlled not only by her husband, but also by her entrenched belief that she must figure out Roger.

4

Hallie returned from Chicago determined to show Roger the attention and respect he deserved. She even wrote him a note apologizing for being over-protective of Eric. It *was* all her fault that the trip turned out to be less fun than they'd imagined. She left the note in his briefcase and knew he had read it when he came home that evening with a smile on his face. At dinner he told her he was glad she was learning to understand him. "I so hate those scenes Hallie," he said. "It's much better when you just go along with me without all your fussing. I always have your and Eric's best interests at heart."

"I know Roger. I'm trying to learn what you expect." Hallie felt her belly tighten as she said the words. Somehow, this wasn't right. She felt like she was living with a stranger, and the reality of a lifelong partnership with another person was so unlike the fantasies she'd had as a child. Maybe that was her problem, she thought. She spent too much time clinging to childhood dreams.

Roger was tender and loving with her that night, leaving Hallie to wish all his lovemaking could be so romantic and gentle. Hallie hated to think about the way he'd been when they were trying to conceive Eric. Sometimes it seemed she had no choice but to have sex with Roger and during those months sex was quick; when Roger was done, he turned his back to her. She began to dread hearing him come to bed.

Overall, though, Roger seemed easier to be around. Hallie believed Roger's mood was getting better and better because two of his papers were accepted for publication and his book manuscript was coming along. He worked late most nights and hurried out the door in the morning with a travel mug filled with coffee.

With his success came requests to present papers at conferences, and Hallie found herself looking forward to his trips away. Although she felt lonely at times, Hallie also felt relief when she heard the front door close in the morning. They'd made it through another 24 hours without an incident, she'd think, always hopeful that their worst days were behind them.

Hallie grew to enjoy her quiet days with Eric more than the hours Roger was at home. Sort of a secret life, Hallie thought. She wondered if other women felt safer home alone than when their husbands were around. Each weekday morning, Hallie watched from the window and when she saw Roger's car pull away, she curled up on their overstuffed couch with Eric on her lap and watched the morning shows and then the women's talk shows on television. She paid close attention to marriage counselors and psychologists, always looking for ways she could make her life with Roger better.

One morning, Hallie heard a psychiatrist talk about the challenges of being married to what she called a "difficult" man. The description of the kind of man the doctor talked about sounded much like Roger, and Hallie felt encouraged to learn she wasn't the only woman with a moody, temperamental husband. But, as the program continued it was clear that wasn't exactly true. The therapist suggested challenging the so-called difficult man's bravado and drawing a line that he couldn't cross. She even talked about teasing the bad-tempered man. Hallie couldn't imagine standing up to Roger when he called her stupid or ungrateful. And sadly, it was out of the question to tease Roger. He barely had a sense of humor about the world in general, let alone about himself in particular. Tears filled Hallie's eyes when she realized she was too afraid of Roger to tease him or challenge him when he spoke harshly to her. She had to find a different way to heal all that hurt inside her husband.

Just after Eric's first birthday Roger came home and picked up Hallie and swung her around. He was ecstatic over his great news. He'd been offered a job as head of the neuroradiology department at a small hospital. They would be moving to a city in a neighboring state. "I can finally run my own show. I don't have to answer to that clown anymore. He's such a loser—and that wife of his. What a competitive bitch."

Hallie had long since given up hope that he'd change his mind about Sue, the woman Roger almost always referred to as a bitch. As far as Hallie could see Sue spent most of her time trying to see that disadvantaged women in the community had prenatal care. She also lent her name to a new organization in town that was working to establish a women's shelter. Hallie wanted to argue, to defend Sue, but she pushed those issues aside and instead asked Roger about when they would move. She was excited, too. Hallie was glad for a change. Maybe in a new hospital, she and Roger would make more friends and now that he was going to head a department perhaps they could buy a house. It felt good to have new dreams and a fresh start.

* * * *

Hallie bounced Eric on her lap as Roger rose to introduce his family. "We're looking forward to becoming active in the church and the wider community here," Roger said, "just as we were in our former home." Roger looked relaxed and happy as he glanced around at the congregation.

Despite the beauty of the church itself, including the blue and red stain glass windows and the intricate carving on the altar, Hallie still had a difficult time adjusting to being a Catholic. She'd been raised in the Baptist church but before Eric was born Roger had insisted she convert. Hallie couldn't figure out why. He hadn't talked much about the religion of his childhood, yet as soon as Eric was born, Roger had told her they were going to church that Sunday morning. After the mass, he'd taken her by the hand and introduced her to the smiling young priest. "We're so happy you'll be coming to our catechism classes, Hallie. Your husband told me you were so eager to become part of our community."

Roger squeezed her hand so Hallie just nodded and said she had enjoyed the mass. As they walked home with Eric happily bouncing around in the carrier on Roger's back, he'd told her he'd made the arrangements for her to begin morning religion classes. "They have a babysitter there, so you won't have to fret about Eric. It will be good for Eric to be around some other babies." Hallie had thought the same thing, but when she'd mentioned it to Roger he had accused her of being lazy and not wanting to take care of her own child.

Despite what he'd told this new priest, Roger had not been particularly active in the church, even after Hallie had completed her classes and was officially a Catholic. But now that they were settled in their new city, Roger apparently planned to change all that. This was news to Hallie and on the way home from mass Hallie asked Roger if he intended to join the men's group in their new church. But he snorted and said, "Of course not. They're just a bunch of guys who do maintenance jobs around the place. I'd never hang around with them. I offered to help with parish growth and planning for the future. That's where they need someone like me."

Hallie had to put her hand over her mouth to keep from making a remark about the maintenance jobs in their new house that Roger would neither do himself nor hire someone else to do for them. Meanwhile, she spent her days scraping old wallpaper off the walls of their bedroom, a room that flooded with light each morning. It was the one thing that made Hallie happy they'd bought the house, despite the work ahead.

She told no one, however, that Roger had picked the house by himself on a visit to the new city. He'd told her he'd bought the house after he came home. "You'll love it," he'd said. "It needs work, but we can do it—or, on my new salary, I'll hire a contractor." Hallie had yet to see Roger lift a finger to help and when she'd asked about a contractor he'd thrown back one of his remarks about how ungrateful she was. "You seem to think we're made of money. It won't kill you to get your hands dirty."

Hallie didn't know if they were made of money or not because she never saw the checkbook. Roger gave her grocery money and she asked him for money if she needed clothes for Eric or herself. Roger chose their doctors and told her when to make appointments, just as he told her when they were going to go out to dinner or rent a movie. Usually, he arranged to go shopping with her and if he was in a particularly good mood, he bought her more new clothes than she expected or sometimes even wanted. Roger joked with the sales clerks and bragged about his beautiful wife. But Hallie had grown weary of the way he talked to her in public and then, once they were home, so often turned cold and called her ungrateful.

Still, Hallie had reason to hope. As they settled into their new home, Roger seemed happier than Hallie had ever seen him. Eric was growing into a beautiful toddler and on Sunday mornings Roger proudly carried him to the daycare room in the church and glowed when people hovered around and admired the baby. Hallie joined the women's group at the church and invited a couple of women over for coffee to talk about a holiday bazaar they were planning for the church. She also became acquainted with a neighbor. Ginger, a lively young woman with a baby boy just Eric's age, was taking some time off from her teaching job. She welcomed the company of another woman, and for Hallie's part, Ginger was like spring air, fresh and sweet.

"I've so wanted a new friend," Hallie said one morning as they sat with coffee and the cinnamon rolls Ginger had brought with her.

"That makes two of us," Ginger said. "Being a mom is great and all that. Don't get me wrong. But I get tired of picture books and Sesame Street. I need adults. Bob is great, but women friends are nice, too"

"Tell me about Bob," Hallie said. "Have you been married a long time?"

"Actually no," Ginger said. "We lived together for years and decided to get married after the baby was born."

"Really?" Hallie was surprised. Roger would have something to say about that, she thought. But then again, he wouldn't know, because she wouldn't tell him.

"Does that shock you?"

"No, no, Ginger. I was just thinking about how strictly Roger and I were raised—I was a Baptist, and he was raised as a Catholic. I guess we just never made it into the modern world in some ways."

Ginger just shrugged and went on to talk about Bob, a man she called the love of her life and even more impressive to Hallie, her best friend. After she left, Hallie indulged in fantasies about what it would be like to have a husband who was truly a friend. By the time Roger came home that evening, Hallie had figured out ways to talk with Roger like two adults. She'd tell him about her day. She'd ask for his advice about the remodeling work. She'd ask him about the interns and residents he supervised. They'd talk, really talk.

That night Roger asked her to bring his dinner into his study. "I have to proofread a paper tonight. It has to go out first thing in the morning. Just my luck, I have one of dumbest secretaries in the whole place."

"I could help you proofread the paper after dinner," Hallie said. "Let's just relax and enjoy our meal."

"Relax. Right. I just finished telling you how much I have to do tonight and the first thing you do is tell me to relax."

"Look Roger, I only meant that I could help you." Hallie was surprised at her tone of voice. She sounded almost angry. She could feel her heart pounding.

"Get out, Hallie. I don't have time for your whining."

"I'm not whining. Don't tell me I am, Roger."

Roger lunged at her and raised his hand in the air. Hallie felt herself flinch, but he stopped himself before he struck a blow. Instead, he took her arm and pulled her to the kitchen. "My dinner, Hallie. In the office."

Hallie fixed his plate. She inhaled deeply and exhaled slowly. She wouldn't give up. "This was a bad evening," she muttered to herself as she dished a ladle of stew over the bed of noodles. "I made a mistake. I should have read the signals. Another night. I'll try another night. He didn't hit me." Hallie hated to be grateful for that, but she was.

* * * *

One afternoon Ginger stopped by and Hallie invited her in. She was making her own pasta sauce and the smell of garlic and tomatoes filled the kitchen.

"Wow," Ginger said, "you're good. Homemade pasta sauce."

"It's one of Roger's mother's recipes. I make it for him once or twice a month."

"Lucky guy. Keep quiet about that around Bob. He'd be jealous. We end up with Chinese take-out or burgers—or chicken on the grill in the summer when we want to stay outside all the time."

"That sounds like fun to me." She and Roger had a barbecue once. They'd entertained the planning committee at their new church and their families. The two parish priests had come, too. Roger had helped her set out the bowls of potato salad and chips and the fruit plate she'd spent a couple of hours preparing. Hallie had felt great in a sundress that Roger had given her for her birthday the summer after they were married.

Hallie had thought the barbecue was a big hit. Roger had seemed almost jovial and although he usually hated smoking, he had accepted a cigar from one of the men and puffed on it as if it was something he did every day. He'd been quiet after everyone left, but Hallie hesitated to ask if anything was wrong. She assumed he was tired and didn't care to talk. Later, when he'd come to bed, he turned to her and said, "All in all it was good day. I think those people like us well enough. But later this week, I'm taking you shopping and getting you a new dress. I had no idea you still had that ugly dress I bought you."

"I felt good in it. Two of the women admired it. You never said it was ugly—you always liked it."

"Well, times change. I can make a real name for myself in this city and I want my family looking good. That dress looks terrible on you.

"Okay, I'll put it in the pile of things I'm saving for the church holiday bazaar." Hallie turned to go to sleep, disappointed that she'd done something to mar their good day. Still, she'd only worn the dress because he'd given it to her.

"Hallie, Hallie—earth to Hallie. You're a million miles away."

"Oh sorry, Ginger. I was just thinking about a barbecue we had when we first moved to the neighborhood."

"Hey, why don't you and Roger come to our house for dinner sometime. I can make pasta and a salad—you can bring your sauce."

"Well, I-I-I'm not sure when, you know, when we c-c-could…" Hallie stuttered and stumbled as she tried to think of a reason they couldn't come.

"Hallie, it's okay," Ginger said. "You look pale. I'm sorry if I made you uncomfortable. We can talk about it another time."

"Oh, it's just that Roger likes me to check everything with him," Hallie said quickly. "He works late at the hospital so often that I never make plans without talking with him."

Ginger nodded as if she understood, but Hallie couldn't help but notice the worry in her eyes.

* * * *

"One of the neighbors asked if we could come for dinner some evening. I said I'd check with you." Eric was in bed and they were having a late dinner alone.

"Who? Which neighbors?"

"Ginger and Bob—two doors down. Ginger seems awfully nice. Their baby is just a little younger than Eric."

"No. I don't want to get tight with the neighbors."

"But I thought you wanted to become part of the community and all that…"

"Let me handle it. I know the people we should get close to. It isn't good to be cozy with neighbors. Take my word for it."

Hallie tried to figure out how she'd explain this to Ginger without losing her friendship. She needed a friend, even if she couldn't talk to her about Roger.

"I know the people we need to meet. Do you understand me?"

"Not exactly Roger," she said. "In any case, I would like to have some couple friends."

Roger's face softened. "I know. I'm sorry I've been so preoccupied. But you can't make friends with just anyone. I have a respected position in this town and I don't know anything about Ginger and Bob."

Hallie decided to tease just a little. "That's why I wanted to have dinner with them. Isn't that how you do find out about someone? Anyway, Ginger says Bob manages a music store—

he's been in the music business one way or another all his life. He sounds like fun."

"She's telling you only what she wants you to know Hallie. Trust me. I'll find us some friends." As an afterthought, he said, "And they won't manage dinky little stores for a living. You have no judgment, babe."

The next day Ginger called and the two women took the toddlers to the park. As hard as it was, Hallie decided to tell the truth, or at least part of it. "I asked Roger about your invitation," she said, "but he's so focused on his job and his book manuscript right now that he said we just can't make social plans."

"No problem," Ginger said. Her voice was warm, making Hallie glad she'd said something.

"I guess Bob is more laid back about things, huh?"

"Oh sure. He's an easy going type."

"Roger seems to feel so much pressure all the time–I guess you'd call him a Type A personality." Hallie tried to keep her voice light, but she was ashamed that she thought she needed to think up excuses for her husband.

When they walked home, they stopped in front of Ginger's house and continued chatting. From the corner of her eye, Hallie saw Roger's car pull into their driveway. Her heart started to beat hard and she felt a familiar fluttery nervous feeling in her stomach.

"Hallie? What is it? You look like you've seen a ghost."

"Oh nothing. I need to go though. I have to start dinner. Roger's home early."

"Okay. I'll see you later then. Or, I could walk with you and meet him. How about that?"

"Uh, not today. Another time." Hallie hurried down the sidewalk and met Roger just as he was going up to the side door.

"Who was that?"

"Ginger. The woman I was telling you about."

"I thought we agreed not to see them."

"We agreed that we wouldn't socialize as a couple with them."

Hallie felt the acid in her throat. This was going to be bad. She could tell. "I want to keep her as a friend."

"Well, aren't you the fancy lady now," Roger said as he followed her into the house. "I work all day and instead of doing your work in our home you go off with some woman with nothing better to do than waste time."

"We were at the park with the babies Roger. Please. Both of us work hard. We're mothers at home. That counts for something."

"Oh, you *poor* thing. You have so much to do." Roger threw down his jacket and headed into his office. "Let me know when dinner's ready."

Hallie tried to stop her hands from shaking as she set the table and took warm bread from the oven. She tucked Eric in the highchair and called Roger. When he came to the table he ate in silence. But over coffee he started to talk and within seconds he had tears in his eyes.

"Roger, what is it?" When she saw the tears, her fear melted. Roger didn't look angry. He looked hurt.

"Oh Hallie. I need you so much. You don't have any idea how much. I'm under so much pressure and what keeps me going is the thought of you and Eric here in this house. That's what I work for all day. You and Eric, no one else. Promise me you'll never leave me—never."

Hallie saw the tension and fatigue in his eyes. "Oh Roger, I wouldn't leave you. Having a woman friend—just a neighbor—doesn't have anything to do with you or my job here." She reached out and covered his hand with her own.

Eric started to fuss in his highchair and Hallie turned to tend to him. But Roger held her hand and pushed it down hard on the table when she tried to move.

"I need to tend to Eric. What are you doing?"

"Everything else comes first. Is that the way it is? Some bitch named Ginger. And now Eric. My, my you've had a busy day."

"That's not how it is, Roger. You are always first. How can I make you understand that?"

Eric was screaming now, trying to climb out of a highchair he was rapidly outgrowing anyway. "Please Roger…"

"Okay, babe. We can finish this later. I'll see you later in the *bedroom*." Roger gave her a seductive look and loosened his grip on her hand. Hallie almost sighed out loud. She'd have to have sex with him, she thought, just so he'd know he came first. Hallie wished he'd stay in his office and work on his paper until he fell asleep at his desk. But that wouldn't happen. It never happened that way.

Hallie put Eric on the floor and began clearing the dishes and cleaning up the kitchen. She let her thoughts drift to Ginger. What was she doing at this same moment? Hallie imagined Bob coming home with Chinese food and Ginger setting out plates while Bob picked up the baby. He probably asked about her day and they sat together at the table and talked back and forth. Maybe they snuggled on the couch and watched a movie or a favorite show together. Hallie wasn't sure what they did together in the evenings, but she was certain Ginger was not afraid of Bob; Hallie also guessed her new friend didn't need to have sex with her husband just to prove her love.

Hallie was deep in her fantasies about her new friend's life when she felt pressure on the small of her back as Roger pressed her into the sink and ran his hands up and down her hips. "Right here, right now babe," he said.

"What about Eric? He might see us." Hallie felt tears form in her eyes. She hated this helplessness and at that moment she hated Roger.

"He's right here playing with some blocks on the floor. He doesn't know what we're doing. Just stay still and he'll be fine."

Roger reached under her skirt and pulled down her panties and spread her legs with his hands. He said nothing as he thrust himself deep inside her. With her hips jammed against the counter, Hallie bit her lip to keep from crying out in pain. She was bound to have bruises on her pelvic bones from his roughness. Hallie turned to look for Eric, but Roger yanked her back by her hair and pulled her head up. "All mine," he whispered in her ear, "you're all mine."

Getting to Work

What Can We Learn About the Cycle of Abuse?

Hallie returns from Chicago determined to do whatever it takes to make her marriage work. This is a "mind" decision, however, and notice that "body" messages are telling her how dangerous her situation actually is. Her "belly tightens," but she refuses to pay attention. In abusive situations, important red flags always appear. Like Hallie, many women choose to ignore them, or at least they believe they are pushing the symptoms away.

We also see Roger cycle into a calmer, loving stage. Following Roger's huge explosion, we can see the short-term steps in the cycle:

- Hallie so easily takes the responsibility for Roger's rage. She has let him "off the hook," so there is no need for him to wrestle with his own internal critical messages.

- Roger can now become loving again because he has "let off steam" and calmed his own anxieties.

- Roger is more certain than ever that Hallie will stick by him and he will continue to have his "victim" to control and feed his narcissistic power hungry ego.

We have seen this cycle before, and we can view it metaphorically as a dance. Roger leads the way with his need to calm his insecurities, which Hallie now expects. She tries to meet that need with her reassurance, but also by going along and continuing to placate his moods. This dance has become the "norm," even though it is very dysfunctional. However, the situation feels familiar (even "normal") to Hallie because it is what she experienced growing up with an alcoholic father. Familiarity equals security, at least in her unconscious mind. Before she married, if anyone had asked Hallie if she would have put up with such abusive behavior, her answer would have been a determined no. She probably would have been shocked by the question. What she believes in her conscious mind can be very different from the messages that "live" in her unconscious mind. Make no mistake, those unconscious messages are driving her behaviors and decisions.

New Messages Seeping Through

Although she's isolated, Hallie relaxes when Roger leaves for work and she feels safe in her house with Eric. We see her listening to others talk about their relationships, but she notes that living with Roger is too scary for her to even try what other women in her perceived position have suggested to do. At first, she believes she's learning that other women face what she does and she's reassured. As she quickly learns, her first impression is deceptive because her situation is far more dangerous. It frightens her to think that Roger is not merely a "difficult" man.

Still, in the process of trying to save her marriage and understand Roger, Hallie looks at her situation more objectively. Watching TV programs about relationships is important, because she has some basis for comparison and she is gaining information in a safe, non-threatening way. Hard as it may be to accept, Hallie has been so focused on solving Roger's problems that she doesn't realize that she is being abused. She wants this marriage to work so badly that she has been living in a cloud of denial.

Where are the Role Models?

Hallie doesn't yet realize that Sue is a powerful role model. Given Hallie's background and her nursing profession, she would naturally admire a woman who is helping abused women and is working in the community on women's health issues. Of course Roger must insult Sue because her abilities and her power threaten him.

As we see, Roger announces that they are moving without consulting Hallie. Relocating is an important event in a couple's life and when healthy give and take exists, a couple makes this decision together. Roger sees Hallie as his property and since he "owns" her, she will go wherever and do whatever he says. He believes making these decisions is part of his duty, and Hallie does nothing to negate that belief. Roger also has a driving need for self-importance, so he grabs at a chance to "run his own show" at a new hospital. The fact is, it is likely Hallie would have happily gone along with Roger's desire to move.

We can see another example of "ownership" when Roger pressures Hallie to convert to Catholicism. (It could have been any religion, by the way. If she'd been Catholic, he would have been driven to get her to go to the Baptist–or Methodist or Lutheran–church.) Notice that he squeezes Hallie's hand when she meets the priest. He is sending the message to go along with him. Roger trained Hallie so well that he only has to use body language to control her. At this point, Hallie may not like it, but she still believes it is part of the "compromise" of marriage.

Hallie Becomes Annoyed

Hallie finally shows some irritation over the way Roger dictates the schedule and defines her job. To an outsider, it would seem as if Roger has defined her as his slave. We see this in the following ways:

- He dictates that she work on their house when he doesn't lift a finger or hire a contractor.

- He doles out money for necessities and makes her account for every penny. She has no checking account, no savings account of her own, and she knows nothing about their finances. This is one of the most powerful ways to control her.

- Making her financially dependent on him gives her the message that he can literally stop clothing and feeding her and Eric at any time.

Can Life Be Different?

When Ginger enters Hallie's life, she has a golden opportunity to observe the way a woman enjoys life when she takes care of herself and chooses a healthy partner. As she cautiously reaches out to Ginger, she imagines her new friend's life, which provides a contrast to her own. Over the long haul of Hallie's awakening, Ginger plays an important role. We see Roger pick up on this and he immediately berates her for "wasting" time with Ginger; in his distorted view of things, any friend of Hallie's would threaten his hold on her.

If it were not so dangerous and tragic, the Good Samaritan persona that Roger presents to the outside world and in the community and church would be laughable. In psychological terms, this persona is what we refer to as a *reaction formation*. Roger uses the adopted persona to cover up the dangerous, devastating side to his personality and is used as he tries to fool himself as well as outsiders. Hallie does see how ludicrous it is when Roger acts superior about doing maintenance in the church. He sees himself as too important, because after all, he's a leader.

Of course Hallie is confused. She lacks familiarity with personality structure, so she can't understand what he is up to. To Hallie, he seems like a split personality and she chooses to feel sorry for him. Roger is aware of his abusive ways, but he sees no reason to apologize because he believes it is his duty to control.

Sadly, most women in abusive relationships believe that if the abuser doesn't hit them, things must be getting better. Hallie doesn't yet understand that Roger doesn't have to hit her all the time, because he already has demonstrated that he is capable of physical brutality. She is under his control now, so he only needs to assume a threatening posture, send her an angry look, tighten his voice, laugh derisively, or destroy objects. The control is complete whether he hits her or not. But she considers it such a positive sign when his responses are only verbal that she sees this as a sign of hope that her life with Roger is coming together.

What Will People Think?

We have seen that Roger sees his family as the vehicle that defines who he is to the world, hence, he decides what Hallie should wear, for example. In psychological terms, Roger is far too enmeshed with Hallie and Eric; this fools Hallie because she can see the enmeshment as "proof" that Roger cares about them, even when the ways in which he shows this supposed love hurts them. Because she still believes he cares, she is willing to cover up for him, explain and justify his behavior, and protect his reputation.

Hallie never had an example of two healthy individuals who encourage each other in life and support their partner's chosen path. To her, family enmeshment seems like loyalty, even if it manifests in unpleasant ways. In this type of family structure Hallie will never be good enough for Roger because one of his main roles is being her judge and teacher. In order to hold on to his fragile sense of self, he must have that type of control over someone.

Hallie takes on the role of protecting Roger's reputation. Roger knows how to convince her to feel sorry for him, and she wants to keep him from harm. In a way, blowing the cover of helpful family man and rising professional would be harmful. She doesn't argue with the priest or tease Roger about helping with the remodeling work. She senses he is too fragile to hear the truth, even in a teasing way. Because she doesn't want to harm him, she finds a way to take on a protective role for herself. As long as she is his victim and his protector she unconsciously knows that he will stick around and make her world feel familiar to her. She can count on the fact that he will be unpredictable, full of rage, loving at times, and always ready to use her because that's what he needs to survive. Until she understands that her unconscious messages tell her to be a burden and someone's victim, she will not choose to change.

We see Roger again cycle into the "little boy" stage in which he is very needy. This appeals to Hallie because this is the only time she feels some control in their lives. She doesn't realize that this neediness is just another way of controlling her.

Sexual Control

Sexual control is often the most powerful way to abuse women. Roger becomes a perpetrator–a virtual rapist–when she's most vulnerable. Unfortunately, an abuser may coerce sex, as Roger does in the kitchen, and a woman goes along after some mild protest. Hallie hates this, but she doesn't see it as a form of rape, even though she admits that the sex was forced on her. This is another instance that triggers her speculation about Ginger's life.

When a woman is afraid to say no, what does that say about the relationship? Many women are raped by their husbands or mates. It may not take on the look of typical rape in all cases, but it is coerced sex no matter how you dissect it. These men are sending a clear message: you are mine and no one else will have you. The covert message is: I can make you do whatever I want. At this point, Roger has Hallie exactly where he wants her.

5

Roger picked at the chicken and pushed the steamed carrots around on his plate while Hallie mopped up the spilled milk and comforted Eric with soothing words. "It was just an accident, darling, no big deal." Despite her words, Eric's tears continued to roll down his cheeks as Roger sighed and smirked with disgust.

"Quit babying him, Hallie," Roger said. "Apparently, he's not old enough to hold a cup of milk without spilling it. From now on, I want him to eat in the kitchen before I come home."

"Roger!" Hallie was shocked and for once, she didn't try to hide her own disgust with his attitude. No matter how badly he treated her, Roger had always given his son love and affection. But Eric was three now, and Roger was growing increasingly impatient with him.

"We are entitled to have an adults-only dinner. Once he learns proper table manners he can eat with us."

"He spilled a cup of milk, for God's sake. It isn't about *manners*." Hallie finished wiping the table and went into the kitchen and tossed the dishcloth into the sink. Exasperated. Fed up. Rarely did Hallie allow herself these feelings. But more to the point, Roger's behavior wasn't normal. No matter how she tried to rationalize his behavior toward her, she couldn't let him hurt Eric. She had to find a way to keep Eric out of their problems.

Roger came into the kitchen as Hallie began rinsing the plates and soaking the pots and pans. He leaned against the counter, coffee mug in one hand and Eric perched on his hip. "I'm sorry, Hallie. I guess I'm expecting too much." His voice was soft and gentle. "Our big boy here just needs a little more time to be good dinner company, I guess." He kissed Eric's cheek.

Despite Roger's soft voice, it hurt Hallie to see Eric looking tense in Roger's arms. He was curling his blond hair around with his fingers and staring intently at her. He's afraid, Hallie thought. Eric wants to get down and come to me, but he's afraid. She wished Roger would go into his office and shut the door and leave them alone. Roger was trying to be pleasant now, but it felt false to Hallie, as if he were forcing himself to take on a pleasant voice. No telling what would come next. Since he wasn't yelling, she risked explaining herself. "I think having dinners together as a family is very important. I would like to have him eat with us, at least most of the time."

"I agree babe," Roger said, "and like I said, I'm sorry." He put Eric down and kissed Hallie's cheek. "I have some work to do." With that, he left the kitchen and went into his office.

Eric came to Hallie and hugged her leg. She didn't know what to make of Roger's quick attitude change. Perhaps his work with the church was helping a little. "So, let's clean up the table, Eric," she said, "and then I'll read you a story."

Later, when she was taking a hot bath, Hallie cried tears of relief. Roger actually apologized to her and tolerated her anger at him. They had not had a bad fight in over a month, but Hallie hadn't felt any better until tonight. For the first time in many months, the knot in Hallie's stomach loosened and when she took deep breaths, she felt the muscles in her face relax.

* * * *

Roger called at noon to remind her about her appointment. "I'll see you in front of the hospital at 2:00. Don't be late."

"I'll be there." Hallie hung up the phone and finished dressing Eric. She was going to Ginger's for a quick lunch and leaving Eric with her while she went to the doctor's office. Although Roger refused to get together with Ginger and her husband as a couple, he had backed off about her friendship with Ginger as long as it didn't spill over and interfere with his time at home. Roger usually arranged to have time off to drive her to routine appointments and they took Eric along. She didn't like that Roger insisted on being there during her appointments, but this time she was glad he'd be with her when they heard the results of her recent tests.

Her headaches had been going on for years and Hallie had learned to live with nearly constant indigestion and bouts of diarrhea alternating with constipation. But in the last year, her periods had become irregular and some months she bled heavily for well over a week. During her last checkup she told the doctor she wanted to get to the bottom of the problems rather than continuing to treat the symptoms. She didn't care much for the doctor and would have preferred one of the other partners in the practice, particularly one of the women, but Roger said Joe Park was the best. She was always stuck with whatever doctor Roger chose, and Hallie imagined that was probably typical of most doctor-husbands.

Although she could never mention it to anyone, she had noticed that Ginger not only seemed happier than Hallie ever had felt, she was healthier, too. There was something about Ginger's robust health that Hallie couldn't help but think highlighted her own lack of vitality. Since Roger had been relatively content since they'd moved, Hallie decided this might be a good time to address her own health concerns. She wanted to feel better and get back some of her old zest for life.

While some women worried about extra pounds, she had trouble keeping her weight up to normal. But Roger always said he liked her thin. "I don't want you fat like that cow Ginger," he said one day. That stung Hallie. Ginger was hardly a cow. She was strong and athletic and it hurt her to hear Roger talk about her friend that way, but she held her tongue. No sense fighting over the insults Roger liked to throw Ginger's way.

Roger had not arrived when the nurse called Hallie's name, so she went alone into Dr. Park's office, relieved to have a conference with him without Roger listening in.

"Good to see you Hallie," Joe Park said, "and you'll be happy to know I've got great news. Your blood studies are normal. Your GI series show no change."

"You're saying it's just all part of what you call irritable bowel syndrome."

"Right. Not much we can do about that. The usual medications. Millions of people with the same problem. And we'll set up an appointment with a Fred Perkins–the best ob/gyn man we have around here."

"But what is at the root of it? Why am I getting worse?" Hallie didn't want to see Fred Perkins. She'd met him once at a hospital reception and he seemed distracted and cold.

"We can't say for sure," Dr. Park said, "but my guess is that stress is probably the culprit. Not easy being a stay-at-home mom ya' know. But you can see Fred just to rule out anything serious"

"But I love being home with Eric." Hallie blurted her response. She would have tried to talk more about her confusion but Roger's knock on the door shut her down.

Dr. Park and Roger greeted each other like old friends. They chatted about the hospital and mutual acquaintances and by the time Roger settled into the chair next to Hallie, she began to wonder if Dr. Park would ever turn his attention back to her.

"Seems like what we have here is all about stress, Roger," Dr. Park said. "Like so many moms I see.

"That's what I thought," Roger said. "We'll just have to teach my girl to relax." He reached over and patted her hand. "Maybe it's time for a little vacation."

"But, I don't think this can possibly be about staying home with Eric," Hallie said. "Like I said, Dr. Park, I love my time with him."

"Well Hallie, the tests don't lie," Dr. Park said. "There isn't anything seriously wrong with you. That's great news. Many women have headaches. And people of both sexes have these digestive problems. We'll treat the symptoms, but you can help yourself with some stress management."

Roger leaned back in his chair and threw up his hands. "Joe, I have to take some blame here. You know I put in long hours. Being a doc's wife is no picnic."

"True. You have to think of that, too, Hallie." Dr. Park looked intently at her. Then he stood up and Roger followed his lead. "Roger is a rising star around here."

Apparently, Hallie thought, my appointment is over. At least Fred Perkins hadn't come up. She hoped she could make her own appointment with one of the women gynecologists she'd met at the hospital. But she couldn't shake her angry feelings toward Dr. Park and his empty assurances that she was fine. In fact, Hallie's stomach churned and a wave of nausea came over her. All the way home in the car her hands clenched the wheel as she thought of all the things she wished she had said to Dr. Park. But another voice came through and told her to grow up and cope with what was on her plate. By the time she pulled into Ginger's driveway, Hallie was trying to talk herself out of a headache. She wouldn't give in to it. She'd fix a great dinner and turn herself around. No more complaining.

Ginger was in the backyard with the boys. Eric had his shoes and socks off and was running around the grass. Hallie started to say that Roger didn't allow Eric to run around barefoot, but she stopped herself. She didn't see the harm in it. It was good to see him giggling and whooping it up with another child.

Ginger greeted her with her usual exuberance. "Eric is such a great kid," she said. "I love having him here. So, what's the word about you? I hope it's good news."

"Well, they tell me I'm fine–that all my symptoms are just stress."

"I see. Well, at least that's something you can work on, huh?"

"I suppose, but…"

"What?" Ginger looked genuinely concerned.

"They act like it's some mom-at-home syndrome."

"They? Who's they?"

"Oh, Roger and Dr. Park."

"Roger was there–at the doctor's office with you?"

"Sure. He always comes with me to appointments. One of the things that goes along with being married to a doctor."

"Really? I've never heard that," Ginger looked puzzled.

Hallie turned her attention to Eric. He ran toward her and begged to stay a little longer.

"Can you stay for coffee?" Ginger asked. "And how about some cake. You need some meat on your bones."

"Thanks. We can stay a little while. I'd love some coffee and cake."

Hallie watched the boys while Ginger fixed snacks and coffee. They settled at the picnic table on the patio.

"I have great news," Ginger said. "I'm pregnant. I just found out."

Hallie was surprised. Ginger had never said anything about wanting another child. "Why that's wonderful," she said. "I don't want to be nosy, but have you been wanting this to happen?"

Ginger threw her head back and laughed. "Well, to be honest, we didn't plan it at all. But, there's a saying about a baby being unplanned but not unwelcome. That about sums it up. Accidents happen and once we knew we were excited."

"How wonderful for you. You're lucky, too. Roger *hates* surprises. He wouldn't like that kind of news." Hallie regretted saying so much. But once the words were out she couldn't take them back. "We're still thinking about another child," she quickly added.

Ginger looked as if she wanted to say something, but had changed her mind.

Hallie decided to change the subject. Just thinking about Roger's reaction to an accidental pregnancy made her stomach flutter. "I'm thinking about calling my mom to see if I can arrange a visit. I haven't seen her in so long."

"That sounds nice—it's always good to get away and see family. We're thinking about going up to New England to see our folks this fall. We'll camp all the way."

"That sounds like fun. I always loved camping out." Then Hallie laughed out loud.

"What? What's so funny?"

"I was just thinking," Hallie said, "about the time Roger agreed to go camping. It was just after we found out I was pregnant with Eric. He borrowed a tent and some gear from another doctor and we took off to the mountains in North Carolina. It was fabulous— at least I thought so. But Roger hated every minute. He thought every mosquito in the state was headed his way."

"That bad, huh?" Ginger chuckled.

Hallie felt good to be able to tell an amusing story about Roger. Ginger had so many funny stories about her husband. She always told them with such affection in her voice. "By the end of the weekend, I knew that Roger and I wouldn't be camping out any time soon. But he did say he'd try it again when we could afford a camper. It was sleeping outside that did him in." Hallie laughed. She knew in her heart though that Roger had been so good-natured about the weekend because he was still so excited about her pregnancy. The story made her nostalgic for that Roger.

Hallie fixed steaks on the grill that night for her and Roger and a hot dog for Eric. She was happy after her visit with Ginger, who always had a positive effect on Hallie's mood. But Roger was quiet during dinner and Hallie couldn't draw him out. He went straight to his office and she soon heard the sound of the television. Hallie concluded he was tired and wanted to be alone. She gave Eric his bath and put him to bed. She walked past Roger's office toward the living room. Suddenly, his door flew open and before she knew what was happening, she felt his forearm wrap around her neck. She could breathe, but just barely. "Roger…"

"Do you know what I was thinking about while I was sitting alone in my office."

Hallie shook her head, unable to speak.

"Of course you don't know. You're a stupid ninny. An ungrateful bitch." He yanked at her neck harder.

"Telling a colleague of mine about how *stressed* you are. You…poor…little…thing. Such a hard life."

Hallie shook her head. "No…no…I didn't."

"Oh, a liar, too." Roger pushed her forward and into the kitchen and pinned her against the sink. "Well this is what I think of liars." He reared back and swung his arm out and slammed it into her back.

Hallie felt her body weave back and forth and she grabbed the sink to get her balance. "I am not a liar," she whispered. But Roger had already left the room.

There wouldn't be a mark on her, Hallie thought bitterly. She could call the police. She could report him. Isn't that what some women did? But she couldn't prove anything. Besides, there had to be a better way to get through to Roger. Nauseated and weak,

Hallie vomited up her dinner and took a handful of antacids. She swallowed two aspirin in hopes of stopping the building headache before it kept her up all night.

Hallie turned on the water in the shower and stepped in. She let the water cascade over her shoulders and pour down her back. It ached so from the blow. Hallie picked up the bar of soap, and as she lathered her body with it, she allowed herself the sarcastic thought that Roger even controlled the brand of soap they used. She didn't even like it, but Roger insisted she buy it because it was so cheap. She almost laughed out loud when an image of Roger checking the soap in a colleague's house came into her mind. If one of the other doctors used a different brand, then he'd want to change and use that one, too. He'd never admit it, but he was intensely concerned about these little things he associated with status.

Suddenly, the water turned hot, nearly scalding her. She scrambled to turn the water off, but Roger's arm reached out to grab her wrist. "Stop," she screamed, "the water is burning me."

"Oh, really?" He gripped her and pushed her under the stream. She struggled and slipped around on the wet floor.

Finally, Roger turned off the water, pulled back the curtain, and perched on the edge of the tub. Naked, covered with soap, and still stinging from the hot water, Hallie wrapped her arms around herself and huddled in the corner. "Please go away and let me finish my shower. Please."

"I thought I'd show you what real stress is. You studied psychology, didn't you? You didn't learn much, but you know that extreme heat and cold are stressful. You want to talk to Park about stress, I'll give you something to talk about."

"Roger, listen to me. I didn't…"

"Shut up, you slut, you bitch." Roger pulled her out of the tub and sat her on the edge. "Let's see how stressed your skin will feel when the soap dries. Give you something else to talk to Park about. Poor little Hallie."

Hallie put her face in her hands and cried. Roger stood over her and waited. The air in the bathroom seemed to close around her and waves of nausea rose. Just as Roger planned, the soap dried and her skin itched. Eventually, he tired of watching her and left the bathroom and slammed the door behind him. Hallie couldn't risk getting back in the shower, but she took a cool washcloth and wiped off the soap. She put on a nightgown, wrapped herself in a blanket, and curled up in the corner of the couch, discouraged to think about how many evenings she'd spent this way. Mentally exhausted, she fell asleep.

* * * *

"Hey sleepy head, wake up." Roger was gently stroking her cheek.

"What time is it?"

"Past our bedtime," he said.

Hallie sat up and looked into her husband's face. His eyes looked so kind, so loving. It made no sense. "Can we talk just a minute?" she asked.

"Sure."

He agreed as if talking to her were the most natural thing in the world. Hallie couldn't figure this out, no matter how hard she tried. "It is so important to me that you know that I did not say one word to Joe Park about stress. *He* told *me* that my symptoms resulted from stress. I *argued* with him. I love being home with Eric. It's insulting to hear him act like being a mother is responsible for all my health problems."

Roger held his head in his hands and rocked back and forth. He looked as if he might cry. "Oh Hallie. Why, why didn't you say something sooner?" His voice was anguished. "We'll find you another internist. Park's obviously an idiot."

"I tried to talk to you, Roger. I tried." Tears of frustration and anger welled in Hallie's eyes. Why did he always have to hurt her first and let her explain later?

"Let's not talk about it anymore. I made an appointment for you with Perkins. He can get you in next week."

Hallie started to protest. She didn't want to go to Perkins. "I'd rather go to Joy Feldman—all the women I know like her."

Roger started laughing as if what she'd said greatly amused him. "You have got to be kidding. Joy is an incompetent bitch–a real ball breaker. You'll go to her over my dead body."

"But... but... I don't like Perkins."

Roger gently put his hand over her mouth. "Do you think I would send you to someone I don't trust. I know him. He's good. Feldman is out of the question. Trust me on this."

Hallie sighed and felt her body go limp. Roger drew her against his chest and she was afraid to pull away. The next morning before he left for work, Roger said he had a surprise for her. "I want you to call your mother and arrange a visit. Call the office and tell Joan when you want to go and she'll make all your travel arrangements for you."

"Oh, Roger, I've been missing my mother. I'd love to visit. But I can make the arrangements. I don't want to bother your secretary with that."

"No trouble. Her job is to keep me happy." Roger laughed as if he'd made a joke.

Hallie's mother was thrilled that she'd be bringing Eric for a visit. "I'll arrange some time off and we can spend whole days just catching up," she said.

When Hallie hung up she called Roger's office and talked with Joan. Roger's secretary sounded a little annoyed and Hallie was about to apologize but thought better of it. Roger was always reminding her that she was an important doctor's wife and that made her important to people like Joan. Maybe he was right.

That afternoon when she and Ginger took the boys to the park Ginger remarked that she seemed excited.

"I sure am. I'm going to see my mother. We'll have such a good time. She's made quite a life for herself since she left my dad a couple of years ago. She's like a new person."

"They divorced late in life I take it."

"I don't usually talk about it, but my dad drank a lot. His alcoholism ruined any chance of a happy family. My mother took it for as long as she could–too long really."

Ginger looked sympathetic. "I've known people who lived with alcoholics and it can be rough all right."

"I always said I would never marry a man who drinks. Thank God Roger has no taste for it. I couldn't handle that."

Hallie had thought a lot about her mother's choices. Since she'd left Hallie's dad, Nina had blossomed into a radiant woman. She'd found a job as a receptionist, which suited the outgoing personality she'd developed. Or, Hallie wondered, had she always been like that but had been forced to hide her own light?

"What about your dad? Is he still alive?"

"He found himself a new woman who will take all his abuse," Hallie said. "I send him a note a couple of times a year, but I never hear back from him. I'm just glad my mother got out of it while she still has some good years left." Hallie hoped her mother still had some years. Not long after she'd left Hallie's dad, Nina had discovered a lump in her breast. Surgery and chemotherapy followed, and so far, she'd had no recurrence.

Hallie kept talking, but she noticed that Ginger didn't look at her, or comment on anything Hallie said about her parents. Hallie felt her shoulders tense and she was conscious of the aching spot in her back that had taken the full force of Roger's blow. An image of herself huddled in the shower flashed through her mind, too.

Hallie regretted ever saying anything about her parents and her father's drinking. It upset her to remember the way her father treated her mother, but even more, it upset her to face, even for a minute, that more often than she cared to acknowledge, Roger treated her the same way. Sometimes she was sure Ginger could see inside her and knew more about her life than Hallie wanted her to know.

That night, Hallie took some aspirin to relieve the nagging pain in her back. She had so many things going through her head. Talking about her mother made her think about her father and the way he looked when he drank. And Hallie thought about Ginger and it made her sad that her mother had never seemed as happy as Ginger, never looked as relaxed. Hallie hated to admit that she herself never looked as happy or relaxed either.

In the middle of the night, Hallie woke up in a cold sweat. The dream that roused her from a deep sleep was unpleasant, even frightening, but she couldn't recall what was in it. It was almost dawn before Hallie went back to sleep.

Getting to Work

What Can We Learn About the Cycle of Abuse?

We now see Hallie standing up to Roger for Eric's sake. She will not do this for herself—most likely because she still carries the message from childhood that she is not worthy enough to fight for. Why, she wonders, does Roger behave in such an infantile way about what is literally spilled milk? Overall, Roger manages to stay calm, but he sees Eric's behavior as defying him, rather than behavior and mishaps typical of three year olds. If he were working with a young child in his office he undoubtedly would understand that this is normal behavior. But situations with Eric are different, in part because they are too close and too personal for him and he can't remain objective.

Roger's reactions are related to his lack of real ego strength, which is why he takes trivial events so personally. If someone or something in his life is imperfect, he sees it as a personal slap. For Roger, people and events fall into two categories: for him and against him, black or white. Roger can't see the gray areas of life.

Roger is mired in narcissism. The world not only should focus on him, but his rage is justifiable because he believes he can live without having to be responsible for his behavior. Typical of individuals who see their own needs as paramount, the targets of their revenge are the people closest to them, in this case, Hallie and Eric. He rages at the people with whom he feels the safest, and the ones he is quite sure will not abandon him.

What About Eric?

Even though he's only three, Eric is tense around Roger and shows his fear through his body language. Up to this point, Hallie believes that Eric is for the most part unaffected by Roger's hostility, including his name-calling and the way he orders Hallie around. However, even very young infants pick up on the quality of the energy around them. They can sense tension in their caretakers. That may sound vague, but most of us have the capacity to sense mood changes. We know the difference between a warm, loving atmosphere and a cold, tense one. Indeed, although Hallie is in denial about this, the atmosphere in her home changes the minute Roger walks in the door, even when Roger is in a good mood. Eric senses the underlying fear and feels it himself. Even infants begin to form messages about whether they are in a safe world. Ideally, caretakers and parents take on the job of making sure these infants feel safe.

If children pick up on the message that their homes, and hence the world, is tension-filled, rather than exciting and safe, they respond and change their behavior in order to protect themselves. They could become unhealthy reckless risk takers or too frightened to try anything new. Likewise, they might feel the need to be perfect in everything they do, or too disillusioned to attempt to live up to their abilities.

The only thing Hallie is doing by keeping Eric in this atmosphere is providing him with a home and food. The negative lessons he's learning include:

- he must put up with whatever life gives him in order to be secure.

- his anxiety levels may rise and he'll find a release for them through rebellion of some kind, including, anger, depression, drug use, poor school marks, trouble with the law, mental instability, and so forth.

- treating someone abusively, especially a spouse, is acceptable.

Eric, like all children, and certainly like Hallie herself, will imitate the behaviors he sees in mom and dad. Because he is not learning to respect himself or others, and individuality is not encouraged or accepted, he may grow up and choose a mate who will do the same "dance" with him as he sees Hallie and Roger doing.

Roger's Public Face, Hallie's Private Symptoms

We see Roger going to the doctor with Hallie. In most cases we would see this as an indication that a spouse is being supportive and caring, but in Roger's case it is part of the web of control he continues to weave. Naturally, he wants to be sure that Hallie doesn't tell her doctor about his abusive behavior, and he does not want anyone, especially another man, to have more control over Hallie than he does. To Roger, seeing a woman doctor is out of the question because it undermines his need to degrade other women and convince Hallie that these professional women are not acceptable on any level.

Roger is jealous of anyone Hallie comes in contact with because he fears they will "show him up" in Hallie's eyes. Roger probably knows that an assertive woman would be far too self-assured to be fooled by him or to stay with him for long. This doctor, and other women like her would not be a player in the "dance" of abuse. So, Roger just has to put her down. Since he could never have such a woman, he has to tell himself she's worthless. On a more practical level, he probably realizes that she may pick up on Hallie's symptoms being related to some abusive trauma. In general, Roger is driven to degrade anyone Hallie likes, from her neighbor, Ginger, to a woman doctor, who Roger immediately labels a "ball breaker."

Roger also puts on the charm, so to speak, when he adopts a chummy, collegial attitude with the doctor and even takes some blame for Hallie's symptoms. This is a hollow display, however, and is, in essence, a man-to-man encounter in which Hallie is little more than an object to discuss.

Illness is All Too Common Among Abused Women

Hallie's physical symptoms are typical of the *battered woman syndrome*. I have heard women complain about the same problems over and over:

- headaches,
- depression,
- anxiety,
- indigestion, including diarrhea, constipation, colitis, and so forth,
- fatigue/exhaustion,
- substance abuse of all kinds, including smoking, alcohol abuse, overeating/obesity, prescription drug abuse, illegal drug use.

My clients say that their medical doctors are treating their myriad symptoms, but they have no knowledge about their home situation. Today, doctors are more aware of the battered woman syndrome, but unfortunately, many do not take the time to dig deeply enough to find it. Many women will not volunteer the information because they are ashamed and believe that they are to blame.

In Hallie's case, Roger has the doctors completely fooled. He shows them his professional, good-citizen side who wouldn't hurt anyone. In this atmosphere of camaraderie, they may never think to question each other's integrity. As a result, Hallie's doctor does not look further than *Roger* leads him; Hallie cannot convince him that something else is going on. She is dismissed and discounted–another message that Roger has total power over her life.

Economics and Abuse

Many individuals, including physicians and psychotherapists and even battered women, are surprised to learn that abusive behavior occurs just as often among those in the higher socioeconomic circumstances as among the poor and disadvantaged. In fact, some statistics indicate that the incidence is even higher among the middle and upper classes. Once and for all, we can dispel the myth that education and money prevent abuse.

In addition, the mates of more educated, influential, wealthier individuals appear to be more reluctant to ask for help than those of lower socioeconomic status. Several reasons are offered to explain this:

- Wealthier women fear no one will believe them because the more professional man often hides his abusive personality behind a sophisticated façade.

- Even if they are taken seriously, they fear no one will help them, because their abuser often has considerable power in the community.

- They are ashamed to tell anyone because often they are viewed as too intelligent to stay in such a situation.

Domestic violence, just like substance abuse and addictive behavior, has absolutely nothing to do with intelligence. Hallie is intelligent and educated. She is not unlike millions of women who are trying to live a normal life in spite of abuse. Rich or poor, abused women stay because they are trying to live out introjected powerful messages that they must stay and that they have no choice. In addition, a wealthy woman knows her life and her children's lives will change financially, often drastically, for the worse, if she leaves.

False Hopes and Empty Dreams

Hallie so desperately wants the loving family she never had that she's quick to believe it is possible for Roger to change. We see her crying with relief when they have an argument and Roger actually apologizes to her! Sadly, this represents a phase in the cycle of violence, the calm phase after the explosion or "letting off steam."

Notice, too, that when Hallie stands up to him, Roger backs down. Clearly, this does not always work, but remember that

Roger's greatest fear is that Hallie will abandon him. Her assertiveness kicks him into the "boyish" phase in which he wants to please her. This is similar to the way he would have tried to please his *mother*; after all, he had to be sweet and cute once in a while so that she would stay around.

This phase is not without inherent danger, because Roger's rage is unpredictable. He may go into the "fear of abandonment" phase or he may rage uncontrollably, also out of fear. Hallie has no way to predict it and by now she understands this.

In this chapter we also see Hallie getting in touch with other messages in her blueprint. For example, she has a positive childhood message that says: "I have what it takes to be strong." She learned this while growing up because she often had to be strong for herself and her mother during her father's drunken rages. In other words, it was a message learned under the duress of negative conditions, but it has the potential for positive application.

Note that getting acquainted with Ginger gives her a safe place to allow positive messages to come out. Ginger is a good role model to show her what being strong looks like and provides Hallie with a picture of herself as a strong woman. It is important that she have a "safe harbor" in the form of a safe person. She can be comfortable with Ginger, even if it is too scary to confide in her about the abusive conditions in her life. At least she is giving herself time and space to let down her defenses long enough to allow stronger messages to come through.

When Hallie slips and tells Ginger more about Roger than she consciously planned, she feels guilty about betraying his secrets. Of course, a part of Hallie desperately wants to tell someone; she wants to cry out for help. She then tells an amusing story about Roger to take the focus off his "bad" side. Hallie takes pleasure in this because she truly loves the caring, fun part of Roger. Because he shows her this side intermittently and randomly she is drawn even closer to him.

It may sound paradoxical, but *intermittent* positive reinforcement is much more powerful than constant, *steady* positive reinforcement. We tend to try to elicit positive reactions when we experience them only intermittently; hence, the powerful hold of someone being nice to us one minute and unpredictably nasty to us the next. Hallie keeps trying in order to receive that positive message, even if she fails much of the time.

Hallie's Confusion

It is a common misconception that alcohol or drug use is the cause of abusive behavior. However, the potential to be abusive is already there and the substance may escalate it, but it does not cause it. Hallie is naively relieved that Roger doesn't drink. But as Hallie talks about her parents she is beginning to realize some truths about her own situation. We do not yet know the content of Hallie's disturbing dream, but it is common for battered women to experience a recurring dream, or perhaps more accurately, a recurring nightmare.

If you are in this situation, it can be very powerful to look at your parents' history and see how your path resembles theirs. In her mother, Hallie now has a role model for healthier living, but only after she left Hallie's father. Her father serves as an example of the way abusers will go on to another victim when the one he is with no longer plays the game. This begins to show Hallie her deep-seeded fear of losing Roger if she stands up to him.

Unconsciously, we tend to choose partners who have characteristics similar to our parents. Familiarity equals security and security is one of our basic human needs. By telling Ginger her parents' story Hallie begins bringing to her conscious mind what she has kept in denial for so long. This is truly a first step in changing her life.

6

Hallie saw the stack of flyers sitting amidst piles of free newspapers and notices about upcoming community events. She picked one up and folded it in half and slipped it into her handbag before perusing the other papers and flyers on the table. She also took a notice about a newly-formed women's book group and another that announced a series of lectures at the university. Each lecture dealt with a different issue relevant to the community, from education to water quality. Hallie wished she could go to similar programs at home, and she'd so love to join a book group. She'd then come across a brochure for the community mental health center. Hallie held it in her hands, disturbed by the variety of feelings rushing to the surface. On one level, she desperately wished Roger would agree to see a therapist, but she was much too afraid to bring it up. She could hear his derisive, mocking response to that idea. On another level, Hallie realized she wanted nothing more than to *work* in such a place. She longed for the professional connections, the feeling of contributing to something greater than her own narrow life.

If she mentioned the idea to Roger, he would remind her about her important service work in the church, and even more significant, he would say, she was holding down the fort at home, which allowed him to work hard to make a major contribution in his field. He never tired of telling her about his latest triumph—the medical world was listening to what *he* had to say. Every paper accepted and every lecture he was invited to give proved that. As Roger saw it, Hallie mused, her *important* work was taking care of him so that he could be a big shot. That sounded disrespectful but Hallie had finally begun to wonder if Roger ever would change.

For several minutes, Hallie allowed herself to leave Roger behind and live in a different world, a fantasy life she drew for herself in vivid color. She imagined herself in an apartment, not necessarily in this town, but in one like it: medium size, a diverse population, prosperous enough to have a good public school for Eric. So, maybe she wasn't qualified to work in a community mental health center. Surely she could find a job in the local hospital, and when Eric was older she could take some classes, look into a master's degree. Hallie felt her heart beat faster as a vision of her life became clearer. She'd buy second hand furniture and repaint it, she'd put plants in every room, maybe she'd join the Y or a health club and swim, or she'd…

"Mommy, *Mommy.*" Eric tugged at her slacks, bringing her back to the moment.

Hallie took a couple quick breaths to bring herself back to the reality in front of her. "What sweetie?"

"Ice cream? Can I have ice cream?"

Hallie was about to say no. Roger didn't like Eric to eat ice cream in the middle of the afternoon. He frowned on most snack food and desserts altogether, except for the cookies and pastries he especially liked. Hallie laughed out loud as she said, "Yes, darling, yes. Let's have some ice cream. Two scoops each." She didn't have to worry what Roger thought. He was hundreds of miles away.

Her mother had needed to work that afternoon and she dropped Hallie and Eric off in the small downtown area. For the first time in what seemed like years, Hallie browsed in shops and walked along with Eric at a leisurely pace. She'd never once checked her watch or worried about dinner. Finally, she'd ended up in a bookstore-café, where Eric immediately pointed out the ice cream counter. Eric mulled over all his flavor choices for what seemed like hours. Hallie didn't care. Eric had a bright, eager expression she longed to see more often. Eventually, he chose double-chocolate fudge and a flavor that sounded odd to Hallie, cherry pie. But Eric was happy when they sat at a table by the window and licked their cones and chatted about what they saw outside.

Hallie was almost finished when she realized that she was eating ice cream without giving a thought to her supposedly bad stomach. The doctor had told her to avoid foods that upset her stomach, but that included just about everything. She and Eric had been with her mother for two full days and so far, she had eaten everything in sight. Hallie had a strong feeling that a couple of scoops of chocolate chip ice cream were not going to hurt her.

When they were done, they started down the street to the park to wait for her mother to pick them up. Being with her mother had started a chain of thoughts that traveled back and forth between past and present. While Nina had never been a beautiful woman, she looked so happy and serene it startled Hallie. Even living on a receptionist's salary, her mother managed to have a full life. She volunteered at the senior center and had joined a walking club. Nina called her tiny one-bedroom apartment her palace, which considering its size and hodge-podge of furniture struck Hallie as funny. Ironically, though, her mother meant it.

The mother Hallie knew during her childhood and teenage years had shown perpetual tension in deep lines around her mouth and eyes. One day, Hallie had heard a thud against the wall of her parents' bedroom and minutes later her mother had hurried out of the room and down the hall as she wiped blood from a cut on her mouth. Then there was the day her mother ended up with hideous purple bruises on her upper arm; Hallie could close her eyes and see her father dragging her mother across the kitchen. He had pushed her out the back door and locked her out. He wouldn't allow the kids to open the door and Hallie spent the afternoon bringing him cans of beer. The next day Nina had smiled brightly and said the *misunderstanding* was over.

Thank God, Hallie thought, Roger didn't drink. At least with Roger there was hope that he would–or could–change. Still, sometimes when she looked in the mirror, she saw a woman who looked older than most women still in their twenties. She saw a woman who lived with at least mild nausea most of the time. Then, too, it unnerved her when Nina kept asking how she was. "Are you sure you're okay? I hate to say this, dear, but you're so thin and pale. Have you seen a doctor?"

Hallie had tried to reassure her mother that she'd been to the doctor. Apparently, stress was the cause of everything, from headaches to constant digestive problems to heavy periods. The gynecologist had given her hormones to straighten out her periods, and now Hallie felt bloated and her headaches were worse. In a way though, she was glad to look even a little heavier. It made it easier to convince her mother she wasn't really so thin.

When they reached the park, Eric ran to the sandbox and Hallie settled on the park bench. She opened her handbag and looked at the brochure for A Path to Hope, an agency that helped women who were victims of domestic violence. A phone number was printed on the bottom. It wouldn't hurt to call, she thought. No one needed to know. But what would she say? Roger provided a good life for her and Eric. True, he was moody, unpredictable. Things were getting better, she thought. In her head, Hallie calculated the days that Roger came home reasonably content. Since their move Roger was generally happier most of the time. Of course, Roger rarely seemed truly happy, not in the lighthearted way that Ginger or her husband appeared to be. But as Hallie shifted around on the bench to find a more comfortable position, she hated the realization that her back still hurt from the heavy blow Roger had delivered a couple of weeks ago.

Hallie felt a surge of courage as she admitted that even if Roger's angry and violent outbursts came less often, they had escalated over the years. She thought back to spending her wedding night locked in the bathroom of the cabin in the woods. That was a far cry from forcing sex on her in the kitchen. *She would call that number*, she thought, *it couldn't hurt.*

✝ ✝ ✳ ✳

"Have you ever considered calling the police?"

"No, not really."

"Is there a reason that you have chosen not to involve the police?"

"Well…" Hallie took a minute to face the questions posed by the counselor. These were questions she had been avoiding for years. She was angry with herself for making the call in the first place. She hadn't thought it through before she impulsively picked up the phone and dialed the number while Nina was at the park with Eric. "For one thing, Roger is a prominent doctor in the area. It might ruin his career if the police were involved. Besides, if I did that…" She let her voice trail off.

"Do you think that would end your marriage? Are you afraid of that outcome?"

Hallie tried to find the words. Finally she blurted, "I'm afraid he'd have me committed to the psychiatric ward." It horrified her to think such a thing, but once she said the words, she could see that reality ahead just as clear as the water in the glass in front of her. Roger would convince his colleagues that she was unstable and he'd have her under psychiatric care. Besides, he'd already threatened to take Eric away. "He'd take our son and convince a court that I'm unfit."

"Have you talked to a lawyer?"

"No," Hallie said, "I don't have money of my own."

The crisis counselor listened patiently while Hallie told her about Roger and his mood swings. In a kind tone the woman had asked what she meant by mood swings. With her heart filled with shame, Hallie had told her that Roger had hit her, pushed her, torn up her clothes, and destroyed things in their house. She stopped short of telling the counselor that Roger had raped her or slammed her back so hard it still ached weeks later.

By the time she thanked the counselor and said goodbye she had made a commitment to call the legal aid agency when she got home. She would find out if an attorney would talk to her. She also agreed to read a couple of books about battered women. Hallie still winced at the term. She thought of battered women as poor women or women who walked around with black eyes and broken bones. Batterers were men like her father; batterers drank and became dangerous because alcohol changed their behavior. Her father had never brought flowers home or planned a cruise ship vacation, as Roger talked about just before she'd left.

Men who were true batterers didn't pamper their wives, did they? Roger might bring home a negligee or perfume when it wasn't even a holiday. At times, Hallie thought, Roger's behavior could be called indulgent. It was so difficult to sort out. But Hallie knew for certain that Roger's behavior didn't seem truly normal. Normal behavior did not need to be hidden. She remembered her mother putting layers of make-up over bruises; she remembered her own grandmother telling Nina that marriage was, as she put it, "no bed of roses." Hallie had said that to herself a million times, with, she realized, the same tone of resignation she'd heard in her grandmother's voice. Divorce, Grandma had always said, was not an option. That's what Roger said, too.

Hallie felt a headache coming on and she took some of the medication she'd brought with her "just in case." She couldn't go over and over this in her head anymore. She'd rather fantasize about a job and an apartment and a school for Eric. She wanted to go back to the café and sit across from Eric and eat ice cream. Hallie's headache subsided and she leaned back on her mother's couch and began to plan the furniture she would buy for her new apartment. The life she imagined was very pleasant.

* * * *

"Hallie. Hallie. Wake up, dear. Lunch time."

Hallie felt her mother's hand resting gently on her shoulder. "I must have fallen asleep. I'm sorry."

"No problem. You probably needed the rest."

"How was the park?"

Nina frowned ever so slightly, but said, "Okay. I'll talk to you about it later."

The three sat down at the table and ate peanut butter sandwiches. Eric happily hummed to himself and swung his legs back and forth. The sandwiches tasted good to Hallie, especially since her headache was gone. Hallie had noticed the inexpensive food in her mother's refrigerator and pantry. How often, she wondered, did her mother eat peanut butter sandwiches just to save a few dollars. She didn't know exactly how much money Roger made, but she was sure they had more than enough and could afford to make Nina's life a little more pleasant. Hallie wished she could send her mother a little money now and then, or buy her a new coat for the winter. She felt guilty thinking about a cruise next winter when her mother was scraping by.

After lunch, Nina used the influence only a grandmother could have to convince Eric that he needed a rest. "Even if you don't sleep sweetie," she said, "a rest will give you so much energy for the rest of the day." She led him into her bedroom and Hallie smiled when she heard Nina tell Eric he could rest on the big bed.

When Nina came back she poured them each a glass of iced tea. "There was a incident in the park, Hallie. I think you should know about it."

"My goodness, tell me."

"A little boy, no older than two, tried to take Eric's shovel and bucket and Eric pushed him and threatened to break his arm."

"Oh no." Hallie could barely breathe. She could actually feel pain in her own arm as she thought back to one of the ugly kitchen scenes. Roger had turned on her and yanked her arm back. Eric had seen it. "No, no. I just can't believe it."

Nina looked thoughtful and serious. "I pulled him away quickly. No harm was done. But it reminded me…" She stopped in mid-sentence and looked away.

"Of what? What did it remind you of?"

"It reminded me of Jimmy. He started acting that way and, well, you know what's happened."

Hallie thought about her older brother and his reputation as a fighter. Nina didn't like it, but her father had taken a certain pride that no one could push *his son* around. "Are you saying Jimmy bullied other kids when he was just four?"

"Uh huh. I'm afraid so. When I heard the tone in Eric's voice it took me back so many years."

"I haven't seen Jimmy in a long time. Marlene sends birthday cards and a gift for Eric at Christmas. I do the same for Cindy." Marlene had married Jimmy shortly after she found out she was pregnant with Cindy. Then they'd moved to Cincinnati to find better jobs. But for all practical purposes, Hallie barely knew her niece or her sister-in-law. In truth, she barely knew Jimmy. She'd always been a little afraid of him.

"Was…was Jimmy imitating Dad?"

"Of course, Hallie. He learned to be a bully from the best of them."

Hallie heard the bitterness in her mother's words. She leaned back in the kitchen chair and closed her eyes.

"You can close your eyes, Hallie, but that won't change anything."

Hallie's tears started slowly, but built into deep sobs. She covered her face with her hands. Nina moved her chair around the table and put her arm across Hallie's shoulders.

When Hallie had cried herself out, she went into the bathroom and washed her face with a cool cloth. When she came back out, she saw that her mother had moved into the living room and had set the pitcher of iced tea on the coffee table. Nina patted the seat of the couch and said, "Sit down and tell me what's going on."

Hallie settled on the couch next to her mother, but when she started talking, she found herself going on and on about Ginger and Bob. She told Nina about Ginger's big smile and hearty laugh. She told her about Ginger and Bob's evening walks around the neighborhood and the way they cooked outside and sat around and talked to each other. With a feeling of deep shame, she told her mother that Roger called Bob a loser because he wasn't ambitious and had time to waste having barbecues with his family. Hallie talked about Ginger's unexpected pregnancy and about the camping trip the couple planned. "She's the only friend I have and Roger calls her a cow and her husband a loser. Ginger doesn't say anything, but I know she's insulted that we don't invite them to our house or accept their invitations."

"It must be difficult to see such a happy couple." Nina's matter-of-fact voice lacked even a hint of judgment.

"It is. I have spent so many years believing that I just have to try harder. But it seems like Ginger doesn't have to try at all. I know that's not true. She must have to work on her marriage some, but they have fun. And I don't understand. Roger doesn't even drink, but the way he acts…"

Nina's expression turned from puzzled to angry. "I was *so* happy when you married Roger," she said. "A professional man with a good background, and thank the good Lord, a teetotaler. I thought you'd get away from the family and have a completely different life. How could we have been so fooled by a man?"

"Oh no, it isn't exactly like that." Hallie didn't want her mother to think Roger was a bad man. He was insecure. A part of him was a little boy. He needed to grow up. "He does provide for us so well."

"Hallie, you're so thin you look ill. Roger regularly insults your one friend, a neighbor you can see only during the day when he's gone. He even chose your *religion.* Now we can see that Eric is picking up his nasty, bullying ways. Don't you think I see what's happening?"

Hallie didn't know what to say. Her mother had never talked this way before.

"Promise me you'll think about what your grandmother and I went through. Promise me you won't believe there's no way out. That's what I believed–my marriage to your father felt like a stranglehold, not a relationship."

Despite her pain, Hallie let out a quick laugh. "I've never heard you use the word relationship before. We always used the word marriage, but we never talked about an actual relationship with a man."

Nina just shrugged and left the room to check on Eric. Alone with her thoughts, Hallie felt bombarded with information she had to process. She felt her chest tighten and another headache was starting. She went to her handbag and fished around for the bottle of medication.

"Another headache?"

"I'm afraid so." She swallowed the pills with a glass of water. "I know what we're talking about is important. But I need to think about it. I can't give up on Roger yet. I just can't."

Nina hurried over to her and hugged her. "I know, Hallie. You are determined to try everything. But I want you to know that if you decide to take Eric and leave him, I won't think you've failed."

* * * *

Roger was waiting when Hallie and Eric walked off the plane. Hallie saw that he was all smiles and held a red balloon with ERIC printed in big black letters. He hugged Hallie and scooped Eric up in his arms. "I've missed you both so much," he said, "and I've got knock-your-socks-off news."

Hallie wanted to believe in Roger's buoyant mood. No matter what doubts she had, she had decided she was going to be happy and pleasant, so she started by asking about the good news.

"I've been invited to speak at *two* international conferences, babe."

Hallie got caught up in the excitement as Roger described the conferences in Germany and Japan. He would travel alone and attend both conferences in one trip. Hallie felt a little flutter of excitement in her stomach and then immediately was ashamed because what she was excited about was being alone with Eric while Roger was away.

"And I've saved the best news for last. I've booked our cruise— a family cruise. Seven days, with stops in St. Thomas, Antigua, and St. Martin's, just to name three of the ports we'll see. There's childcare on the ship and you and I will have the time of our lives."

"Oh, Roger," Hallie whispered, "that sounds so wonderful. We *will* have the time of our lives."

Roger took them out to dinner and for once, didn't spend the evening in his office. He was tender with Hallie and helped her put Eric to bed. Later they made love and he told her how much he missed her. "This house is so empty when you're not in it." Just before he fell asleep, Roger said, "You know, maybe it's time to have another baby. I've been thinking about what Father said about family life during mass last Sunday."

Hallie's heart started to beat a little faster. She dreaded what Roger was going to say, but she had no choice but to listen. "What was that, Roger?"

"He said that bringing up a family was the true calling of a married couple. He talked about the team of husband and wife, mother and father. It made me realize what a good team we are, but I also was caught up short. I've been selfish."

Hallie was curious about what would come next.

"Before we were married we talked about having a big family. I know Eric isn't enough for you, or for me either. You're a good mother and each year, I become a better provider, so I want you to stop using birth control." Roger laughed when he added, "About time we were good Catholics anyway."

Roger gave Hallie one last hug before he rolled over to his side of the bed. Hallie's head was swimming. Roger would be leaving in six weeks for his conference and three weeks after that they'd be leaving on a cruise. She was surprised that he actually wanted to have another baby, especially since he acted like Eric was a nuisance, except when he wanted to put on a show of being so devoted to his son. On the flight home, Hallie had thought about her fantasy life in a small apartment with Eric. But as she headed back to her real life, tears flooded her eyes as she realized her fantasies were becoming all mixed up with the realities of her life. She longed to tell Roger she changed her mind, that another child wouldn't be right, at least now. She had a strong urge to shake his shoulder and talk to him, but in reality, she was afraid. All that sweetness could turn to rage in a matter of seconds. She couldn't risk it.

That night, Hallie dreamed that she was running down a dark hall and something was chasing her, but at first she couldn't see it. She ran faster and faster to get away from it and in the dream Hallie felt her heart pounding fast and hard. She turned her head and saw that whatever was chasing her had long blond hair, hideous hair that looked like a thick wig. Finally, Hallie hit a brick wall with a terrible thud. She had no choice but to turn around and when she did, the thing with the wig came closer. It had a long gleaming knife in its hand. Terrified, with nowhere to escape, Hallie reached up and yanked the wig off. It was Roger! Hallie sat up straight in the bed. Had her own screaming wakened her? She didn't know, but she got of bed and ran into the bathroom and shut the door.

A minute or so later, she heard Roger's voice through the door. "What happened? Are you sick?"

"No, no. I just had a bad dream—a whopping nightmare."

"Oh. Well, come back to bed now. I hope I can get back to sleep. I have an early meeting."

Hallie didn't want to get back into bed with Roger, but if she didn't, she knew he'd blame her for his lack of sleep. If his meeting went poorly, that would be her fault, too. She splashed cool water on her face and then reluctantly, returned to the bedroom and slipped in beside Roger.

Getting to Work

What Can We Learn About the Cycle of Abuse?

In this chapter, we can see glimpses of Hallie's family history, and we—and Hallie—begin to realize that she is repeating familiar family dynamics in her marriage. This is typical; most people do choose partners based on their own family's characteristics. A person who shows many of the same traits of our mother and father will be attractive to us on a certain level simply because these traits are familiar. They are what we grew up around, so they seem normal.

The familiarity is important for other reasons, too. During childhood we absorbed the message that to marry someone like our parents (or the people who raised us) would give us the opportunity to replay our childhood and have more of what we liked, but equally important, fix what we didn't like. This is an unconscious process, and it becomes an unconscious goal to resolve those childhood issues, even if we cannot consciously name them.

In addition, whatever we experienced in childhood is still familiar; therefore, it provides a type of security. Because we "know" it, we think it is better than choosing the unfamiliar. The deep human need for security sends a message that "different" could be "dangerous." When I worked in an agency that dealt with sexually abused children and their families, I was amazed to see that the children would not only want to protect the parent who had abused them, they wanted to return to their homes. As I came to understand, what they were familiar with, no matter how horrific, at least gave these children a sense of security. Going into a foster or adoptive home was an unknown, which frightened them even more than their parents' behavior.

A Crack in the Cycle

Family dynamics repeat themselves until someone has the courage to interrupt them. That crack in the cycle may come in any number of forms. In this chapter, Hallie starts experiencing inklings of her independent, professional side. With little or no difficulty, her imagination begins to soar—she can see herself operating as an adult with independent agency, meaning that she can make decisions and run her own life. It may seem odd, but women whose objective conditions include dire poverty, no education, health problems, and a complete lack of power to make choices, are not much different from affluent women who are like the proverbial princess who is locked in a tower. She may have nice clothes, but she doesn't choose them. Like Hallie, she may be ill, but is not free to seek care.

In a sense, Hallie's trip to see her mother is like being released from the tower. The time away from Roger provides space to focus her energies on her own goals, not just her ongoing job/goal of keeping Roger happy and under control. Being in another environment also shows her another way to live and in her heart she thinks, "Just maybe I can live differently, and I am capable of making a choice." *When we want to get a different perspective, it is important to change our surroundings, if only for a day or a few hours.*

Painting a New Picture

You may want to change, but you aren't sure where to begin. It is important to gain a clear picture of what change will "look like." This means visualizing a fantasy and allowing yourself to live it a few minutes every day. Try your vision on for size as if you're deciding whether to buy a particular dress. Get used to the picture and see what you like about it and what you don't want to keep. How could you change the fantasy to make it perfect?

As a second step, begin to *live* your vision, taking it one step at a time. Bite off a small piece that you can handle at the moment. For example, Hallie is starting to think about her work as a nurse, which Roger has never allowed her to do. She can work on her vision by gathering information about techniques she'd need to learn if she were to return to the nursing field. She can read articles about nurses and file that information away for future use. By taking these steps she is no longer allowing her professional interests and competency to stagnate, and she is sending a message to herself that she can grow. This in turn increases her self-confidence and self-esteem.

Hallie's next possible step may be a little bolder. For example, she could talk to the nursing director of a hospital or the nurse in charge at a doctor's office. She can gather ideas about possible work environments and working schedules. An employed person would simply call this updating information about the field, which is something everyone in any profession must do. Hallie is not making a commitment, but she is exploring direction. She can continue searching for new ideas and carrying out tasks as they feel safe and comfortable to her.

What is Roger Afraid Of?

Hallie knows that Roger shows no understanding for her needs and desires to grow professionally, but she may not understand the reasons he fears her individual need to grow. Like many abusive men, Roger knows that if she gets involved with something or someone outside their home, he is likely to lose her as his victim, which may mean that she will abandon him. In addition, Roger's involvement with his profession and career means that he is not willing to share the work of raising Eric or of taking care of the house. Roger insists on complete freedom to pursue his goals and in order to do so, he has to believe that Hallie should be happy with staying home. After all, he reasons, he makes a good living. Of course, he controls every penny.

Roger's way of life is quite stressful, and he punishes Hallie for the stress he places on himself through his compulsion about his career. He blames her for his burned out feelings while she "sits at home." Roger sends mixed messages about the role he expects her to fulfill, so it is no wonder she stays confused and on edge.

Constructive Anger

We see Hallie allowing her anger and other disturbing emotions to surface. She sounds cynical when she says that Roger sees her role as leaving him free to be a "big shot." She is annoyed to think that she can't send her mother a new coat or a few dollars. It bothers her to hear him talk negatively about Ginger. While she is away from home, she is allowing the negative thoughts about Roger to surface. As we've seen, she rarely expresses any of these thoughts in his presence.

Anger is often healthy in that it gives us good information about what is wrong in our life and we need not fear our anger as long as we get the messages we need from the emotion. What we *do* with anger can be either constructive and healthy or dangerous and unhealthy. Roger's anger is dangerous because he lets it control him and he uses it against others, specifically Hallie and by association, Eric. But Hallie's surfacing anger is an integral part of the process of self-examination. She can use anger as a tool to provide the motivation to improve her life, and the life of her child.

The Body-Mind Connection

Did you notice that Hallie feels better when she's away from home? She surprises herself by eating ice cream, which she associates with her supposedly "common" digestive complaints. In this different geographic and more important, emotionally peaceful, environment, her physiological ailments begin to subside. This is extremely important information and Hallie needs to listen to the messages her body is sending.

Unfortunately, many people do not take seriously enough the information the body routinely sends about what is healthy or unhealthy. However, it is our job to listen to body messages and not just pass off symptoms as the "same thing that Aunt Betty had," and so forth. We know better than anyone else what is healthy for us. So, why do we look outside ourselves for the information that we think will make us happy?

Unconsciously, Hallie wants to be healthy and happy *only* if Roger approves. However, Roger will never approve because that is, frankly, beyond his capabilities. Nothing is ever good enough for him, including Hallie. What he gives from his "self" is subjective information about himself and this has very little to do with Hallie. For her part, she is too insecure to believe in her own good sense to know what is best for her.

We could argue that Roger brainwashed her into giving him total control over her. It is true that he did engage in undermining talk that in a sense brainwashed her to second guess everything about herself. However, she was a willing partner in the relationship dynamic because her childhood messages told her to give over the control of her life. Ultimately, she believed it was her *duty* to believe Roger when he said he knew what was best for her and even openly expressed the idea that he could "teach" her to understand him. She could then learn to treat him in such a way that made their life work. Of course, this is an illusion.

Hallie is slowly learning that 1) there is no way to win with Roger, and 2) she has had to sacrifice everything to even attempt to win his acceptance. In addition, the definition of acceptance has changed. At one time, she wanted to build a true partnership with him and her goal involved convincing him that such a thing was possible. However, acceptance to Hallie now means some level of peace and quiet, and is defined not in terms of kindness but in the absence of emotional or physical assaults against her.

Hallie's dream is instructive, too. She'd had a bad dream before, but she couldn't remember it. This time, she has a horrific dream and she won't be able to wipe its images away. Nightmares are common among battered women. So much of the time Hallie represses her fears, but at night, their reality surfaces. We can expect her to have this dream—or others—more frequently.

The Pattern is Learned

Hallie's mother has delivered negative messages in the past, but she has changed and now her life stands as a positive role model for Hallie. Nina urges Hallie to consider the possibility of leaving Roger. This is a change, because in childhood, Hallie experienced her mother as a submissive caretaker to Hallie's abusive alcoholic father. She has visual images of her mother's injuries and she can remember the sounds of abuse in her childhood home. Hallie absorbed these sensory details.

As we learn, Hallie sees the changes her mother made after leaving her father. Of course, Nina's lifestyle changed financially and being alone has not always been a bed of roses. However, her mother had the courage to leave and start over with very little. In the process of building her new life, Nina has developed self-confidence, strength, adventure, and most of all, freedom and peace of mind.

In numerous ways, Nina forces Hallie to look at the way Eric is negatively influenced because Hallie has stayed in the marriage. Over and over I have heard women say that they protected their children from the knowledge that the father/husband is abusive. This is part of an old myth and does not reflect more sophisticated knowledge about the various ways children form impressions about the emotional atmosphere in the home. The fact is, children pick up on the truth and consequently, imitate their parents' behavior. You *cannot* hide the truth from a child who is living in an environment of abuse. Children, even infants, are extremely sensitive and intuitive. They know when someone they love is being hurt and they know when someone they love is abusive.

If abuse is going on in your home, you cannot lie to your children and expect them to believe you just because you are an authority figure. Sadly, the actual message they receive is that they cannot *trust* you to tell them the truth. Furthermore, they then learn that the world is not safe for them and they cannot depend on you. More than likely they will become angry and disillusioned and then begin to believe it is their job to protect you. Adopting this role takes away the freedom to be a child. As children of abuse grow older, they eventually become angry about *their* losses.

If your children are teenagers, you may wonder why they don't respect you for "protecting" them from their abusive father all these years. This is how you see it, after all. But they will wonder why you didn't leave or get help in order to protect them and yourself in more concrete ways. You see, they know that shooing them off to their bedrooms—or sending them down to the basement or even hiding them in the closet—is not true protection. And so, you will have repair work to do. I do not say this to discourage you or make you feel bad about yourself. It is better to be empowered and take care of these problems rather than putting a false "good face" on what has happened.

Life Father, Like Son?

Imagine how astonished Hallie is to learn that Eric has been mean to other children. Her sweet little boy behaved like a bully in the park? How can that be? Hallie has been naïve and somehow convinced herself that Eric has not witnessed the violence. In actuality, he has seen bullying and violence in his home, and he has reached the age when he thinks it's okay to mimic his father's actions.

Such are the messages children learn from their parents. Adults have the ability to distinguish right from wrong but children do not have that sophisticated brain function until much later. So, they have no choice but to copy what they see and hear. They know when something hurts but they don't label it as right or wrong, nor do they understand the consequences of their actions. As the years pass, problems with Eric are likely to increase. This isn't a phase he will naturally pass through. Ironically, if Eric begins to have difficulties in school, Roger is likely to use it as another weapon against Hallie.

Fantasies Versus Steps and Plans

In reality, sometimes it is not safe to just up and leave. When that is the situation, as it is in Hallie's case, women must be smart and secretive. I often hear women say that they feel sneaky doing things behind their husband's back. This comes from another childhood message and produces guilt when we feel sneaky. That message worked in childhood, but as adults, it is damaging when applied to dangerously abusive relationships, especially when we know the abuser will neither change nor let us go. As you will see, Hallie eventually must resort to being sneaky in order to make healthy changes in her life.

Earlier I suggested that you use your imagination to visualize a new life for yourself and your children. I used the words fantasy and fantasize, and it is necessary to allow yourself to create a vision of life as it could be. However, using your imagination to create a life in which you act, rather than reacting, is not the same as daydreaming about someone rescuing you from your hard life. It's one thing to work to create a vision, but it is entirely different to spend time in mindless fantasy that is not followed up with action. So, while it is healthy for Hallie to think about having a job and an apartment and perhaps even going back to school one day, it must go hand in hand with taking action steps.

Hallie was sneaky, in a healthy way, when she contacted agencies where she talked to an individual specially trained to help battered women. Most communities have these agencies, which often offer free groups to attend, and many are associated with shelters that offer temporary housing for battered women and their children. Hallie will find the possibility of support, friendship, financial help, and trained individuals to guide her through legal steps.

Like Hallie, if you make these calls, you soon will learn that you are not alone. It takes courage to take first steps, so reward yourself when you do it. When that criticizing voice comes in and tells you that you are a traitor to your husband or that he is going to kill you for doing this, tell it to hush and concentrate on the voice that says how brave, smart, and resourceful you are. If you're not accustomed to hearing that voice, as with most women who are in abusive relationships, then force yourself to make up a voice that you can use for encouragement. Write encouraging notes to yourself and carry them in your pocket. Then, when you hear the critical voice, pull out your note. Through practice, you will find the positive voice quickly. Eventually, positive "self talk" will come to you automatically.

Hanging on to Hope

Hallie is fooled into thinking that fewer angry outbursts is a sign that Roger is improving and will sustain these apparent changes. Naturally, Hallie holds on to this belief because it reinforces her sense of hope. However, this is deceptive and Roger actually is cycling through another stage of power. This stage comes down from the aggressive stage. He can "afford" to be quieter because he knows he needn't rage as much because he has instilled enough fear that all he has to do is *look* as if he might rage to maintain his control. Hallie always carries a fear of the rage. As she becomes a little bolder and asks for more, or relaxes her hypervigilant attitude, Roger will find an excuse to rage again and reestablish the iron fist of control.

It sounds contradictory, but periods of calm act like a powerful tool to maintain control over a victim. Roger is in essence setting up games in which Hallie flips back and forth between happiness, is afraid to trust that happiness, then gets angry when the happiness goes away, and finally feels humiliation and guilt for causing the abusive partner to make the happiness go away. These games give Roger all of the power and control he needs to keep Hallie his prisoner. In fact this is exactly how prisoners of war are treated. As time passes, Hallie will probably begin to doubt her own sanity. Roger baits Hallie with kindness and love and then switches to abuse when she is "off-guard." She's confused and deeply hurt, and most of all, as hard as she tries, she just can't figure out how to avoid the games and the cycle they produce.

Danger is Not an Illusion

A person who can carry out such obsessive rituals is dangerous. Roger's behavior is not caused by any external person or thing. It isn't about work, pressure, kids, or financial stress, although batterers will look for a million reasons. These individuals have a personality disorder that can only be treated by professionals trained to handle these cases. Even then, many cannot be helped at all. We may think they have been *cured* of this disorder because they may be able to control their rage for long periods of time, even years. But at some point most of them will fall back into the dangerous behavior.

It is important to differentiate individuals with this dangerous personality disorder from the person who rages, gets it under control before doing much harm, which means he has not physically harmed anyone. This type of person usually apologizes and feels genuinely remorseful and because of this, is often willing to see that the behavior is destructive. These individuals are willing to learn healthier ways to interact and behave.

Just because the rage does not turn to physical abuse, this type of person can still be frightening to live with. If you are with someone who scares you, I recommend that you seek professional advice to help you determine how dangerous this person may be and the type of help you need. Just as Hallie called the agency to ask questions, you can call a hotline or an agency to ask about these issues. Most communities have a hotline and you can remain anonymous when you call.

Who are these Batterers, Anyway?

It is sad but true that batterers come in all descriptions. They may be unemployed or marginally employed or they may be physicians or corporate executives. They may have almost no education or they may hold doctorates. These dangerous personalities are not formed because these individuals were impoverished children or spoiled rich kids. All these men use battering and abusive behavior to control through fear.

Based on my professional experience, women in the lower socioeconomic groups tend to ask for help much more readily than women living in more advantaged socioeconomic conditions. I believe that the latter groups do not seek help for fear that their partners are so powerful in the community that no one will help them. In addition, these women have the most to lose financially if they leave the relationship. Furthermore, they also fear losing custody of their children to their partner. Indeed, they view their partner as powerful enough to convince courts that they are unfit, crazy, hysterical mothers. Abusers with high-status jobs, money, and professional power often threaten to do just that if their wives threaten to leave. Or, these men, who see themselves as so powerful, will threaten to literally drive their wives crazy, and the women often believe this threat because by then, they may feel crazy at times.

When women feel threatened they may convince themselves to stay until the children are grown. Tragically, as we all know, some of these women, and sometimes even their children, don't live long enough to reach their goal. We know that great damage has been done and Roger believes that he can do whatever it takes to control Hallie. As we follow Hallie through her life with Roger, is there any doubt that she and Eric could end up as a story on the evening news?

7

"Your husband is *cute*." The saleswoman's voice was high-pitched, nearly a squeal. "He has such good ideas about cruise clothes. We don't see many husbands like yours."

Roger was pulling colorful skirts off the racks and matching them with cotton shells and T-shirts the clerk picked out. Hallie's stiff neck ached and she wanted to scream each time she spotted Roger winking at the clerk. These shopping trips with Roger had turned into nothing more than a platform for him to be a show-off, and, Hallie noticed, almost every saleswoman swallowed his act, especially the young women. Hallie thought back to her early years with Roger when she'd been flattered that he took such an interest in her clothes. She rarely liked what he picked for her, but other women seemed envious that he was so interested. She also remembered what happened when he turned on her, and irrationally blamed her for *his* choices. He'd shredded more dresses and pantsuits and even sweaters than she'd care to count. She'd been forced to watch him with her own eyes.

Eric was getting restless in the chair where Roger had put him and told him to stay. Instead of snapping at him, as he would do at home, Roger picked him up and teased him about helping Mommy be even prettier. Eric looked uncomfortable and curled his hair around in his fingers. Hallie noticed he did that every time Roger picked him up, even when he talked in that phony, charming way. The saleswoman teased about Eric being shy and she beamed at Roger. "What a dad," she said, looking Hallie's way.

Hallie smiled and agreed, aware that every minute of their shopping trip was torture for her. If Roger deserved an Oscar for his performance, then so did she. No one could possibly see that she had caught on to Roger's public charm. What Hallie couldn't figure out was why it had taken her so long to realize that this charm was an act. Sometimes she felt just as stupid as Roger accused her of being. In the guise of showering her with attention, he managed to choose every single article of clothing she wore. In sad and bitter moments, Hallie remembered the hated wedding dress.

Hallie noticed an older saleswoman watching her younger colleague fawn over Roger. Her mouth was curled in a cynical smirk, but when she saw Hallie looking at her, she quickly changed her expression and smiled. Hallie wondered how many similar glances she'd missed over the years.

Later, as they strolled through the rest of the store Eric spotted Ginger and Judy, another friend of Ginger's from the neighborhood. Eric became excited and called out to her. Hallie had tried to steer Eric away and out of sight, but she hadn't pulled it off and Ginger and Judy came toward them and greeted them with laughs and smiles. "I keep getting bigger and bigger," Ginger said, "so I'm on a mission for more clothes."

"I think you look fantastic," Roger said. He nodded to Ginger and Judy. He sounded kind and gentle.

"I do, too," Hallie said. "You really *are* glowing!"

"We're loading up on cruise clothes today," Roger said. "Hallie's a knock-out in some of these things." He explained that he was leaving town soon and wanted to take Hallie shopping before he left. "Some men don't like shopping with their wives, but I think it's fun."

"Lucky Hallie," Ginger said. "Bob happily sent me off with Judy."

Hallie watched Ginger studying Roger. She's probably surprised he's being this chatty, Hallie thought. She hoped that wouldn't encourage Ginger to issue another invitation.

Later, in the car on the way to the restaurant for lunch, Roger started in on Ginger. "My God, that's one ugly woman," he said, "and such a cow."

From his car seat in the back, Hallie heard Eric begin to chant, "Ginger cow, Ginger cow, Ginger cow."

Hallie twisted around in her seat. "Eric! Stop that. You will not say those things about Ginger."

Eric stopped, but he began giggling and Roger laughed along with him. "Hey, son," he said, "we know a cow when we see one, don't we?" Eric laughed even harder. "See Hallie, our boy has some taste. We know a cow of a woman when one crosses our path."

Hallie's eyes flooded with hot tears of frustration and hurt. He had won, she thought. He would now start using Eric to taunt her. And so he did, all the way to the restaurant. "Ginger cow, Ginger cow," over and over again. The big shot doctor doing supposedly innovative work was teaching his son to call a grown woman a cow. If Hallie hadn't been so heartsick, she would have laughed in scorn—and out loud, too. She was fed up with making excuses for him. She resolved to tell Eric he was not allowed to make fun of other people.

Hallie had trouble falling asleep that night and when she did, images of her brother disturbed her dreams. He stared at her, saying nothing, but his mouth was stretched into a sneer. Sweating and frightened but fully awake, Hallie sat up in bed and thought about the way he and their father had ganged up on her. They had teased her about being flat-chested, they teased her about being short, but most of all, they taunted her about being shy and tongue-tied. "Cat got your tongue, cat got your tongue?" Years had passed, but at that moment, she hated both of them. Hate wasn't something she often allowed herself, but she didn't care. They were cruel and hateful.

Hallie felt a twinge in her lower abdomen and threw back the covers and tiptoed to the bathroom with her fingers crossed. Please, let it be my period, please. Hallie's eyes filled with tears of joy and relief when she saw the spotting. A month had gone by and she wasn't pregnant. Now that Roger wanted a baby, Hallie was grateful that her periods lasted well over a week, and even the heavy bleeding served as a protection from sex she didn't want.

Suddenly the room flooded with harsh florescent light. She looked up and saw Roger standing in the doorway. "No baby, huh?"

"No, Roger. I'm sorry."

"When we get back from our cruise I'll make an appointment for you with Perkins. We will get everything checked out."

"It's only been a few weeks, Roger, just since I came back from Mom's."

"You're right," he said. "I guess I'm impatient to get a little one started." His tone was matter-of-fact, neither angry nor pleasant. "I'd hoped you'd get pregnant before I left for my conferences."

Impatient to look good to the priest, she thought. They got back into bed and in a few minutes, Hallie heard Roger's soft, steady breathing. Only ten more days until he left for Europe.

* * * *

Hallie moaned with pleasure. "Oh Roger," she sighed. She hated faking orgasms, but she'd been doing it for years and had learned that it was easier just to pretend. Not that Roger couldn't be a good lover. He knew how to be tender and passionate, but now that all he thought about was getting her pregnant, he was obsessed with quantity. Hallie was exhausted from his demands, and no matter how hard she tried to accept the idea of a new baby, she was terrified by the thought of becoming pregnant. Her cherished memories of her first pregnancy were her only consolation. At least for those few months, Roger had cared enough to show her the side of himself she fell in love with.

"I sure hope you got pregnant tonight, Hallie," Roger said, as he rolled away, but held on to her. "It's important to me."

"Me too," she said. She threw an arm around him and kissed his chest. "Me too." It was too easy to lie, she thought, entirely too easy.

The next morning she helped Roger pack for his trip. She'd taken his suits to the cleaners and ironed his shirts perfectly. Every piece of his clothing was clean and even his neckties were lined up on the back of a chair so he could make his final choices.

"Some men have wives who do all this for them," he said, "but no, not me. I married a fashion ninny."

"Roger, what a tease you are. For years, I've offered to pack for you, but you won't let me."

Roger shot her a snide look. "Is that what you really think? That I *want* to waste time folding my clothes? That I want to do *your* job?"

"You can't say I didn't try to learn what you wanted?"

"Sure, sure, you tried. In your own stupid little country-girl way, you tried."

Hallie left the room to make their coffee and Eric's breakfast.

"Did you hear me Hallie? You're a stupid hick!" His voice boomed through the house.

"I heard you," she shouted back. "I'm making coffee. Eggs or cereal?"

"I'll eat at the airport," he yelled from the bedroom. "I need to get out of here. I just can't be around this stupidity another minute."

Hallie watched the clock. He had a 10:45 flight. It was 7:30 and the airport was only fifteen minutes a way. There was still plenty of time left for a real blowup. Keep your mouth shut, she said to herself. Just hang on.

She glanced at Eric who had screwed up his face and was mumbling "stupid hick." Hallie felt a wave of nausea, but she didn't say anything. When Roger was gone, she'd talk to Eric about the disrespectful name-calling he'd picked up from his father. She disliked violating the idea of presenting a united front, but she'd tell Eric his father was wrong. She had ten days of peace ahead and couldn't wait until it started.

Roger came into the kitchen with the wall calendar from his office. He threw it on the kitchen table and grabbed a mug from the cabinet. He poured himself some coffee and said. "Take a look at the calendar."

Hallie stared at it, unsure of what he wanted her to see. "Yes? What should I be looking for, Roger?"

"Can't you tell?" He looked genuinely puzzled, as if it should be obvious. "See the check marks and the red zeros? I'm keeping track of your periods in red and these checks keep track of when we have sex. The way I figure it, we may have made a baby last night."

"Could be a little early," Hallie said, "but you may be right." She smiled up at him. "I hope so, Roger. I sure hope so."

Roger took her hand and led her back into the bedroom. "Once more for insurance," he said. He unzipped his pants and let them and his briefs fall to his ankles. He wasn't aroused and Hallie wondered how quickly she could get this over with. Eric was sitting in the kitchen. She didn't want him walking in on them.

"Roger, what about Eric? He's in the kitchen and..."

"He'll be fine. Close the door."

With her heart beating fast, Hallie closed the door and began caressing Roger in hopes that she could arouse him quickly. She closed her eyes and tried to relax as Roger pulled up her nightgown and roughly stroked the top of her legs and buttocks.

Relieved that her efforts were working, Hallie went along with Roger as he led her to the bed and climbed on top of her. He pushed himself into her and she almost gasped with the pain. She wasn't ready for him.

"Not turned on?" His voice was loud in her ear.

"I...I...I just need a little more time."

Roger rolled off of her and pulled up his pants. "You bitch. You have time, but I don't."

"I know, but I can't just..."

"If you really cared about me, you'd be eager for it. You'd be begging me to fuck you. I'll be gone for ten days and all I'm doing is trying to give you a baby now. I can see how much I'll be missed around here. Well fuck you."

"Roger, I know, but..." Roger didn't usually use language like that. He criticized people who did, especially women.

Roger pushed her against the wall and cupped her face with his hands and squeezed her cheeks. "You still don't know how good you have it. Ungrateful, stupid bitch." Roger let her go and grabbed his jacket and picked up his bags. She quickly checked on Eric. He'd left the kitchen and turned the television on in the living room. She turned it off before Roger saw it and she shushed Eric when he started protesting. "We'll go back in the kitchen now," she whispered, "and soon we'll go visit Ginger."

Roger set his bags by the front door and came into the kitchen. He tossed a handwritten list on the table. "I will try to call you on these days. I've figured out the time difference and I expect you to be here for my calls."

"Where can we reach you? Do you have emergency numbers for me?"

"My office knows where I'll be. I don't want you bothering me over stupid little things." Roger took an envelope out of his jacket pocket and set it next to the phone schedule. "This is all the money you'll need for the next ten days. I want an accounting when I get home. And maybe by the time I get back you'll be grateful for the privileged life you have. Some women would kill for a life like yours."

"Oh Roger, I have always appreciated what a good husband you are. I'm proud of you and I love our house. I'm so happy with the car you gave me. I *am* grateful. Because of you I can stay home with Eric–and the other babies we'll have one day."

Roger's face softened a little. He leaned over to kiss Eric goodbye and he wrapped his arms around Hallie. "I just wanted to give you a baby," he whispered. He held her close, but it was a gentle hug.

They both startled at the sound of the doorbell. He let her go and opened the door. The limo driver greeted him and picked up the bags. Roger gave her a quick wave and closed the front door behind him. Hallie waited until the limo pulled out of the driveway before she ran into the bathroom and buried her face in a towel and let the tears come. She felt like crying for days, but she made herself stop. She didn't want to face Ginger with a face red and blotchy from crying. Hallie dabbed a cool wet cloth over her eyes. Then she grasped either side of the sink with her hands and braced herself as she leaned over and stretched her back. She let her head flop forward and felt the muscles loosen in her back. "I am such a liar," she said out loud. "I have become an amazing liar."

Hallie went back into the living room and turned on the television for Eric. While he watched Sesame Street, she picked up a yellow legal pad from the kitchen counter and started writing. At first it resembled a list. But then her quick scribbles became whole sentences and soon, she'd written paragraphs. She started with her feelings about a new baby, her fears of bringing another child into their family. She wrote about the things for which she was genuinely grateful and then she admitted how often she lied just to avoid Roger's outbursts. She had never done this before, and she had to stop in a few minutes. The words she'd written frightened her; she had to face her dilemma in small pieces.

Eric skipped into the kitchen and pulled a chair next to her. "Let's go to Ginger's," he said.

"We will, darling, we will. But I want to do something first." Hallie sent Eric back to the living room and she pulled out the Yellow Pages and searched for the number. When she saw the words "domestic violence" she let out a deep sigh. A part of her still held on to the idea that these services were meant for poor women, not for women who lived in nice houses and drove cars their doctor-husbands had given them for their birthdays. Then Hallie thought about her phone conversation with the counselor. She had faced her fear and made that call and she would do it again. She wrote the number on the top of a fresh page on the legal pad. Then she looked up Planned Parenthood. Maybe she could avoid becoming pregnant without Roger ever finding out. Hallie wasn't sure she could be that deceptive, but it wouldn't hurt to look into it. She found that number and wrote it under the first number. Finally, Hallie looked up the listings of Catholic churches. When she found one she figured out was clear across town, she wrote down that number, too.

She'd taken the first steps. She pulled off the sheets from the pad and considered where to put them. Her mind went wild thinking about the possibility that Roger's flight had been cancelled and he could come back home. She snickered at her own paranoia, but she still resolved to hide the numbers and her writing in the trunk of her car. Quickly, she pulled on jeans she liked and slipped her feet into sneakers. It wasn't normal, she thought, to take such pleasure in wearing clothes and shoes her husband hated. It wasn't normal to be so relieved to see him close the door behind him, knowing that he'd be gone for over a week. Sadly, she wouldn't miss him.

Getting to Work

What Can We Learn About the Cycle of Abuse?

Hallie is beginning to realize that she is living with an enemy. Her defense mechanism of denial has broken down and she is allowing herself to really feel the reality of her plight, plus the fear that goes along with it. It may seem ironic, but she loves Roger and wants her marriage to work more than anything. Hallie wants what she did not have as a child—a happy, pleasant, loving, and respectful relationship. She vowed to find it as an adult and has failed to do so; in that sense she feels failure and shame.

In spite of her deep desire for a good marriage, she is facing the reality of her fear of Roger. She has learned to second-guess him, but she also knows how unpredictable he can be. She is angry with him and with herself for not being able to pull off a successful family life. Now she must see the truth: she has no control over making Roger change and in fact, she is seeing him get worse. Roger is demanding more and is degrading her more. This is bound to happen as he begins to suspect that Hallie's denial mechanisms have broken down.

What Roger Knows

A part of Roger, to some extent an unconscious part, is able to perceive Hallie's changes. We notice that Hallie is not quite so vulnerable, at least emotionally. Earlier, Hallie reacted with deeply hurt feelings and confusion. We see that Hallie has seen through his charming façade with strangers, for example. In addition, she appears increasingly clever, which makes him hurl insults to diminish her. Maybe he can't put his finger on it right away, but he no doubt suspects that Hallie doesn't always react honestly and may choose words that do little more than attempt to appease him. Initially, the changes in Hallie cause Roger to step up his attempts to gain more power over her.

This is a critical stage, because it can be a danger point for Hallie and Eric.

For her part, Hallie senses that Roger may notice changes in her, so she uses the only tool she has to take care of Eric and herself: Hallie lies; she tells him what she knows he wants to hear in order to keep him under control. She believes that lying is not typical of her and so she feels guilt and sadness over it. This behavior lowers her self-esteem because it goes against her own value system. However, her instincts tell her that she must behave in a manner that allows her to survive. Even though Hallie doesn't believe in lying and deception, she has actually engaged in calculated behavior all along. She has lied to herself, hidden her true feelings from Roger, and almost every day of their marriage, she has tried to figure out how to step around him.

Why Doesn't She Pack Up and Get Out?

To individuals who do not understand the battered woman's syndrome, it may seem impossible to figure out why Hallie stays with Roger. However, Hallie remains too scared to pick up and leave; at this point, she wouldn't know how to go about taking that kind of step. Like many women in a similar situation, she must spend time digesting new doses of reality before going on to the next step. Sure, she has seen through so much of Roger's behavior and she is self-protective enough to know that having another child is not advantageous to her, regardless of what Roger might think.

It's not uncommon for battered women to continue to try to save the marriage, even when they have accepted the unpleasant truth about their lives. In fact, typically, women try to leave seven to nine times before they actually stay away for good. This may seem like a sign that the women are weak, but that isn't true. Leaving a violent, abusive marriage is an internal process, not just an external act. As we've seen, all Hallie's energy has been directed to her marriage, and bad as it is, it may represent the strongest part of her identity. It is no wonder that a part of her is reluctant to believe that her dream cannot come true.

Old Dreams, New Grief

In spite of her willingness to stay, Hallie has begun grieving the loss of her relationship with Roger and, even more important, the death of a dream. Like so many women, she had dreams about family life and she tried to match the childhood fantasies with the reality. Hallie's dreams began in childhood and she has nurtured that dream for many, many years. This is a strong component of her Lifetime Messages Blueprint. She will not give it up easily, but instead, will put herself in harm's way to fulfill it. It's almost an addiction. Hallie is living in an excruciating place where it's still too difficult to leave and almost impossible to stay.

What Eric Knows

As we've seen, the "public" Roger displays Hallie like a trophy. He also adopts a parental role, which fulfills his need to be a care-taker to someone who adores him. To a stranger, the public mani-festation of this attitude may masquerade as amusing affection. The private behavior reveals Roger's obsession with control, even ruling over her body, seeing it as his to use and abuse as his whims desire. In Roger's reality, Hallie's body is his to make pregnant if he so desires. She is his object, not a human whose spirit can be crushed. Roger is apparently completely unaware of what she goes through when he degrades her; even his teasing is devastating. Roger cannot see any of this because his one and only goal is to *always* keep her under control and unsure of herself. And all along, Eric sees and absorbs all of it.

Hallie is breaking through her well-defended naivete when she agonizes over the harsh reality of Roger's influence over Eric. Roger can manipulate this small boy to go against Hallie through hurtful teasing. To this point, she has protected Eric from Roger and stood up to him for Eric's sake. She reasons that Eric is only a child and does not realize that Roger's taunting and teasing hurts her. However, she has a vulnerable, scared heart and unfortunately, some of her strength has come from the unrealistic belief that Eric is her ally.

When one parent relies on a child to be a friend or ally, the child may respond and try to fulfill that role. However, this is an unfair expectation and has consequences. Eric knows Roger is his father and Eric has a connection with him, although even as a toddler Eric feels unhealthy energy between Hallie and Roger. Instinctively, Eric may sense Hallie's need for protection and Roger's authoritarian control. Even preschoolers may begin forming and taking on a role as protector. He attempts to placate his father as he also strives for approval. Like all children, Eric wants approval from both parents.

Unfortunately, Eric has been robbed of much of his childhood. We can see that he cannot relax and just be a child. He senses the lonely desperation in his mother, while at the same time seeing his father's swings between phony charm and sneering sarcasm. Even though Hallie would give her own life to protect Eric from Roger—or from anyone who might threaten him—Hallie is just waking up to the reality of the pressure Eric is under.

The Blueprint Leaves Clues

Clearly, Hallie's Lifetime Messages Blueprint has influenced Hallie's decision to marry Roger (or a man similar to Roger). In her dreams, she remembers her brother and father's emotional and verbal abuse. The message is two-fold: first, all men will see her as unattractive, shy, and tongue-tied, and second, she must choose her partners in life who will carry on that message and allow her to live it to its fullest. Hallie's attraction to Roger shows us that we tend to choose what feels familiar, even if it's unhealthy, because familiarity carries less risk than going with the unknown. We believe the familiar will help us feel more secure. As Hallie chooses people in her life to help her perpetuate this belief system, her self-esteem and self-confidence continue to plummet until she truly believes she deserves cruel treatment.

In various ways, Roger continues to send the message that Hallie is unattractive. Together with his threats, insults, and his nasty teasing, he continues to tell her that she must be shy and remain unable to speak her mind. Because Hallie believes it is her job to make him happy and figure him out, no matter what, his paranoid narcissism keeps her focused on anticipating his every reaction. Hallie has become totally out of touch with her own needs and feelings. This is the way her father and brother wanted it, and now Roger is fulfilling that role.

Signs of Hope

We can see glimmers of hope when Hallie takes small steps toward becoming informed and protecting herself. Taking steps to prevent an unwanted pregnancy, even if it means deceiving Roger, represents Hallie's determination to stay safe. Relative to what she will have to do later, these may seem like beginning baby steps, but they are important nonetheless because acting on her own behalf begins to build Hallie's self-confidence and self-esteem.

8

Hallie picked up the receiver and started to dial the number. She lost her nerve and hung up, but a few minutes later she worked up the courage to try again. She'd had Sister Dorothy's phone number for two days, but she hadn't managed to complete the call. Still, Hallie mentally calculated what she'd accomplished in the two days since Roger left. She'd made an appointment at the family planning clinic and she called the hotline for domestic violence and talked with a counselor.

Although the counselor, Naomi, had encouraged her to come in to talk about her options, Hallie had said no. She was far too afraid she'd run into someone she knew from the church or, even more horrific to contemplate, the hospital. But during their conversation she'd told Naomi that she planned to see a priest, and the counselor had suggested that Hallic see a nun, Sister Dorothy, instead. Many of the women who called the hotline saw this nun, whose training enabled her to be a spiritual counselor. Now all Hallie had to do was make the call.

Even with the anxiety about going behind Roger's back and secretly taking the birth control pill, which is what Hallie planned to do, she spent many relaxed hours alone with Eric. She'd slept better than she had in years, once Roger's late night call was out of the way, that is. Just as Hallie had expected, Roger's first call came at the precise time he'd written down. The list he'd given her was almost comical in its detail.

Unfortunately, Hallie thought, she had put Roger's list of call times and instructions on the kitchen counter next to the phone. Ginger had seen it when she came over for coffee. "What's this?" she'd asked. Ginger then quickly apologized. "I'm sorry, I didn't mean to be nosy."

Hallie had laughed and said, "No problem. It's just that Roger is so organized. He feels better when he has everything planned, even down to the phone calls." That sounded stupid, even to her, and she wondered if Ginger was convinced by her light tone. That list also included instructions about what to have in the refrigerator for Roger when he came home and a checklist for the way he wanted his closet rearranged. No wonder it looked odd to Ginger. What a relief it would be, Hallie thought, to just tell the truth.

The desire to speak the truth, to stop watching every word, to let light wash over the ugliness that she hid behind the walls of her home provided the final push. Sister Dorothy answered on the first ring. Hallie was conscious of her stammering and the nervous tone in her voice as she told Sister Dorothy that the counselor at the shelter had recommended she call.

"Would you like to see me in person?"

Hallie nearly cried at the kindness in the simple question. "Yes, I would very much like to see you. But I don't have access to money of…"

"Not another word about money. Just come in. And Hallie, are you in danger right now?"

The question stunned Hallie. She had an urge to deny that danger was an issue at all, but a stronger impulse took over, a drive to tell the truth propelled her. "My husband is in Europe on business–he's speaking at medical conferences, actually. So I'm fine at the moment."

"Well then, you'll want to come in soon. Would tomorrow be okay?"

Hallie sat at the kitchen table and wrote down her feelings about her marriage in order to prepare herself to talk with Sister Dorothy. She found herself writing a history of the marriage, complete with her hopes and dreams, as well as the confusion that had taken over her life. That night, she sat up and waited for Roger's call and heard the false pleasure in her voice when she greeted him. She asked question after question about London and the conference and even about the hotel food, all in an attempt to avoid his interrogation, which is how she'd come to think of Roger's questions, even the simple ones. The next morning she and Eric drove across town and Hallie soon saw the large white frame house Sister Dorothy described. It had several therapists' offices and Sister Dorothy was listed as a spiritual director on the sign out front. That comforted Hallie, although she wasn't sure why, except that she often felt a deep soul sickness, as if she'd lost the connection to her own spirit.

Hallie began to cry the minute she walked into the small office. Sister Dorothy didn't appear surprised, but simply passed her the box of tissue and then distracted Eric by giving him blocks and puzzles to play with at the child's table set up in the corner. Hallie thought about how different Sister Dorothy was from the handful of nuns she'd seen as a little girl. Those women wore long black habits that covered them head to foot. A woman about the same age as Hallie's mother, Sister Dorothy wore a plain navy pantsuit and a crisp white blouse and what Hallie thought of as sensible, comfortable shoes. Her walls were filled with books and her desk in the corner was piled high with legal pads and notebooks with pens and paperclips and post-its sticking out. Hallie concluded Sister Dorothy was a dedicated and busy woman.

"I'm not sure what brought on all these tears," Hallie said.

"Many women weep from relief when they come here. Sometimes they talk about healing tears."

"I feel more like I'm cutting myself open," Hallie said. She hesitated, but she knew there was something Sister Dorothy should know. "Um, I'm not sure if this matters, but I used to be a Baptist. I became a Catholic only because my husband–uh, Roger–insisted. But I miss my old church so much." Hallie hadn't been aware of how much she missed it until that moment.

"Doesn't matter at all to me. The work I do isn't about a specific belief." Hallie would always remember how Sister Dorothy explained that she would work with her to find the kinds of help she needed and she assured her that her job was not to judge or make decisions for her.

"I've been so embarrassed about what's happened to me–to my marriage."

"Why don't you start at the beginning."

Hallie pulled out the sheets she had written the night before, but once she started talking she didn't need them. The stories were linked together by a common thread, which Hallie later thought of as her reflexive defense of Roger and the marriage: "He doesn't mean…" or "He's just insecure…" and "He really loves us…" But Hallie also heard the anger rise in her voice and soon she was crying again, and these tears felt like rage. Her angry tears intensified when she repeated what Roger had said about Ginger and how Eric had mimicked him and started calling Hallie's one good friend a cow. Of so many things that cut through her, why she wondered, did that one thing hurt so much?

Sister Dorothy listened and didn't interrupt until Hallie finished an abbreviated version of her marriage, right up to the morning Roger left for Europe. And she ended with a question: "Can this really be normal?"

Hallie wasn't surprised when Sister Dorothy said "no" in a voice just above a whisper. "But it isn't about what is normal," she said. "It is about what you know to be good for you and what is hurting you and your son."

Hallie listened while Sister Dorothy gently said, "Step back and listen to the story of Roger and Hallie's marriage as if someone else is telling it. If you heard this from a friend what would you think?"

Something shifted in Hallie and it frightened her. She had the urge to get up and run. "You think I should leave, don't you? But I can't. I won't."

"I'm not trying to tell you to leave," Sister Dorothy said. "Let's look at steps you can take to improve your situation."

By the time Hallie left, she had a list of books that Sister Dorothy recommended and suggestions about communicating with Roger and another list of how to prepare herself to stand alone if necessary. The next day she drove to the other side of town and saw a nurse practitioner who gave her birth control pills. Hallie felt ashamed that she lied about her income. Some women in the waiting room were truly poor, and there she was, a doctor's wife with no money of her own.

Hallie wrapped the pills in plastic wrap and took them down to the basement and hid them in the storeroom at the bottom of a carton of her old books and papers from nursing school. "They ought to be safe enough here," Hallie said out loud. Most of the time, Roger acted as if he'd forgotten that they'd met while she was a nursing student and when he did remember, he belittled her education. She took her first pill, and felt a surge of elation ripple through her body. And like she had at other times, Hallie felt odd that these simple things brought such profound relief. She had a long way to go to feel normal again. She so hoped Roger would be willing to make the journey with her. Ever since her appointment with Sister Dorothy, Hallie had been practicing different ways to approach Roger and ask him to see a marriage counselor with her.

On Sunday morning, Hallie took Eric by the hand and together they walked the half-mile or so to the Baptist church. When Hallie thought about it, she was willing to compromise on the issue of religion. She would remain a Catholic for the sake of unity, but she'd like to attend a Baptist church now and then and she couldn't see what objection Roger could have. She had become accustomed to his objections over just about everything, but perhaps in the neutral environment of marriage counseling he would be more open to her ideas. On the walk home Hallie hummed the old hymns that had meant so much to her. Eric carried the picture he colored of children from all over the world. As soon as they got home, Hallie lifted him on a chair and let him tape the picture to the refrigerator.

That afternoon while Eric napped, Hallie sat on the patio and read a book about women and self-esteem and the tendency of many women to submerge their own desires to please a man. Sister Dorothy had told her about it and Hallie checked it out of the library. Now Hallie saw herself on every page. Odd, she thought, that when she visited her mother, she could envision a life that included her own accomplishments, a life with meaning. Most especially, she'd seen herself living without worrying about the minute by minute demands of one person. The minute she'd arrived back home, she again found herself immersed in the difficult life with Roger. Sex she didn't want, a schedule over which she had no control, chores dictated by her husband's whims. In between, when Roger was away, for an hour or a few days, the real Hallie came out from behind a veil of fear and really lived. It was ironic, Hallie thought, that in some ways her life was no different from the women in the Middle East, who had to hide behind a literal veil and had no choice but to live under the control of men. How different was it, she asked herself, to live in fear, first of her father and then of the man who pledged to love her and cherish her?

By the sixth or seventh day of Roger's trip, Hallie realized she was eating everything in sight. More important, she wasn't thinking about what would upset her stomach or give her a colitis attack. And she'd not had a headache since that day in Sister Dorothy's office when she had so much to face that her head started to pound. She ate the same food she fixed for Eric, topped off with cake or cookies for dessert. She checked her weight each day on the bathroom scale though, for fear her healthy appetite might lead to a few extra pounds. She would like that, but Roger wouldn't. But as she ordered burgers and shakes at the drive through window, she resolved to worry about it another day. Besides, she would burn off calories cleaning the house.

The day before Roger came home, Hallie ran down the list of things she had planned to do while he was away, and overall, she felt satisfaction over the progress she'd made. She hated having to keep the birth control pills a secret, but she promised herself that as soon as she and Roger were in marriage counseling and ironed out some of these serious problems, she'd stop taking them. She also planned to talk to Roger about a job. She'd circled part time nursing jobs in the paper and put the list with the piles of odds and ends mail and papers in the kitchen. It was amazing how flexible hospitals were willing to be in order to hire and keep good nurses on staff.

She called Sister Dorothy as planned and described her plan to approach Roger about marriage counseling. Sister Dorothy was pleased that Hallie had read a couple of books she'd recommended, but Hallie heard the concern in her voice when she said, "Please be careful, Hallie. Protect yourself and Eric. Don't be surprised if Roger reacts badly to the suggestion that you believe the marriage could use some work. Remember that you have choices."

"I know. He'll probably tell me I'm ungrateful." Hallie didn't add "bitch" to the description because she was embarrassed to admit he'd say that. "But I will keep at it."

At first, Roger seemed like a changed man, or at least an almost changed man. He played ball with Eric in the yard and grilled chicken on the barbecue. When the sun went down, they put Eric to bed and curled up on the couch and Roger told her that other doctors had praised his papers and many of his older colleagues were more interested than they used to be in the field of neuroradiology. "It was great, Hallie, just great. I felt like my work was finally being appreciated by important people." He squeezed her shoulder and kissed the top of her head.

Hallie wished he would quit while he was ahead, but he couldn't resist finding fault with someone. At the second conference the head of a radiology department at a medical school in the Philadelphia area had talked to him about establishing an institute for brain imaging. "Once my book comes out next year," he said, "I'll be on my way and nothing can stop me."

"Are you seriously thinking about Philadelphia then?" Hallie's sense of adventure kicked in. She liked the house and she'd miss Ginger, but she was always ready for a change.

"Nah, not on your life. We can do better than Philadelphia. Anyway, I can't work under that whore. Heard she got the job because she fucked the right guys."

"Oh Roger."

"I'm serious. She's a whore." Roger had a light tone in his voice, and that was a change, Hallie thought. It was as if he were joking about the department head. "But speaking of fucking…" Roger gently laid Hallie back and reached under her skirt.

Hallie didn't like to hear Roger talk like that, but at least his touch was tender. They made love on the couch and for the first time in months, Hallie relaxed into the experience. She closed her eyes and said a silent thank you for the pill. Tomorrow night, she said to herself, she would talk to Roger about marriage counseling.

The next night it was after ten when Roger arrived home. He'd eaten at the hospital and he went right to his study to work on a new paper. The night after that he came home in a good mood, and leaned against the kitchen counter while Hallie made a stir-fry shrimp dish on the stove. She wasn't sure how he happened to be shuffling through her papers on the low desk next to him, but as she was spooning the rice onto their plates she heard him say, "What are these ads, Hallie? I see red circles around want ads for nurses. You can't be serious."

"I was going to talk to you about that. It was just an idea—part time work. Now that Eric's older, I thought…"

"You thought, you thought. I spill my guts out to you the other night about how much progress I'm making and now you hit me with this?"

"I don't see what one thing has to do with the other. Just give me a chance to explain…"

"Typical little Hallie—always trying to explain."

"If you wouldn't interrupt—just hear me out. I have some things to say."

"Well, well, well," Roger said, his voice filled with sarcasm and scorn, "I have a few things to say right now myself."

The next thing Hallie knew, her nose was bleeding and the skin on her cheek burned hot. She ran out the back door and onto the deck, but he caught her elbow and spun her around. "Don't you dare walk away from me."

"I'll do what I have to do to protect myself," Hallie yelled.

"Why you stupid slut."

Roger shoved her in the middle of her chest and she lost her balance. She fell backward and tumbled off the front of the deck. Pain shot through her arm and shoulder. She managed to roll over on her back, and when she opened her eyes her vision was blurred. But she did see Roger on one side of her and a crying Eric on the other. "Don't cry, sweetie," she said. "Mommy's okay."

"Baby, are you really okay? You took quite a fall."

"Fall? That's what you call it?"

"I'm sorry Hallie, but really, if you hadn't run out like that…"

"No, Roger. I'm not covering this up. I think my arm is broken. I can't move it. And it's because you shoved me."

Roger rolled her to her good side and eased her up. "You have to go to the hospital. I realize that, but I want you to tell them you fell."

Hallie thought for a minute and realized that maybe, just maybe, this was her chance to get Roger to marriage counseling. For once, she had a bargaining chip. "I don't think so, Roger," she said. "I don't want to lie about this, not to myself and not to anyone else."

"Hallie, please, I'm going to beg you. I know you're angry. You're in pain. But this kind of thing could ruin my career. Please, please, think about our future."

For the first time Hallie heard fear in Roger's voice. She hated how pleased it made her, but she liked this unfamiliar sense of power. "I want something from you Roger."

"What? What more could you possibly…"

"It's not about things, for God's sake. It's about *us*. It's about our life together. I want to go to marriage counseling. I don't ever want to be afraid of you again. I want to be able to talk to you, really talk." Hallie felt woozy, as if she were going to faint.

Roger's voice sounded like it was coming from the end of a long tunnel, but she heard him say, "Okay, Hallie, okay." Then she heard him direct Eric to walk calmly to the car and felt him lift her body. She leaned all her weight against him as they made their way to the car.

She was alert enough to hear Roger tell the story of her fall to the ER doctor, who, she realized, was no doubt an acquaintance of his. If she hadn't been in so much pain, she might have had the energy to resent the respect he received from the staff, and by association, merited the extra attention given to her. "I'm not sure exactly how it happened," Hallie said. "One minute I was going out to the deck to get the table ready for dinner and the next minute I was on the ground."

"We have got to put the railing on that deck," Roger said. "We've been talking about it since we got here. It's only about a foot and a half, and we don't let Eric go out there alone anyway." He looked relaxed as he sat in the chair next to her. "Looks like you'll have your arm in a sling on that cruise we're taking." The doctor and nurse both laughed. Hallie wasn't sure why.

"I guess so," Hallie said. She didn't want to look at him. It was odd, she thought, that in the midst of this pain, she felt a kind of euphoria. If this is what it took to get Roger into marriage counseling, then so be it. She hung on tightly to a small sense of victory.

Getting to Work

What Can We Learn About the Cycle of Abuse?

We finally see Hallie taking steps toward autonomy. Through good, healthy anger she is realizing that Roger is abusing her. It may seem amazing, but many women do not realize that their husband's/partner's behavior falls into the category of true abuse unless and until they are sent to the hospital. This episode represents a real eye opener for Hallie. Yes, she remains too frightened of and loyal to Roger to expose his abuse at this time. However, she is taking steps to protect herself and Eric.

Why is Hallie so afraid someone will find out about Roger's behavior? Would it not be a relief if he were exposed? Unfortunately, this usually is not the case. Battered women often have been so isolated and so brainwashed by the emotional, mental, and physical abuse that they doubt themselves. Hallie's efforts to explain and rationalize Roger's behavior show that she still doubts her perceptions and her ability to make healthy decisions. She even doubts her own sanity—maybe Roger really is right about everything.

Hallie is so vulnerable to Roger's control and dominance that she feels simultaneously secure and terrified. If someone finds out about the dynamics of the relationship and tries to help her, Hallie does not trust that the person, whoever it is, would be capable of defeating Roger. Hallie experiences Roger as all-powerful; though her perceptions are distorted, he is the only person she trusts to do what he says he will do. That is her history with him.

In a way, Hallie is trying to retain some control over what will happen next in that she wants to decide how much information about her life with Roger she can safely expose and when she'll expose it. Hallie has allowed the possibility of leaving Roger into her consciousness, but at this time, few or no options for safety remain. This is one reason she holds out so much hope for counseling.

As we can expect, Hallie fears change. Fear is a natural human reaction to change appearing on the horizon. Imagine her fear when she realizes that if she walks away from her marriage, she will have only herself to rely on for protection and security, which are basic needs she and Eric have. With her self-confidence so undermined, her fears will loom very large. Consider that at this point Roger can literally control her from thousands of miles away. Hallie believes he will know when she is not following his written and verbal orders.

Finding Her Strength and Spirit

A part of Hallie knows she can be independent and strong. This is the component of Hallie's personality that is as fearless as a rebellious child. When a battered woman can get in touch with that part and let it dominate, she rediscovers her creativity and her spirit. This is linked with the universal concept of spirituality, not any particular religion or religious belief. Until Hallie can recognize her longing for spiritual connection and get in touch with her creative spirit, she will shut down and allow herself to be victimized.

Each of us has a deep-seeded sense of a powerful energy that guides our lives. We have the choice to tap into this energy or to ignore it. Our natural spirit is connected to a belief that we have power to determine our destiny and to take charge of our lives.

Our own spirit can be viewed as the essence or spirit of who we are and is linked to our belief in our power to survive.

Spirituality forms the basis of any faith system, and guides our choices about the way we act on that faith. Hallie is familiar with an organized religious group, but some women may choose meditation and contemplation. No spiritual system ever devised calls for an individual to become a victim of another person. In other words, we are *not* victims unless we *choose* to be. Hallie will never break free of Roger until she embraces the reality that she has choices.

Part of life involves learning from traumas that come our way. We endure these events and usually find ways to deal with them, and when we are spiritually healthy, we take action rather than simply *reacting* to them. Hallie's actions, although they may seem small, show she is becoming healthier because she is acting on available options. Looking at it another way, the "old" Hallie might have spent the two weeks Roger was gone very differently. For example, she might have curled up on her couch and relaxed into the peaceful atmosphere in her house. In other words, she could have stayed in denial, perhaps fantasizing about the "good" Roger. Instead, Hallie has regained enough of her spirit to take actions on her own behalf.

Deep within, we know if our lives are healthy or unhealthy, and as adults, it is our responsibility to do something about our situation. If Hallie remains a victim, then she negates her spiritual power. We think of our human identity as most important, but we are first spiritual beings and we're going through a human existence in order to learn how to be deeper spiritual beings. As we take each step and expand our knowledge, we have the power to choose what we do with this knowledge.

Hallie remains in this abusive relationship because she has lost sight of how important and powerful her spirit is. Before she can or will fight for herself, she must regain this connection with and love for her spirit. For a variety of reasons, she has allowed Roger to dominate her spirit to the point that she believes she is incapable of gaining anything better, much less deserving a different life. Her own childhood set her up for this. Her alcoholic and abusive father broke her child spirit; her co-dependent and enabling mother taught her that it is more important to appease others than to fight for her own spirit.

Religion versus Spirituality

During therapy sessions with abused women, I have often found that religious beliefs have prevented them from connecting with their spirituality. For example, one of my clients tried hard to abide by the teachings of her religion, which can be summed up as "turn the other cheek, pray for your marriage, and always remember that the man is head of the household." She worked to align herself with those beliefs and she ended up physically and mentally devastated. She couldn't live with the disparity between what her spirit knew and what these superficial and misinterpreted beliefs dictated. As a result of a breakdown, she was admitted to the hospital for several weeks of intensive psychotherapy and physical rehabilitation.

The physical body will reflect what Hallie called "soul sickness." Hallie suffers physical and emotional symptoms from Roger's abuse. The symptoms lessen when he is gone. However, physical illnesses she has also result from her lifetime messages blueprint, which contains a strong admonition that she must make this marriage work. Herein lies an important clue that helps answer all the prevailing questions about why women don't leave at the first sign of abuse. Like Hallie, many women hold deep beliefs that they must prove their ability to keep a marriage together because they could not, as children, help their own parents keep the family intact. Hallie couldn't heal her parents' marriage, but her mother eventually left. Even if she hadn't, Hallie would still feel the pressure to fix her marriage and succeed where her parents failed.

Hallie is a well-to-do doctor's wife, but she has little or no money. She sees poor women at the clinic and feels guilty that she's lied about her income. In actuality, it isn't her income at all. Roger believes the money is his and he gives and takes away.

One of the most powerful ways to keep a victim controlled is to provide just enough to keep her alive and, at the same time, deprive her of anything more, especially the freedom to exercise a choice, even one as simple as picking out some clothing. As this continues, women may believe they are incapable of taking care of themselves and their children, so they try to cope by staying married. Hallie knows that she cannot provide for Eric the way Roger can. However, we know that Hallie is a woman with skills. She can take care of Eric, but she needs to absorb that knowledge.

As Hallie begins to take steps toward autonomy, her self-confidence and self-esteem will rise, because the rebellious and creative child within her is activated. As I've said, Hallie is aware of the way her body reacts to Roger's absence. When she visited her mother, she also noted the lack of physical symptoms. These are powerful body messages and will guide her, if only she will listen to them. The mind and body are one—not separate entities. They work together to give us information about the way we are living. Hallie has ignored the messages before, and doctors she has seen colluded with her, and Roger as well, to ignore physical messages. Over time, we can expect to see physical illnesses if we ignore the messages our bodies send. Unfortunately, too many physicians prescribe the latest new drug to deal with ulcers, colitis, headaches, insomnia, weight gain or loss, addiction, and so forth, without looking into the cause. Yet, these same doctors know that these illnesses can be symptoms of stress or psychological disorders.

As horrible as it is, the trip to the emergency room has opened Hallie's eyes. Even though she does not expose Roger, she finally realizes the extent of the danger in her environment. The combination of the emergency room experience and the visit to Sister Dorothy provides a growing sense of support. Emotional and physical support are extremely important to everyone regardless of their situation. Sister Dorothy gives Hallie's confidence a boost and she feels capable of accomplishing healthier changes.

Note that Sister Dorothy is not pushing Hallie to leave Roger. If she did, Hallie might become frightened, which could prompt her to end the session and never return or call the spiritual counselor again. Hallie needs to remain in control and at this point she is still willing to believe that Roger will change and will go to counseling with her. Of course, it would be ideal if he could truly change and sustain the changes. So, while Hallie does not believe she needs to walk away from the marriage, she does understand that she must take some positive actions for Eric and herself. Using the threat of exposure may not be the best way to approach Roger, but it is the only effective way she has. Regardless of the outcome, Hallie has taken a critical step on the path to healing.

9

Hallie adjusted her straw hat, but she still squinted in the bright sun. Ever since they'd arrived on the ship, Roger said over and over, "This is the life, Hallie, this is the life." But Hallie wasn't so sure that cruise ship life suited her. She spent most of her time finding patches of shade, trying to avoid the heat and getting sunburned. On the other hand, wandering around the cruise ship was like visiting a big city with shops and game rooms and something new to see around every corner. Hallie and Eric spent hours exploring and taking in their surroundings.

Thankfully, Eric enjoyed himself playing with other kids on the cruise. Much to Hallie's delight, he'd taken to the swimming pool like a fish in a pond. She settled into the deck chair at the shallow end of the pool, making sure Eric could still see her. He still tended to worry if she went too far away. Roger either teased or berated her, depending on his mood, about coddling him, which annoyed Hallie since he was the one who wouldn't allow Eric to go to preschool. He didn't even let her take Eric to the playgroup at the church. No wonder Eric was reluctant to let Hallie out of his sight for more than a few minutes.

Hallie picked up her book, but she only pretended to read. With her arm still immobilized, it wasn't easy to hold the book anyway, and besides, she had other things on her mind, especially Roger's promise to go to marriage counseling. Although Hallie didn't like holding it over his head, he was undeniably responsible for her broken arm, and the only way she could reconcile what happened was to continue to see it as an opportunity to turn their marriage around. She didn't intend to waste this chance. So, as Hallie sat by the pool, she mentally prepared a list of things she wanted to discuss with Roger in the presence of a neutral third party. The first item was certainly Roger's refusal to send Eric to preschool. His excuse was that he wanted *her* home. Why? Supposedly because he could concentrate and do his important work only if he knew she and Eric were safe at home. That was ludicrous, Hallie thought, and she definitely wanted to talk about it. And for her, the way he continued to insult Ginger in front of Eric was another important issue.

Now, Hallie thought, she had something else that just wasn't fair. The first full day on the ship, Roger met Ed, a real estate developer from Florida. At first Hallie was relieved that Roger hadn't dismissed him as a "loser," as he did with most people. She was happy Roger had a tennis partner he enjoyed, and for some reason, he found Ed's wife Kimberly acceptable, too. But last night when they were alone in their cabin after dinner, Roger berated her because she couldn't play tennis, and he added golf, too. "Even if you hadn't broken your arm, we would have missed a chance to play doubles with Ed and Kimberly, because *my* wife doesn't know how to play." When was she supposed to learn to play tennis and golf, she wondered?

At one time, Hallie might have apologized to Roger for not being an available tennis partner, or she might have teased him a little. But last night she'd simply shrugged it off and tried to avoid any exchange over such a trivial issue. He wasn't satisfied with that, however. Apparently, to Roger, tennis was hardly a trivial matter. It would have been funny, Hallie thought, if Roger weren't so touchy.

"What you fail to understand, Hallie, is that we are *finally* going places. Speaking at international conferences is paying off. I told you we could go to Philadelphia, but I'm holding out for better."

"I know, Roger," she'd said. "I'm excited about your career, but what does that have to do with my inability to play tennis?"

Roger just laughed. "Hallie, when we move, we'll be *expected* to join a country club." He threw up his hands and said, "As strange as it might sound to you, I have to improve my golf game just to fit in. So is it too much to ask that my wife at least *try* to act as if she cares about getting to know the right people?"

Hallie always had detested these conversations about the so-called right people, the men Roger considered important. "Don't they have swimming pools at country clubs?" she'd asked. "I'd rather spend my time swimming than learning a game I never wanted to play in the first place." Hallie surprised herself with the strength in her voice.

"Oh really. Well, never mind. Suit your stupid little self. I wouldn't dream of imposing on you, even if it meant helping my career."

Roger had rolled over and gone to sleep, but Hallie had stayed awake and marveled at how such a small thing could become so big to Roger. Then she thought about what she really wanted. Of course she wanted Roger to respect her. That was basic, but she also wanted what almost everyone thought of as a full life, which included friends, companionship in her family, and when Eric started school next year, meaningful work for herself. Somehow, spending afternoons playing tennis or golf didn't match her picture. Besides, she thought bitterly, if she did end up frittering away hours at the country club, Roger would call her lazy, ungrateful, and a loser. Why was it she could never win? Hallie wanted to talk with a marriage counselor about that, too.

Hallie slathered more sunscreen over her arms and legs, and hoped Roger would change his mind about looking for a new job in Florida. For some reason, this cruise had sparked a yearning in him for the water and tropical weather. At breakfast that morning, he'd talked about moving closer to the ocean and learning to sail. Hallie felt her stomach tighten at the thought of spending weekends with Roger on a boat. The fact is, she was afraid to even think about another situation in which Roger would shout at her and call her names. Between contemplating tennis, golf, and sailing, Hallie ended up anxious and afraid that Roger was forcing more adjustments on her. But then she warned herself not to look so far ahead.

When they had come home from the hospital the night he'd pushed her off the deck, Roger apologized again, but told her he wanted to wait until after they came home from their cruise before they started counseling. "That's only a couple of weeks away," he said, "and besides, I need time to do the research to find out who would be the right person for us to see. He has to be someone across town."

Hallie hadn't been surprised that Roger preferred a counselor who wouldn't have heard of him. But she had other concerns, too. "I had hoped to see someone next week," she'd said, "and I'd just as soon go to a woman as to a man."

"Next week is too soon, sweetheart," he'd said. "And you have to trust me to choose the best person—I want someone topnotch, and if that happens to be a woman, then fine. The reality is, though, the best people around here are men."

Hallie had bit her tongue to keep from blurting out something to the effect that his statement was ridiculous, undoubtedly untrue. However, she accepted that she had lost that round, but she didn't intend to lose the fight. At least that's how she'd thought of it. But it so often seemed that she barely had a chance to get used to one thing before along came something else. Now, all Roger did was talk nonstop about moving to Florida and joining a country club and living the good life in a place that was sunny and hot all year round. The whole subject made her head pound.

* * * *

The morning of their fourth day on the cruise, Roger told her to call Ed and Kimberly's cabin and invite Kim to meet her at the buffet lunch. He also told her to leave Eric in the childcare center so the two women could get to know each other without having Eric interfere. "Please try to be sociable with her. Ed is an important man in south Florida. He has connections and could help me find the job I want. And he can tell us about the best areas to buy a house. At the very least, he can use his influence to get us into the best country club."

"That's fine, Roger. I don't mind having lunch with Kimberly. Does she know I'll be calling? Have you talked to her?"

"I expected you to call her and extend an invitation, if it's not too much trouble, that is." Sarcasm dripped from his voice.

"Don't talk to me that way, Roger. I'm perfectly capable of inviting someone to lunch."

"What did you say? What did my smart mouth wife say?" Roger grabbed her good arm and swung her around.

Hallie yanked her arm out of Roger's grip. "Get your hands off me," she said.

"Oh, look who's issuing orders now. You think this is the way you're going to fix our marriage?"

"Roger, we can't fix our marriage at all if you take everything I say as some kind of challenge to you."

Roger stared her down, but he didn't grab her again.

* * * *

Hallie tried to like Kim, but with little in common, it was difficult to keep up a lively conversation. Besides, in a loud voice, Kim made nasty comments about other people on the ship. Hallie felt nauseated and barely able to force down small bites of the shrimp salad and fruit she'd taken from the buffet. She nibbled dry crackers just to settle her stomach. She spent most of her time looking around her to see if others were bothered by Kimberly's loud talk. It gave Hallie a headache to even imagine spending time with this woman if they moved to Florida. Or, Hallie thought, if Roger moved to Florida without her, a part of her wouldn't care.

"Are you looking forward to tonight?" she asked Kimberly in an attempt to steer the conversation away from gossip about other women on the ship. Everyone had been talking about the formal dinner and dancing, with a famous singer entertaining, too. Hallie was looking forward to it, too. As it happened, Roger was a terrific dancer. They had been out dancing only a handful of times since they were married, but Roger always rose to the occasion and confidently led her around the dance floor.

"I suppose so," Kimberly said, "but we've been on these cruises before. Same old thing, I'm sure."

"Well, it's new to me," Hallie said, "and I made a lovely gown just for the occasion."

"You made your dress?" Kimberly looked stunned.

"I found some beautiful violet silk. Roger said he liked it." Hallie wondered why Kimberly had such a strange look on her face. Hallie decided it must be her imagination and said no more about it.

Later that afternoon, while Eric napped, Hallie tried on the gown. She couldn't help admiring her own work. She'd taken great care with the design, which emphasized her small waist. The low back showed off her smooth skin. Even better, her grandmother's antique jewelry looked perfect with it. She was getting ready to take it off when Roger came through the door.

"Oh, I see you're wearing the famous dress."

"Not famous now," she said, "but maybe after tonight it will be. I'm so looking forward to this evening." Hallie twirled around and remained determined not to let Roger ruin her mood.

"Famous for making me a laughing stock," he said.

"What? What are you talking about?"

"Hallie, you couldn't keep your mouth shut about *making* your dress?"

"Why should I? You saw the material. You saw the pattern. You wanted me to save money and make the dress myself." Hallie turned around slowly. "And as you can see, it turned out just great."

"Take off the dress, put on regular clothes, and follow me."

"Why?"

"Don't ask questions. Just do as I say."

"I am asking, Roger. I want to know."

Roger reached out and grabbed the scoop neckline and in one fast motion, he ripped the dress down the front.

"Oh my God. Oh my God, you've ruined it." Hallie felt hot tears in the corner of her eyes.

"Quit whining and crying. I told you to get dressed. Wake Eric up. We are going shopping."

"I love this dress, Roger. *You* said you liked it, too."

"Hallie, only stupid women tell rich, influential women that they sewed their dress. After all these years, you're still the country girl. You're a loser, you always will be."

Hallie's heart started to pound. Oddly, though, Roger's cold anger didn't frighten her into silence. Perhaps, she thought, because Roger wouldn't risk hurting her when he was so determined to impress Ed and Kimberly. "I'll go shopping with you Roger. That's fine. You can change your mind about the dress, Roger, but you had no right to rip it up. You ruined my hard work."

"And I'll ruin it all I please, Hallie. Apparently, this is the only way you'll ever learn. Look, sweetheart, I wanted my girl to look good tonight. If you hadn't opened your big mouth, you might have pulled it off, you know."

"What? Pulled off what?"

"Kimberly might have thought you had a designer gown, but now she knows it's just a dress some little mountain girl hick would wear. Are you finally catching on?"

Roger's voice was low and quiet–and colder by the minute, too.

"Sure, let's go shopping in the ship's boutique," Hallie said, in an equally cold tone. "I'll let you pick out my dress for the evening, but I want you to stop calling me a loser and a hick. Maybe some people care about designer clothes and think that making a dress is stupid, but I'm not one of them."

Roger looked surprised. Then he smirked. "Take you away from home and you turn into a smart mouth woman. Too bad you're still so stupid. And you have the same country girl tacky taste as that grandmother you loved so much."

Roger continued to stare at her, his gaze was so cold that Hallie looked away.

"And I'm getting rid of that ridiculous jewelry once and for all." He slowly grabbed the beads and held them in his closed fist.

"No Roger, these beads were grandmother's. You know how much I love them." She put her hand over Roger's and turned her face away. Somehow, though, she didn't care if he did slap her. She had to save her beads. "Please, please," she said to herself, "please let go."

Roger gave one hard yank and Hallie felt the clasp at the back of her neck pop open. "Stop, stop," she yelled. "You're ruining them."

Roger held the beads in his hands and pulled and tugged at them until he had pulled the necklace completely apart and then, without ever looking up, he smashed the necklace with his foot, grinding the beads into the carpet.

Hallie covered her face with her hands and wept. This pain felt different, she thought. This wasn't about Roger and his temper and all the destructive things he said and did. Hallie knew her tears came from a broken heart and a loss that felt so great that for a moment, she wanted to die.

* * * *

Roger waved at Ed and Kimberly. Ed waved back and motioned for them to join him at the bar. "Good to see you two."

"Oh Hallie," Kim said, "nice dress."

"Thanks." Hallie hated the dark green slinky dress, hated the ship, and Kim's phony smile made her long to be home. She'd invite Ginger over and they'd share a cup of tea. At least Ginger was real and not trying to impress people all the time. Hallie put her hand to her throat, but quickly remembered that the beads were gone. Hallie didn't think much about material things, but her grandmother's beads were the only touchstone she had to help her feel close to a woman she had loved so much.

Roger laughed as if someone suddenly had said something hilarious. "I told Hallie that the next time we take a cruise, we'll leave Eric with one of his grandmothers. That way, a lovely silk gown won't end up with a grape juice stain running down the front. Thank goodness the boutique was open."

Ed and Kim laughed along with him. "Oh no," Kim said, "that must have been quite a mess."

Hallie just smiled, but Roger continued his light, charming banter. "Eric tripped over his own little feet and before my best girl here could get out of the way, the juice just flew through the air and landed right on her." Roger turned to the bar and reached for two glasses of champagne.

Liar, Hallie thought. Her dress was ruined because he is so impossibly cruel.

"Here's to new dresses, sweetheart," Roger said as he held up his glass for a toast.

Hallie clinked her glass with his and took a sip of the champagne. Then she turned her attention to the crowd gathering in the room. She hoped the subject of her dress would soon exhaust itself. Roger had told this grape juice story to the saleswoman at the boutique. Oh how they'd laughed over it. He leaned across the counter and put on all his phony charm and soon had the woman bringing out every possible dress. Hallie had been quiet as she watched the scene unfold. By the time they actually got to the boutique she didn't care what dress she wore. The cruise had turned into a nightmare anyway; the dress episode only capped it.

Only to be polite, Hallie commented that she'd ended up with the green dress because it was about the only item in the whole store that fit her. Kimberly and Ed laughed as if she'd made a joke and Roger went along, too.

"Well, again, it's delightful," Ed said in a kind voice. "I hope you'll save me a dance later, Hallie."

"Thanks, Ed, I certainly will." Hallie felt a lift, not so much because of the dance, but because of his tone. She wondered if Ed had sensed her unhappiness and extended his kindness to change her mood. Well, Hallie thought, it worked; she was putting the unhappiness behind her. She took a deep breath and told herself to enjoy the evening, no matter that she hated the green dress, with it's puffy sleeves and long slit up the side.

The two couples had dinner with two other couples at a table for eight. By the time the evening was over, Roger had danced with each of the women. He flirted and joked and poured on the flattery. The women told her he was definitely an above-average dancer. Kim particularly seemed to float around the floor in Roger's arms. As it turned out, Ed was not a particularly good dancer, not that it mattered. Ed also surprised her in other ways. Hallie had expected him to be a backslapping kind of man, and probably a show-off. But as Hallie observed him she saw that he was actually quite sensitive and, she felt sure, he saw through Roger's act. And that, sadly enough, was exactly what all Roger's exaggerated flattery and good cheer added up to.

"What a lucky woman you are, Hallie," Kim said as the two couples headed back to their cabins. "Roger is obviously going places. He told me a little about his breakthrough work in the brain imaging field. You must be proud to be married to such an important man."

"His work is quite new," Hallie said, "and I'm glad to see it getting the attention it deserves." That was the truth. Hallie thought back to the early conversations she'd had with Roger, conversations in which she'd talked about her interest in the budding field. Funny how he'd forgotten all about that. He never asked her opinion and now that he had a secretary, she never saw his papers until they were published. Most of the time, Roger acted like his work was way beyond her comprehension. That was another thing she planned to change.

Roger and Hallie said goodnight to Ed and Kimberly and as soon as they were alone, Roger became quiet. Not exactly brooding though, Hallie realized. Perhaps he was just tired. "It was a lovely evening, Roger," she said, "and once I got used to it, I liked my new dress." That part wasn't true, but Hallie felt pleasant and wanted to reach out to Roger while his mood was good.

"No doubt," he said. His mouth formed a tight grimace. "Ed thought you were quite the little sexy number in it."

"No, nothing like that," Hallie said. Her stomach fluttered. She'd had a nagging fear that dancing with Ed might bring on a jealous tirade. But she also thought she'd had no choice. If she'd refused, Roger would have told her she'd ruined their chances to make a good connection.

"Did you enjoy flirting with him?"

"Oh Roger, I didn't flirt. I was only being friendly, as I assumed you wanted me to be. You told me Ed was an important man and could help you–help us, if we decide to move."

"Nice is one thing, you bitch, flirting and laughing with him is another. Maybe you'd like to go to his cabin and fuck him. Do you think that would help my career?"

Hallie was shocked at her own first thought, which was that Roger probably wanted to have sex with Kimberly. If anyone had done any flirting, it was Roger and Kim. But, of course, she didn't risk saying as much.

"Shut up now," Roger said. "I'm going to get rid of this babysitter, and then I'll show you how much you mean to me."

Roger was pleasant to the sitter and Hallie went into the bathroom and began to take off the dress. Thank God, she thought, no matter how much sex Roger demanded, at least she couldn't get pregnant. The pills were tucked safely inside an empty compact.

The bathroom door swung open and Roger came up behind her. "This is how I like to fuck you, Hallie." He grabbed her breasts and pinched her nipples and then he turned her around pushed her down on the floor. "I hope you get pregnant, you slut, so you won't be out dancing and flirting with other men."

"Roger, I wasn't flirting. I thought I was doing the right thing."

Roger shoved himself inside her. "Do you want a baby, Hallie? Do you?"

Hallie wrapped her arms around his back and whispered, "So much, Roger, so much."

Within minutes, Roger shuddered and moaned and then quickly got up and zipped his pants. "You are a liar and a slut. I don't believe a word you say. I'm going to the bar. Be ready for me when I get back. I want to make a baby while we're on this cruise."

Hallie climbed into bed and opened her book. Hallie wondered why Roger chose to leave. He didn't drink, at least not very often. They'd each had a glass of champagne and then a glass of wine with dinner. That was more alcohol than they usually had at social events. Maybe he wanted to cool off, Hallie thought. Roger had accused her of flirting before; he'd called her ugly names before. She felt calm, but she wasn't sure why. She certainly didn't want more sex, and she had to admit Roger had been right when he called her a liar. She wanted so much to make the marriage work and with marriage counseling ahead, she felt sure that Roger would see how much his accusations hurt her. Still, a part of her no longer cared. That scared her, but it also made her less frantic, less desperate to please him.

By the time Roger came back, Hallie was just about to turn off the light and call it a night.

"Hi beautiful," Roger said. He had two cans of ginger ale in his hand. "I brought us a nightcap." He grinned as if he'd made a joke.

"Great. I'll get us some glasses." Hallie threw back the blanket and got out of bed.

"Been reading?"

"Uh huh."

"Good book?"

"Uh huh."

"*Uh huh, uh huh,*" he mocked. "My you're chatty."

Hallie didn't respond, but handed him a glass with ice and curled up on the bed.

"You must be thinking about Ed."

"No, Roger, I was reading my book."

"At least my stupid little wife knows how to read."

"Roger, please drop this."

"Oh, I'll drop it all right." Roger came around to her side of the bed and picked up her reading glasses. He threw them to the floor and crushed them with his foot. "Now you can think about having sex with Ed. No distractions."

Hallie burst into tears. "I can't believe you did that. My reading glasses, my *reading* glasses. You know I need them." Hallie felt her chest tighten, almost preventing her breathing, as she saw her glasses in pieces on the floor. Of all the things Roger did, destroying her glasses felt like closing off her most important connection to the world. She covered her face with her hands, unable to stop her tears.

"You won't have time to read now that you'll be pregnant," he said. Roger grabbed Hallie's legs and pulled her down until she was flat. And then, without kissing her or caressing her in any way, he shoved himself into her.

Hallie's tears didn't stop because Roger's thrusting caused her so much pain that she cried out. "Stop, Roger, you're hurting me." She struggled to get away from him. She'd never done that before.

"Maybe you think Ed would fuck you better."

When it was clear that Roger had no intention of stopping, Hallie became silent, but the tears continued to flow. She thought about the broken pieces of her reading glasses and longed to be home.

Getting to Work

What Can We Learn About the Cycle of Abuse?

Roger is obsessed with the way others view him; therefore, he constantly strives for perfection. If he sees Hallie as imperfect, then he thinks of himself as imperfect and fears that others will see him as such. Hallie and Eric are possessions to him. His "possessions" define who he is because he does not have a strong enough self-identity to be secure.

Since Roger views Hallie and Eric as "objects" he owns, he cannot allow them to be individuals. Their role to define Roger dictates how they should act and come across to others. To Roger, Eric must not show fear and a normal attachment to Hallie and concern for her whereabouts are potentially signs of weakness. Again, he puts Hallie in a no-win situation because he will not allow Eric to associate with other children on a regular basis. Roger expects Hallie to be of some use to him; hence the pressure on Hallie to act "correctly" around Ed and Kimberly.

In Roger's mind, Hallie is not an individual with her own likes and dislikes. Over and over, we see that her identity revolves around the way she can be used for Roger's benefit. If she disagrees with him he sees this as a personal insult and a put down of him. As we see her begin to voice her opinion more to him, we will also see Roger's abuse escalate. He retaliates like a child and pays her back by degrading her. He hopes this serves two purposes. One is to make her as perfect as he wants to be; the other is to scare her so much that she would not dare to leave him. His fear of abandonment is always of utmost importance.

Hallie will never "win" with Roger because he will always change the challenge for her. He continually sets up situations to use her in order to prove to himself that his deep inner fears and insecurities are true. He sees in her what he fears in himself. The fact is, until Roger is content with who he is (which is unlikely to happen) Hallie can expect more demands for changes in her life because Roger is constantly seeking perfection.

Always on Alert

Hallie has learned to live in anticipation of feelings of hopelessness and helplessness. Because of the way she has been living, any new event or change must be cautiously examined and she must figure out ways to be safe in a changing environment. While on the cruise, Hallie begins to see herself without Roger in her life. (We saw this briefly when she visited her mother, too.) In addition, Hallie realizes that Roger's priorities and lifestyle do not fit who she is. She reacts (not for the first time) to Roger's talk about "important people." Her reactions, although internal and not verbalized, represent a positive step toward autonomy. Perhaps a different environment and mingling with other people allow her to broaden her mind so that she can see herself in a more creative light. Remember that when she visited her mother she fantasized about a life without Roger.

Notice that Roger is startled and hesitates to grab her when she challenges his behavior toward her. By doing this she is refusing to be his victim; hence, she takes away some of his power. (Knowing when and how to do this can be tricky with an abusive person. This will increase the rage in some abusers and so you may put yourself in more danger.)

Hallie has reached the point of not caring as much about pleasing Roger. Little by little, she feels stronger and has begun to think about changing her life. Unfortunately some women get to this point before they have a safe escape plan in place. *(A safe escape plan includes a place to go, a way to get there, and some financial support.)* They are not prepared to protect themselves and their children.

Living with Fear and Blame

Notice that Roger continues to blame Hallie for her broken arm. Hallie knows he pushed her off the deck, yet she does not challenge him. On some level Roger no doubt believes that the whole incident was an "accident" or a "mishap" of some kind that occurred because of Hallie. His response is typical for most chronic abusers. They never accept responsibility for their abusive actions and always blame their victim. Sometimes they are so convincing they have their victims re-framing the event, eventually coming to accept that the abuser's version is true. Abusers have a definite way of persuading others, sometimes even the courts, that their wife or mate is to blame for her own injuries.

Roger is embarrassed that Hallie told Kimberly about her homemade dress. Again, he sees this as a reflection of his inability to buy her a dress, although he was unwilling to spend money on a dress, not unable. Ironically, Roger had not thought ahead. His withholding behavior is habitual, and he had not anticipated meeting a couple he wanted to impress. A man like Roger will immediately blame someone else, so Hallie takes the brunt of his self-loathing.

Odd as it may sound, when Roger tears Hallie's dress, she can adjust because that is familiar behavior. However, when he destroys her grandmother's precious jewelry Roger sends a powerful message to Hallie. Hallie is devastated by his cruelty because she knows he would rip her up—literally destroy her—with the same heartless abandon. She is finally getting the message that Roger's behavior has no boundaries.

Destroying something that has deep meaning for another person is typical behavior among certain types of batterers. Most batterers do follow patterns of abuse. Based on the common patterns I see in my practice, one would imagine that abusers get together to discuss abusive actions. That sounds strange, but most experts in the field have noted both similar patterns of behavior, and similar patterns of escalation among abusers.

The Ugly Jealousy

We can see that part of Roger's personality disorder manifests as extreme jealousy and possessiveness. Roger looks for any sign that Hallie is flirting and thus, harboring a plan to leave him. When she danced with Ed, even though Roger was dancing with other women, this was the proof Roger needed. Here, too, there is no way for Hallie to win. Roger wants her to be a sophisticated woman on his arm, a wife who knows how to make her way socially. She dances with Ed because she believes Roger expects her to "hobnob" with the people he believes can help him look good. We can see that Hallie doesn't care much one way or the other, but finds socializing with Ed pleasant because he is kind.

Roger has forced sex on Hallie before, and he has hurt her with sex before. It started subtly, in that Hallie didn't feel comfortable refusing. She went along to keep the peace, which was abdicating her power. Later, she found she couldn't talk her way out of it. There was no reasoning with him. Roger is becoming desperately afraid of losing Hallie and uses rape as a way of trying to break her into a more willing victim.

Rape is one of the most powerful ways to intimidate and to keep a victim under control. For many centuries it has been used as a tool to control women, as well as degrading and punishing them. Unfortunately many courts today still do not recognize forced sex in a marriage as the crime of rape. Even in states that do recognize marital rape, prosecutors will attest to the fact that it is a difficult charge to prove.

We also see Hallie feeling a sense of "numbness" about Roger. We can see that Hallie no longer thinks much about how she feels about Roger. She manages her life around him, and desperately wants to talk about things that she believes prevents them from having a good marriage. But her feelings about Roger are becoming less personalized. She certainly is beyond the heartfelt sense of loving him so much. The "numbness" we now see appears to be a necessary part of the leaving process, because as long as she loves

Roger, she will not be able to leave. This shift in her feelings, even in what she thinks about when she ponders her marriage and Roger, is an important development.

The Cruelty is not Accidental

Many of a batterer's messages are sent through symbols. When Roger destroys the jewelry, he is "stomping on" something that he knows Hallie considers precious. Likewise, when he breaks Hallie's glasses he sends a message that he can always keep her locked away from the world. Abusive men will use many symbols to keep their message squarely in front of their victim. Their symbols say: "I can break you at any time so you'd better play the way I want." To Hallie, losing her glasses symbolizes the destruction of the one way she had to escape from her increasingly horrible life.

10

"I'll want to see each of you alone," Dr. Richards said. He peered over his glasses and looked at both Roger and Hallie. "I assume that's okay."

"Sure, fine. Sounds like a good idea." Roger stood and reached across the desk to shake the psychiatrist's hand.

This was their third visit and while Hallie was less than satisfied with what had gone on so far, Roger was more pleasant at home and the atmosphere had definitely changed since they'd come back from the disastrous cruise. On the plane home he'd gently told her to call the optometrist and replace her glasses. It was as close as she would get to an apology, but she didn't care. She had been concerned about her glasses because she had no money of her own, and Roger kept tight control on the checkbook and the credit cards. If he hadn't paid for the glasses, she had no way to get them. Not being able to read was unthinkable. In fact, escaping into novels had always been her one pleasure. Roger's control over all the money, she mused. Something else to talk about with the therapist.

According to Roger, Dr. Richards was a psychiatrist new to the area. Roger had convinced him that Hallie suffered from depression. "You know I don't want to prescribe for my own wife—wouldn't be ethical. So, perhaps you can evaluate the situation," Roger said.

Hallie had enough energy and fight in her to know that she wasn't depressed. She had her physical problems all right, but depression wasn't one of them. "I'm sad," she'd said to Dr. Richards, in Roger's presence. "I am not depressed, however."

"Well, Hallie, being sad may be just another word you use for depression," Dr. Richards said.

"I'm a trained nurse. I know what the words mean," Hallie had snapped.

Roger had chuckled. "You can see how much my opinion counts around here."

"Your opinion is all that does seem to count." Hallie watched Dr. Richards pull out a prescription pad and begin to write.

"Hallie, I do tend to go with Roger's evaluation on this. From what he said, the cruise ended badly and before that, you broke your arm. And with long-term sadness over not becoming pregnant, depression would be a likely result." With that, he handed Hallie the prescription. "I recommend you start taking these immediately."

"Indulge me, Hallie, and listen to Dr. Richards." Roger threw up his hands and laughed, expecting Dr. Richards to laugh along with him. Roger became quiet when he saw that the doctor didn't appreciate the joke. Hallie liked that the doctor didn't treat Roger like one of his colleagues. It was a good sign.

Before they saw Dr. Richards the first time, Roger had told her that he didn't want to talk about her broken arm right away. It infuriated Hallie that he still insisted on calling it her accident. She had just nodded, though, and didn't argue. But when Dr. Richards asked why they sought counseling, Roger talked about poor communication and a misunderstanding that occurred during their cruise. Hallie laughed out loud and Dr. Richards had turned to her and raised his eyebrows expectantly. "Why is that funny?"

Hallie felt nervous and suddenly afraid as she said, "I just think it goes deeper than that. It wasn't a misunderstanding. It was another incident in a pattern."

"I'll admit, darling, that I tend to get jealous," Roger said.

"But my glasses, Roger, my glasses."

"That was an accident, Hallie."

"No it wasn't..."

"Wait, wait," Dr. Richards said. "I can't follow the details right now. Let's just agree that we'll work on communication. The specific incidents aren't as important as how and why they occur."

"I agree," Roger said.

Roger had looked for Dr. Richards to glance his way, but he hadn't. Instead, he studied his appointment book and said, "I think we should start with twice a week and then when we're well underway, we can go to appointments once each week. Okay?" He looked to Hallie.

"That's fine with me," she said.

When they got in the car, Roger warned her not to talk about each little fight they'd had. "Remember what he said, Hallie. It's all about communication."

Hallie nodded. She could talk about communication all right, starting with the names Roger called her. Two days later, Dr. Richards opened their appointment by asking them how they solved problems.

"We don't," Hallie blurted out.

Roger laughed. "She's right, I have to admit. I tend to plan everything and by the time I tell her I've made up my mind."

Hallie decided to keep the conversation as positive as possible, so she told Dr. Richards that most of the time she was fine with Roger's decisions. For example she had been in favor of moving and she liked the house. She was thrilled that Roger's work was going well. But she didn't understand why Roger didn't want Eric in nursery school or why he was dead set against her getting a job, even a part-time position, at one of the hospitals in town.

Roger quickly spoke up. "We're trying to have another baby, so it seemed impractical for her to take a job when she'd just have to quit to be home with the baby."

Hallie almost said that she didn't want a child, but she held back. She felt tripped up, too, as if caught in a lie.

"What about that, Hallie?" Dr. Richards looked at her and waited for a response.

"Roger never wanted me to get a job, even before we planned our first baby."

"That's because I knew we'd be leaving," Roger said. "And a residency takes so much time, too. Odd hours and crazy schedules."

"Hallie, how do you feel about having another baby?" Dr. Richards watched her intently.

Roger stared at her and her heart started to pound. Hallie's hands shook as she brushed her hair off her face. "It's just that— oh, I don't know."

"Hallie, you seem conflicted," Dr. Richards said, "as if this subject upsets you."

"No, no, it's not that." Hallie began to cry and Roger immediately came to her side.

"Sweetheart, it's okay. I'm sorry this has made you sad." Roger turned to Dr. Richards. "You see, we've been trying for, well, for several months now and she's upset that she hasn't gotten pregnant."

Hallie glanced up at Dr. Richards. Somehow, he didn't look convinced by Roger's explanation. Their time was up for that day. At least she was reassured that she could see Dr. Richards alone.

Hallie hadn't wanted to talk about her past, her childhood, and all her old fantasies and dreams. She had wanted to unload her hurt and angry feelings over the way Roger called her names and ripped her clothes, and everything else, too, but Dr. Richards seemed more interested in hearing about her alcoholic father and her mother, whom he called codependent. So, during her first individual visit, she dutifully went along with him and told him about her father's drinking and the way he sneered when he mocked her for being small and tongue-tied. She also talked about her mother's bruises and other injuries she'd tried to hide.

When Dr. Richards asked her to tell him more about her mother, Hallie quickly defended Nina and explained that her mother had been terrified of her father and tried to protect her two children from his anger. "He drank all the time," Hallie said. She could hear the sadness in her voice. "I was relieved when I left for college, although I didn't like that my mother was alone with him. Fortunately, not long after, she discovered a lump in her breast. That changed her life. She left him not long after she recovered from her treatment." Hallie spoke of her pleasant visit with her mother a few months before.

"Do you and Roger visit your families often?" Dr. Richards asked.

"No," she said, "we visited Roger's mother once when Eric was a year old, but we've never visited my mother. I really don't care to see my dad or my brother."

"What about other couples? Do you and Roger have friends?"

"A woman in the neighborhood invited us to get together with her and her husband, but Roger said he didn't want to get involved with the neighbors."

Dr. Richards made a notation in a notebook in his lap. Hallie told him about some couples at the hospital and the church, but they weren't exactly friends. "Roger seems to think just about everybody is a loser," Hallie said, making no attempt to hide the bitterness in her voice, although she was sure the doctor already was gaining a clear picture of her isolation. No family around, no friends, except for Ginger, and Hallie had never told her the truth about her life. "That's his favorite thing to call people, including me. He especially makes fun of my one woman friend, Ginger. She's the neighbor he doesn't want us to get involved with."

"Makes fun?"

"He calls her a cow and gets Eric to go along with him."

Dr. Richards frowned and said, "What's it like for you to have so little interaction with family and friends?"

"I feel lonely and isolated. Roger won't let me have a job either."

"You need his permission to get a job."

"Yes, can't you tell? Can't you see that's how it is with him?" She heard the desperation in her voice.

Dr. Richards never answered her question. Their time was up.

* * * *

Roger had all but stopped really making love to her, Hallie thought, as she got up to get a glass of water. Every time they had sex it felt forced and so mechanical, even though he hadn't hurt her, as he had done on the cruise. All he talked about was having a baby and then relocating for a better job and a bigger house. "A fresh start," he said, "a new baby. That's what we need."

They'd each had several appointments alone with Dr. Richards, but Hallie didn't talk to Roger about her appointments and Roger didn't discuss his appointments either. So far, so good, if quiet was good, that is. However, one evening, Roger called and said he'd be working late and to eat without him. "I had my appointment with Dr. Richards earlier, so I have things to do here. Put Eric to bed so we can be alone when I come home. I need to talk to you."

Hallie didn't trust Roger's monotone voice. It was unreal and ominous. Still, she went about the rest of her day as if things were normal.

When Roger got home she offered him a cup of coffee, but he shook his head. He pulled out a chair at the dining room table. "Just sit down."

"Okay, Roger, okay."

"First, it's all over with Dr. Richards. Done, finished."

"What are you talking about?"

"We'll solve our problems by ourselves," he said.

"But you promised. Ever since the night you broke my arm, you promised we'd work out our problems..."

"Let's get one thing straight," he said, "I *didn't... break... your... arm*. That's for starters, but we have bigger things to discuss."

Hallie had not heard Roger quite this way before. He wasn't raging, but he wasn't acting normal either.

"Aren't you curious?" he asked.

"Of course, Roger. Please, what is this all about?"

"We'll call it your obsession with your petty little career."

"What do you mean?" Hallie asked.

"I thought it was a mutual decision that you not work." Roger said. "But Dr. Richards must think otherwise because he asked me how I felt about your working! Why would he ask me that, Hallie?"

Hallie laughed. "I don't know. I guess he wanted to hear your answer. Why are you bringing this up now?"

"I guess I finally realized how truly ungrateful you are. We're establishing some rules around here, Hallie."

"Oh right, as if we don't already have rules." Hallie's voice was filled with the same kind of sarcasm she often heard coming from Roger. She didn't care though, because a sarcastic sneer seemed like a mild reaction to what he'd said.

Roger grabbed her by the arm and headed toward the basement stairs. "Hey, you're hurting me," she said as she tried to pull away. "And where are you taking me?"

"We're going to have a little look at your precious career."

"In the basement? This is crazy, Roger."

"No, Hallie, you're crazy. Remember, sweetie, I have connections. I know crazy when I see it. I can call you crazy any time I please. I can fix it so you spend your life like a blithering idiot in a mental ward."

"Roger, please. Don't be ridiculous."

Roger continued pulling her toward the basement door and when she kept resisting, he picked her up and carried her down the stairs. "Now, I seem to recall some boxes of your worthless school papers and books." Roger set her down and walked around the storage area checking the sides of the boxes. "Ah yes, this is what I'm looking for."

Before Hallie knew what was happening next, Roger held her from behind and pushed her into the pile of boxes. He let go long enough to open the top box and shove her face down into it. "Take a good last look now, Hallie."

"What are you going to do, burn my books?" Hallie asked. Her throat tightened and she broke out into a sweat. It wasn't the books she was concerned about. She never imagined Roger would ever be down here in the basement. Terrified that he'd find the contraceptive pills she had no choice but to go along. Maybe he would burn the books and the pills would burn with them, safely undiscovered.

"I didn't have a book burning in mind," he said. "I think I'll just watch while you tear all the books and papers into tiny, little pieces."

"I don't believe this. Whether you acknowledge it or not, I graduated from college with a degree in nursing. I would like to work, and tearing up my books will not make me forget who I am."

"I'll tell you who you are. You are my wife, and you'll do as I say."

"So, you actually do think I'm your property, don't you?"

"Just get to work, Hallie. I don't intend to be here all night."

"And if I refuse?"

In one stride, Roger came closer and slapped her across the face. "Start."

If I start ripping up the papers, Hallie thought, I could buy some time. So, she picked up the first piece of her research papers and yanked at it until it ripped in two. She picked up the next and the next.

"At this rate we really will be here all night," Roger said. He picked up the carton and turned it over, letting all the papers spill on the floor. Hallie spotted the package in which she'd hidden the pills. While Roger was looking elsewhere, she kicked the package with her foot. It skidded across the floor and into the corner. Roger looked toward it, but quickly turned his attention back to tearing up her papers and ripping old textbooks.

"What have I done except support all the work you're doing in your field? All I asked for is a little respect. But instead, you push me around and make unreasonable demands, not to mention calling me obscene names." Hallie's voice got louder and stronger, and when she looked up, it was just in time to duck before a book Roger threw hit her in the face.

"You have to earn respect, Hallie. No one hands it to you." He looked around the basement, a look of satisfaction on his face. "We're almost done here, I see." Then Roger did a double take on the package in the corner. "What's in that package?"

"Oh, that? I don't know." Hallie had never felt her heart beat so hard. She'd heard of blinding fear, and now she knew what that meant. She weaved back and forth and then steadied herself against the wall. "I don't feel well, Roger. Let's go upstairs."

"In a minute, in a minute." He stared at the package and then looked back at her. Later, Hallie would imagine that her life was going to end in slow motion, starting when Roger picked up the package and began to unwrap the plastic. Just as Hallie turned to run up the stairs she heard him say, "Well, well, well, if this isn't a betrayal of our marriage, our love, I don't know what is."

"Let me explain, Roger, let me explain."

"No, no, I think I'll be doing the explaining. I think I'll be explaining why no one ever sees you leave the house again.

Or, maybe I'll be spending the next few years explaining that my poor fragile wife had a nervous breakdown and has to live in an institution."

"You won't get away with it, Roger. I won't let you."

Roger grabbed her by the shoulders and shook her so hard her neck felt as if it would snap. Then he dragged her up the basement stairs and pushed her toward the sink.

"I'll call the police, Roger, I swear I will. You won't get away with it this time."

Roger dragged her to the bedroom and pushed her down on the bed. He crushed her with his body and when he'd torn her clothes and raped her, he said, "You so much as lift the receiver and I'll see to it you'll never again see the one child you do have. Don't think I can't do it."

Hallie jumped off the bed and searched for her underwear, but before she could find it, Roger grabbed her by the arm and opened the patio doors that led to the far end of the deck off their bedroom. After he slapped her face again, he pushed her through the door and closed the screen. "You leave our yard, and I'll take Eric and hide him where you'll never find him. He's in the house with me, Hallie, only me. I think this little incident will teach you the lesson you've been too stubborn to learn. You will do as I say, and you can forget about ever seeing that bastard Dr. Richards. It's over, all over."

With those last words, he slammed the patio door, leaving Hallie shaking, with her nose bleeding, out in the yard. Hallie crept around the side of the house to Eric's window. Through the gauzy curtain she saw Roger open his door and walk to the window. She tried to hide below the window, but he opened the sash and whispered, "I know you're there. And I won't be far away. I can take Eric any old time I want."

Shivering and cold, Hallie used the sleeve of her blouse to stop her nosebleed. She could feel her eye swell up and her arms felt bruised and sore from Roger's manhandling. But that seemed like nothing compared to the terror she felt knowing that Roger could take Eric away. She tried to talk herself down. He wouldn't walk away with Eric because it would be too hard to explain. She probably was safe for the night. She debated calling the police, or going to Ginger. Unfortunately, after what she'd been through she probably looked crazed. Roger would claim she hurt herself some way, perhaps even tell the police that she tore up her own papers and threw herself down the stairs.

As Hallie watched through the window and saw Eric sleeping safely in his bed, she also rejected going to Ginger, at least not yet. She could be endangering that whole family. But she resolved to tell Ginger what was going on. It was as if a light bulb went on in Hallie's head. Who did she think she was fooling? Ginger knew her life wasn't normal. A normal woman doesn't hide almost everything. It would be a relief to tell her the truth and ask for help. Hallie also decided to call Sister Dorothy and seek her advice. But at home, from now on, she would act as if Roger had been right and she had been wrong. She would, at least for a little while, be contrite; she'd behave like a woman who'd learned her lesson.

Getting to Work

What Can We Learn About the Cycle of Abuse?

Hallie and Roger are finally getting help, or at least that's how Hallie sees it. Roger agreed to seek help only because Hallie had a bargaining chip, her broken arm. Notice though, that Roger never admits that he pushed her off the deck or apologizes to Hallie for any of his abusive behavior.

Roger finds ways to justify his behavior, but because Hallie does not think that way, it is very hard for her to believe that he really does not care how much he hurts her as long as he keeps her around. He is incapable of feeling his own deep pain so he cannot feel others' pain either. Roger has no difficulty rationalizing that she provoked him.

Intimidation Through Threats

Another typical ploy Roger uses is his attempt to convince her she is crazy and an unfit mother. He uses anything from subtle hints to actually labeling her as "crazy." The fact that he is a doctor and quite intelligent adds validity to his accusations. By this time, Hallie no longer believes something just because Roger says it, but she knows that he has the power to make others believe it. This is an important distinction, because Roger is losing the power to brainwash her. Earlier, she was enamored and wanted a husband she could admire and respect. She took Roger's criticisms to heart and tried to improve herself. Little by little, though, she has seen through Roger. His public "show" and his private cruelty are no longer lost on her.

At the same time Hallie begins to tell the truth, she is also deepening her understanding of the kind of power Roger has over her. During these increasingly difficult times with Roger, it is very important that Hallie remain calm and focused. His abuse is escalating and has become so threatening that it would be easy for her to fall apart from exhaustion and terror.

Calling on Inner Resources

At this point, Hallie's most important survival skill involves using her intelligence and resources to outsmart Roger, one way or another. If Hallie "loses it" by becoming hysterical or panicky it could easily look like Roger is right to label her insane.

I have seen women break down and in a hysterical tone they finally spill out all the stories about horrible abuse. They may try to explain it all to the police, doctors, caseworkers, and so forth because they become desperate for help. Unfortunately, the people from whom these women are seeking help may see their irrational behavior and agree with the label of "crazy" that the abusers have used. Those in a position to help may fail to do so because they are unable to hear or see the history behind the pleas for help coming from these women. Tragically, this is especially true if the abuser remains calm and determined while she is losing it.

We can be certain that Roger is capable of being calm and detached should Hallie break down. With his external power, that is, the power Roger holds in the world, he has the capacity to convince authorities that "poor" Hallie is weak and fragile. He could use her medical history against her and it would probably take very little to have her committed.

The Danger Escalates

We now see that Roger is totally out of control and he has probably never been more dangerous to Hallie and Eric. Hallie has had a harsh awakening. She realizes that Roger is capable of getting away with all of his threats, including taking Eric away from her, and perhaps even killing her.

On the one hand, we could say that Hallie has given up. But what is she relinquishing? First, she is letting go of what turned into an empty fantasy. She had an image of marriage in her mind; she had an image of a smart, powerful, successful husband. She believed Roger when he told her that if she "learned" certain things about him, they would get along. She also believed that it was her job to adjust and we saw Hallie tell herself again and again to be grateful. She also held on to great hope that Roger would change.

Hallie has let go of these things, but rather than "giving up," it is important to see that Hallie is facing reality. She will feel a sense of loss, but eventually, what she gains will feel far better than anything she leaves behind. Many women have trouble during this stage because they believe they have failed. After all, despite the advances women have made in our society, for many people, the mark of a successful woman is the ability to maintain a family, quite literally against all odds. So, "facing reality" may be experienced as a failure.

When Hallie is cold and shivering outside Eric's window, she begins to make plans, starting with telling Ginger the truth. When

Hallie resolves to break down the barrier of secrecy with which she has surrounded herself, she is taking a step toward reaching out for help. Some changes take a very long time. For example, it has taken Hallie years to see the truth about Roger and give up the false hope that he will change. But Hallie's realization that she hasn't fooled Ginger, that most likely Ginger has long suspected something is amiss with Hallie's life, comes quickly. Hallie's despair became so great that she could make the shift to remove the social mask she'd been wearing.

Hallie's Choices

In some situations, a battered woman can pick up her children and move, or they can use the safe environment of a counselor's office to say she wants a divorce. How the scenario plays out has much to do with the type of abuser women are dealing with. Some abusers have social control and their children are old enough to evaluate their behavior. These men might accept the situation and, unfortunately, see themselves as "free" and begin looking for their next victim. Roger is not that type, however. It can't be emphasized enough that Roger is a dangerous man, capable of taking Eric and going away or even killing Hallie and setting it up to look like a suicide or even worse, self-defense.

Other than Hallie's mother, who has an impression of the abuse, no one actually knows that Roger has been torturing Hallie, physically, sexually, and emotionally. For this reason, it is important that Hallie move quickly and, most important, secretly, to document Roger's behavior, and then take Eric and run for it.

11

Exhausted and covered with dirt from the yard, Hallie didn't speak as Roger led her back into the house. Thank God, she thought, a new day. She'd huddled outside Eric's window all night, keeping a kind of vigil and vowing to do whatever it took to prevent Roger from hurting Eric. The night had been long and cold, and something had hardened inside Hallie. She had a strange sense that a piece of her had broken off and withered away. If someone had asked her to put words to the sensations, she might have said that illusions died, along with old dreams and hopes. No longer could she fool herself into thinking that she could ever have a loving, meaningful marriage with Roger. She had told other people, including her mother, about Roger's research and all his professional advances, but she saw through him now. He was a fraud, and a cruel fraud at that.

Hallie ran her hand across her face and felt the blood crusted around her nose. She rubbed her arms and felt swollen spots where bruises were forming on the places Roger had held her as he dragged her down the basement stairs and then again when he yanked her and pushed her outside. In just the last few months, she'd suffered all kinds of injuries, including a broken bone. And she felt raw inside as a result of all the rough sex Roger subjected her to in his quest to get her pregnant. Roger had long since left behind even the pretense of tenderness.

As Hallie waited for daybreak, she began to feel an unfamiliar strength, and she also saw a cold, calculating side of herself she hardly recognized. Just as she had made lists of tasks she wanted to accomplish while Roger had been out of the country, Hallie began making new lists of things she must take care of now—and in short order. She'd call Sister Dorothy, she'd seek advice from the crisis line, and once she'd told Ginger the truth, she'd ask for her help, too. Hallie felt the beginning of a plan forming in her mind. And for the first time, she realized how much she needed to break through her long-standing shell of secrecy and tell the truth.

It was almost dawn when Roger had appeared and ordered her to follow him. Hallie stayed silent, not so much from fear this time, though, as from her decision to be smarter than she'd been in the past. Since there was no reasoning with Roger, Hallie decided that her best—and safest—tactic was contrition. He had found the contraceptives, so she had no choice but to behave as if she were so, so sorry to have deceived him. It was a weak defense, but it was all she had.

"Go wipe the dirt off your face and come back out here," Roger said. He leaned against the kitchen counter. "We have some talking to do."

On her way to the bathroom, she peeked in at Eric. He was still asleep, looking so peaceful Hallie almost cried from gratitude for that small blessing.

Hallie washed her face and noted the ugly bruise on her cheek. It was strange, but in a way she was glad it was there. She also was glad she had the records from the emergency room and from the last visit with the doctor when he'd removed the cast. Hallie checked her arms, oddly pleased to see that the purple bruises took on the shape of four separate fingers curling around her right arm. She'd been hiding everything about her life from Ginger, but today, she was not only going to tell her the truth, she was going to ask her to help her document it.

When Hallie returned to the kitchen, Roger was still standing by the counter.

"First, you must stay in today and for the rest of the week. I won't have you making a spectacle of yourself."

Hallie frowned, and immediately started thinking about how she would carry out her plan if he checked up on her all day.

"I will not have you parading around outside looking like an little idiot who can't keep her balance. You look like you tripped over your own feet. First it's the broken arm, and now you've fallen down the stairs. But I won't risk having my clumsy wife out on the street."

"Okay Roger, I'll stay home. No problem. I'm exhausted anyway." Hallie's chest felt heavy and her breathing was shallow. She couldn't wait for him to get out and leave her alone. Just looking at him made her stomach churn.

"Sure, poor little Hallie has so much to do," Roger said. His mouth curled in a mean sneer. "I *will* be calling you periodically during the day. Seems like you can't be trusted to do anything I ask. New rules, Hallie, new rules."

"Whatever you want, Roger."

"Right now, I want to get out of here. I can't stand the sight of you. You're an evil, deceiving, lying bitch. Now it's my job to decide if I want my son raised by a whore like you. Meanwhile, I have patients to see and papers to write. But you wouldn't understand such things, would you? You just sit back and enjoy everything I provide."

The cold distance in Roger's voice was as frightening as any tone he'd ever used before. Hallie felt shivers rush up her spine, but she maintained her calm demeanor.

"So, tonight I'll tell you how we will proceed. But don't even think about leaving this house. From now on, you will do exactly as I say." Roger grabbed his suit jacket, picked up his briefcase, and stalked out of the house.

Hallie waited until she heard his car pull away before she moved. She checked the clock–just past seven–too early to call Ginger. If she couldn't leave the house, she'd have to ask Ginger to come to her. Hallie got out a legal pad and began making notes.

* * * *

"You're telling me this has been going on from the beginning?" Ginger looked pale, almost ghostly as she swayed side to side with little Cindy in her arms. Ginger had given birth while Roger and Hallie were away on their cruise, and Hallie felt terrible burdening her friend with her long, sad story, which had left Ginger looking shell-shocked.

Just past nine, Hallie had called Ginger and told her she had to see her, that it was very important. She also told her she could not leave the house. Hallie astounded herself when she uttered those words. She felt tears sting her eyes, but she talked herself out of breaking down. Focus, she had to keep her focus. Ginger had quickly agreed to come right over. And she didn't ask questions when Hallie asked her to bring a camera because she wanted to take some pictures of the boys with Ginger's new baby. But when Hallie opened the door, she saw her friend's reaction to her black and blue cheek. Ginger had quickly looked away and started talking about the beautiful weather.

"It's okay, Ginger. I'll tell you what happened. In fact, I asked you to come here because I need your help."

Hallie made tea and they went to the back deck where they could watch the boys play in the yard. And after taking a deep breath, Hallie started talking before she had a chance to change her mind. First, she admitted that Roger had hit her, although she decided not to mention spending the night outside. She felt humiliated enough without mentioning that. "It wasn't always this bad," she said. "Sure, Roger always was moody and he had a temper, but I thought I didn't understand him. It got worse after Eric was born, and over the last two years Roger has been more prone to…" Hallie let her voice trail off.

Talking about Roger this way caused stabs of pain—physical pain that seared her chest. Sometimes, the truth hurt, though, and it was even worse when she looked into Ginger's eyes. She continued describing the litany of ways Roger controlled her. She told Ginger that he'd dictated who she saw and even what church they went to. She told her how Roger destroyed her clothes and then chose the new ones. He didn't allow her to have her own friends, and she never had money of her own. She talked about the damage he did in the house during his fits of rage and she slowly built up to talking about his slaps and shoves, and the numerous times he twisted her arm or dragged her around.

When the phone rang, Hallie quickly answered it and checked the time. It was just before eleven. This was Roger's second call.

The first had come in just after eight. True to his word, Roger was checking up on her.

Seeing the frown on Ginger's face when she deliberately kept her voice light and conversational, Hallie realized that her friend still did not quite comprehend what she was up against. Hallie would have to make Ginger understand that she had to keep up at least some of her lies for a little while longer.

"Well Roger, I can fix burgers if you'd like," Hallie said when Roger began talking about their dinner plans. "Or, I can go shopping and…"

Roger sounded friendly, even solicitous when he said, "No Hallie, I'll pick up Chinese food. I'll be picking up food this week. As I said, I *don't* want you leaving the house. No argument now."

"Okay, Chinese sounds great," she said. When she hung up she turned back to Ginger and said, "Let me tell you what I need."

"But, wait…how could you sound so nice on the phone?" Ginger looked perplexed. "What are doing? You could leave him today. You're not thinking of staying with him, are you? Get in your car and drive to your mother's. Just get away."

"No, Ginger, I can't do that. I have to be careful. I never told you, of course, but I called the crisis abuse hotline when I visited my mother. I've talked with people at the shelter here. If I leave now, it could be disastrous for Eric—and for me."

Ginger nodded her head as she attempted to understand.

"I'm making a plan, and I need your help," Hallie said. A few minutes later, Ginger snapped several Polaroid pictures of Hallie's arm and face. Hallie put them in an envelope and Ginger agreed to keep them. Hallie also handed Ginger a sealed envelope and said, "This is some documentation—dates and times—of some of Roger's most serious attacks on me."

"You really think he will try to claim you're crazy?" Ginger asked.

"He will absolutely try to keep me a prisoner by threatening to have me committed. And if I tell him I'm going to leave, he will do everything possible to stop me, including hospitalizing me or…" Hallie looked away.

"Or what?"

"I have no doubt that he's capable of killing me."

"Oh my God!" Ginger frantically looked around as if trying to find the right words. "Then why don't you go to your mother? Get away. Or, you could come to my house. We could hide you."

Hallie pieced together a picture of the steps she needed to take. She had to make Ginger understand why it was imperative that she bide her time and document everything. "And I would never endanger you or your family. I'd never ask you to hide me. It would be too dangerous. If you can call my mother and ask her to get in touch with me tomorrow around noon, that would be great."

Before Ginger left, Hallie called Planned Parenthood and reported that she'd apparently misplaced her contraceptive pills. She talked to the nurse with whom she'd had her appointment and asked if a friend could come in and pick up another three-month supply because she was ill and couldn't go out. "I know it's unusual, but my friend says she is going to be in the area later this afternoon, and could swing by and get them for me. She can explain everything," Hallie said.

Ginger agreed to pick up the pills and keep them at her house. She would bring Hallie a pill each day and she'd come back the next morning to help Hallie with the rest of her plan. Hallie held herself together until Ginger reached over and hugged her. "I'm sorry," she said, "so sorry you have had to go through so much."

"And I'm sorry I've been so silent about my life. The truth is, I should have left him long ago." Hallie felt hot tears start and this time she didn't stop them.

After Ginger left, Hallie began to fix lunch for Eric. She felt good about what she accomplished, even though it had been a humiliating experience to ask Ginger to hide her birth control pills and take pictures of her bruises. Ginger had agreed to keep Hallie's documentation about Roger's abuse, including the truth about her broken arm. Hallie had also noted her contacts with Sister Dorothy and the calls to the shelter.

She went about fixing lunch for Eric and tried to ignore her headache and the growing tension in the pit of her stomach. She had to face Roger, and even worse, she had no choice but to pretend to go along with his rules. Hallie wondered how she had endured so much for so long.

Hallie took Eric into his room and sat beside him and smoothed his hair as he settled on his bed to rest. A wave of exhaustion came over her, but she didn't want to sleep just yet. She felt keyed up and alert, and during these next weeks, Hallie thought, alert was good. Staying alert was essential to her safety and for Eric's future.

As Eric began drifting off to sleep, Hallie looked around the room and weighed what to take with her and what to leave behind. She hated leaving Eric's furniture behind, but she realized she might have to. She would bring Eric's favorite toys, and as for other things in the house, almost nothing in it meant anything to her. Nothing. Sure, she would definitely take the wedding silver because she could sell it and have a little money with which to begin a new life. But over the years, she and Roger had accumulated very little that held any personal meaning. Strange that she hadn't noticed that before. There were no pictures of friends around because they had no friends. Roger had pictures of her and Eric in his office and every year he had a new family photo to send to his mother. It was all for show.

As she looked around, Hallie saw a paper bag in Eric's bookshelf. She didn't recognize it and wondered where it came from. When she picked it up and looked inside she saw it was filled with stones of various sizes and sticks from the backyard. That seemed odd. She wondered when Eric had started collecting sticks and stones.

An hour later, Ginger knocked at the back door. "I thought I should probably not be too visible," she explained. "I've brought the pills. And I asked to talk with the nurse privately. I told her about your plan. She said to call her if you need anything. She also said to be *very* careful, that men like Roger can be even more dangerous if they think you're planning to escape."

"I know," Hallie said, "believe me, that scares me. But I can keep my plan to leave secret. I know I can. The woman at the shelter near my mother's home gave me advice about this months ago–before Roger left on that trip. I wish I'd had the guts to do something right away."

"You were different then, you know."

"Different when?"

"When Roger was gone on his trip." Ginger ran her hand through her hair and looked down at the deck. "I don't know…you seemed so *relaxed.* Now I understand why."

"I felt good then." Hallie told Ginger how she'd enjoyed her visit with her mother, too. "I allowed myself to think about a different life–dream my own dreams–that sort of thing. I could see myself living on my own with Eric. Just being away helped me find a trace of my old self-confidence again."

"I'm glad to hear you have your own dreams," Ginger said.

"In a way," Hallie said, "you helped me without ever knowing it."

"Oh? How?"

"Just by being so normal." Hallie laughed. "You told funny stories about Bob. You looked forward to seeing him at the end of the day. You *look* healthy. I've spent years trying to fend off daily headaches and some days I can barely eat for all the churning in my stomach."

"I have to admit I wondered what really went on here. I guess I thought Roger was, well, *difficult.* I never dreamed…"

"No one ever does," Hallie said. "I wouldn't even allow myself to admit how bad it actually was."

* * * *

"Eric? When did you start collecting stones?" Hallie asked. She and Eric were sitting at the table on the deck. She enjoyed watching him color in a notebook she'd given him. For those minutes, he seemed carefree and happy.

"They're my weapons," Eric said. He didn't look up.

"Weapons? Oh Eric. I don't like the idea of you talking about weapons, even make-believe weapons." Hallie had always said she didn't want Eric to have play guns or any of the violent toys she'd seen in the stores.

"They're *not* pretend. *They're not pretend!*" Eric began to cry and squirm around in the chair.

"It's okay, sweetie, it's okay." Hallie was puzzled by his reaction. "If they aren't pretend, then why do you have them?"

"They're for Daddy. I'll hit Daddy with them."

Hallie tried to hide her shock, but she had to know the full truth. "Why would you do that, honey?"

Eric jumped off the chair. "When he hurts you…" He stopped talking and ran into the house.

Hallie went after him, but the phone rang. It was Roger again. This was his fifth call. Hallie felt torn. She wanted to talk to Eric, but she had no choice but to listen to Roger.

"I'm leaving in exactly ten minutes," Roger said. "I've called in our food order and I'll pick it up. We'll eat inside."

Hallie heard the receiver click as Roger hung up on her, not waiting for her to respond. Then she found Eric sitting on the floor of his room. She crouched next to him. "I don't want you to worry about Mommy," she said. "You don't need your stones and sticks."

"Yes. I want them."

Hallie didn't know what to do. She hated that he felt the need for his "weapons," but she didn't want to take them away if they made him feel safer. "Let's put them in your closet, sweetheart. You'll know where they are, but they won't be right here on your shelf."

Hallie could only imagine what Roger would say if he found the stones and asked Eric about them. She wasn't sure what Eric would tell him. Better to just avoid the whole situation. Still, Hallie felt an ache in her heart to think what Eric knew about his father, and about her, too. She had fooled herself about one more thing. Hallie wondered if she'd ever forgive herself for what had been done to Eric. She pushed the thoughts aside. She couldn't think about that yet. She would address that problem, along with many others, once they were safe.

* * * *

Hallie folded towels while she waited for Roger. He didn't speak when he came in but set the bags of hot food on the counter. "Where's Eric?" he asked.

"In his room," Hallie said. She began opening cartons and emptying the food into bowls.

Roger went down the hall and soon Hallie heard him laughing. A few minutes later, he came into the kitchen carrying Eric. "So, what did my big boy and Mommy do today."

Eric's face became animated when he said, "Played with Cindy."

Roger looked puzzled. "Cindy? Who's Cindy?"

"Ginger's new baby. She and the kids stopped by this morning. We sat on the deck. So, let's eat." She wished Eric had lied or said he forgot. Now Roger knew Ginger had been to the house. He hated that.

Roger put Eric in his booster chair and sat down across from Hallie. "I told you I don't want that cow in the house."

"We were outside most of the time, Roger."

"Oh, like that doesn't count." Roger dished out some rice and broccoli and beef on Eric's plate.

"I don't like this," Eric said. "I don't *like* it."

"Just like your Mommy. Spoiled. You'll eat it."

Eric looked at Hallie with a pleading expression. "Let me cut it for you and then you'll try it," she said in a gentle voice. She looked hard at Eric, hoping he'd see that he shouldn't upset his father. At least though, Roger was no longer asking about Ginger.

It was sad, Hallie thought, that Eric sensed he should stay quiet and not make a fuss at the table. Meanwhile, Roger fell silent. Finally, he looked at Eric and said, "My big boy will have to tell me if he ever sees that Ginger cow around here. You'll do that, won't you?"

Eric nodded, but he quickly looked at Hallie. At that moment, Hallie realized that she'd have to talk with Eric and try to make a game out of not talking to Roger about Ginger.

"I really hate that bitch," Roger said. "She's ugly, and a big fat lazy cow with nothing better to do but hang out here. I can only imagine how bad she looks now that she's finally had that baby. Probably has rolls of fat all over her."

Hallie forced herself to take a bite of food. She wouldn't say anything. It would only make it worse. When they were done eating, Roger took Eric by the hand. "I need to get him away from you," he said. "When I think of what you're filling his head with it makes me sick. Looks like I'll need to monitor things around here much more closely."

"Whatever you say, Roger."

In a high voice he mimicked her, "Whatever you say, Roger. Is that all you can say. Not going to argue, are you?"

"No, Roger, I'm not going to argue."

"I think you're lying. I think you're lying right now." Before he walked away with Eric he said, "I'm putting him to bed. I want you in the bedroom. I'll be in to talk to you."

* * * *

Hallie's heart was beating so fast and hard it felt like loud drums pounding in her ears. She thought her head might explode. As she waited for Roger, Hallie's thoughts went back and forth between her desperate need to get away and a steady stream of self-talk to remain calm. No matter what he did, it would only be a few days longer. Thank God she'd had Ginger take pictures. Even if he killed her in her bed that night, someone would know.

Roger entered the room quietly, but Hallie felt the hostility in the air around him. She might as well have been waiting for her executioner to fire the final shot.

"No one will ever love you like I do," Roger said. He slowly loosened his tie and unbuttoned his shirt. "No one."

"I know, Roger, I know."

"I'm not going to ask why you deceived me, Hallie. Do you know why?"

"No, I don't." She felt like making a run for the door. Only her awareness that Eric was in the room down the hall kept her focused on staying as quiet as possible.

"Because I don't care." Roger lowered his pants and put them across the chair. "What I care about is what you do with Ginger. And I want to know what you told Ginger about us."

"Ginger and I talk about the kids, Roger. We never go anywhere or do anything. We're busy moms." Hallie let herself hope that Roger would make this all about Ginger. She could handle that.

"And?"

"And what?"

"What did you tell her about us?"

"Nothing, Roger. We talked about the cruise a little. But we watched the boys play in the yard. It's what mothers do with their kids." It was hard to keep her voice from rising. What did he want? If she knew, she would give it to him.

"Oh right. As if I'd believe that." Roger quickly walked to the nightstand and ripped the shade off the lamp. He pushed Hallie back on the bed and held the lamp to her face. "I'll ask you again. What did you tell Ginger about us?"

Hallie closed her eyes to protect against the hot glare. The lamp almost burned her skin. But Roger held the lamp with one hand and used the other to pull her eyelids open. Hallie wondered if she could go blind from this. "Nothing. We don't talk about you or Bob. Please believe me, Roger."

"Do you kiss her—do you let her feel you up?"

"What? How could you say such a thing?" Hallie squirmed around; Roger used his knee to hold her down. "You're burning me, Roger. I'll go blind." She tried to turn her head away from the searing light. Her eyes burned, the skin on her face felt as if it were on fire.

"Maybe that's why you don't want a baby, you lying whore. You want to fuck Ginger. How do I know you're not fucking Bob while I'm at work?"

"No, Roger. That's not true. You know it's not true."

"Tell me you think she's a cow. *Say it!*"

"Okay, okay," Hallie whispered, "she's a cow." Hallie would have said anything to make him get the light out of her eyes. "I'm burning up, Roger. Take away the lamp—please, please, don't hurt me anymore."

Roger laughed, but he let go of her eyelids and set the lamp on the nightstand. Hallie closed her eyes but the flashing wouldn't stop. She saw colors and spots and the pain was unbearable. When she finally opened her eyes she saw that Roger had taken off his underwear and had an erection. He hated her that much, she thought. Torturing her excited him. For some reason, that felt like the final insult. No matter what he said and did, he could never hurt her again.

"Open your legs, you cock-sucking whore," he said. His voice sounded like a hiss.

Roger raped her once, waited an hour and raped her again. He never spoke another word and Hallie silently endured the pain because she knew in her heart it was almost over. When he finally slept, Hallie felt a flood of relief. She fell asleep herself, with her last thoughts focused on her next step.

The next morning, Roger told her to stay in. He would be calling her every hour on the hour. He also told her he had to deliver a paper and would be leaving town in two days. Hallie almost cried from relief. Just before he walked out the door, he said, "If you leave this house without asking me first, I'll see to it you never see Eric again."

Hallie nodded. "I understand, Roger. I won't go anywhere. Ever." The numb feeling that came over Hallie amazed her. Telling that lie was so easy.

Getting to Work

What Can We Learn About the Cycle of Abuse?

We now have the opportunity to see Hallie going through a process of change. There usually are four major steps in this process:

1) letting go of old dreams and fantasies, while

2) adjusting to a period of limbo, a stage without definitive knowledge about the next step, and then

3) making a decision to either go back to the old ways and beliefs or to move forward into the realm of the unknown, and finally,

4) moving forward toward the unknown.

As painful as it is, something else has become more important than her dreams of a happy and respectful relationship with Roger and a loving, wholesome family life. The physical abuse and Roger's constant humiliation have gradually erased Hallie's belief that change is possible. Contrary to popular assumptions, this is not an easy step and Hallie must grieve the death of her dreams, the same way she would grieve if a person she loves has died. The dream of a happy marriage to Roger formed the nucleus around which she built her life; her marriage was the largest part of her identity for many years. Now, Hallie must replace her old identity with a new one and that process can feel frightening.

Critical Crossroads

As Hallie decides to let go, she must hang in limbo for a period of time and this can feel like the most insecure place within the entire process. It can be likened to having no country to call one's own or no home to run to when times get tough. For Hallie, it will involve wondering who she is and what parts of herself she can trust. Suddenly, no answers exist and, even worse, Hallie must live with the reality that she may not yet know the questions. Naturally she feels confused, weak, lonely, isolated, distrusting of herself and others, perhaps doubtful about her sanity at times, and filled with a generalized fear of life in general.

This stage can be a dangerous time because if she stays in this limbo for too long, she may find it so unbearable that she chooses a way out before she allows herself to pass through it. For example, some women find the limbo so difficult that they give up the quest for safety and a better life. If Hallie gave up, she could go back to Roger, which in essence, would mean relinquishing her life. Or, she could find another abusive man to take care of her and fight Roger with and for her; this solution has a fairytale appeal to some women. A man appears who becomes a savior, a knight in shining armor; at first she might believe she is being "carried off" from the danger and into some "happily ever after" kingdom. Unfortunately, women who make this choice may find themselves in a situation not much different from the one they escaped.

Tragically, some women dissociate from life and the reality around them. They may become vegetative and emotionally disturbed to the extent that they cannot take responsibility for themselves. A percentage of women do reach this disturbed state and commit suicide. So, for Hallie, it is critical that she let herself feel the pain and uncertainty, knowing it will eventually pass. Trying to stop the pain with unstable reactions will only get her into more trouble or prolong this stage.

Hallie must find ways to secure herself as she experiences this unstable, even risky, phase of change. For example, Hallie could direct her focus to Eric and meeting his needs for safety and security. Another way to enhance her sense of security is to spend time planning for the future. Hallie's earlier daydreams and observations have value now because they can fuel her energy to keep moving forward.

Gathering Internal Resources

In this chapter, we observe Hallie as she decides to take necessary steps to create a better life. We must be careful not to underestimate the degree of courage and perseverance she shows at this stage. Hallie knows that she is moving into the unknown and that the obstacles to a better life could be even worse than what she has faced. For example, Hallie remains at great risk from Roger. If he should "get wind" of her plans, he is likely to lose all control and respond with even greater violence than he did when he discovered the contraceptives. She is right to fear that he would not hesitate to convince others that she is mentally ill and so unstable that she can't take care of Eric. At this point Hallie must hang on to a belief that she *can* create a better life. In addition, she needs to call on her internal and external resources to help her. We can see Hallie slowly regaining her faith in others and trust in herself with each step she takes.

The last stage is moving on and making new decisions about a new life. A sense of relief often accompanies this stage, although a few remnants of fear and doubt remain, which is entirely normal. In terms of "self-talk," Hallie can tell herself the doubts and fears serve to remind her what life felt like in the past and then use these memories as a springboard to jump into more new decisions. This can be an exciting stage if she pushes through the fears and doubts, giving them just enough attention to learn from the messages they send.

Feeling Different

We see Hallie thinking about a kind of hardness she feels. This is good—it is necessary. In order to go through the required stages successfully, women must develop an emotional hardening or feel a numbness come over them. For Hallie, these internal changes represent coping skills—protective mechanisms. Their purpose is to prevent her from feeling so much pain and despair that she crumbles under the weight of it. Because the hardening attitude and the numbness are not who Hallie typically is, she appears a bit startled by the feeling.

Roger may sense this change, and he will see it as a threat to him. However, she has loved him for so long and has tried so hard to make her dreams come true that only a total change in her feelings toward him will save her and Eric from him. Even with all that has gone on, a part of Hallie still cares about Roger and wants her familiar dream to survive. Hallie now knows she must keep that part well hidden, even from her healthier self.

Hallie has allowed new qualities to surface and it provides her healthy anger, determination, and equally important, the shrewd intelligence she needs to get away. Notice her ability to be calculating when she needs to be. She is well aware that she must stay one step ahead of Roger. In previous chapters we saw Hallie try to be calculating in order to appease or please Roger, usually to avoid a scene. That kind of planning was reactive, and led Hallie deeper into the cycle of abuse. Hallie now is calculating on her own and Eric's behalf. She may be second-guessing Roger's behavior, but she is motivated by a desire for a deeper, more profound change. Roger's reactions only matter in so far as they affect her and Eric's safety.

Breaking the Silence Equals Creating Safety

We see evidence of Hallie's new shrewdness when she starts a "paper trail" of Roger's behavior and abuse. She confides in Ginger, and then asks her to take pictures of her injuries. She documents her broken arm by securing her hospital records. She brings Ginger into her plans as part of outsmarting this threatening, dangerous man. These actions result from the good state of mind Hallie created through a combination of anger and fear. Both the energy and the records she keeps will be useful to her in the future when Roger threatens her—and we need to be clear about this: he *will* threaten her.

As Hallie gains strength, Roger continues to use brainwashing techniques. Notice how he reframes his abusive behavior and turns it into *her* clumsiness. His continued degrading remarks are deliberate attempts to regain control over her, because he senses his hold is weakening. Fortunately, Hallie now sees through his tactics and does not let them define her. For example, she knew he had pushed her off the deck. She used that incident to persuade him into therapy, although to no avail; but at that time, Hallie didn't know that her effort would be futile. Now he claims her bruises result from some kind of accident he's invented in his own mind. She is able to "file" this information away as further proof that her new perceptions about Roger are correct. The numbness that Hallie is feeling allows her to focus on these new goals of protecting herself and Eric and resist Roger's manipulation. When she is numb and hardened, no space exists for all the other emotions she has been dealing with.

Reaching out to Ginger is a courageous step for Hallie. It reinforces a message of self worth and from that place of esteem she knows she *deserves* to ask for help. In addition, Ginger's horrified reaction reinforces Hallie's angry conclusions that Roger has no right to treat her as he does. Even more important, however, it's also a smart move. Giving Ginger a copy of her documentation of Roger's abuse reinforces a part of Hallie's plan, a component that will prove useful later on. Notice, too, that Hallie does not agree to just get up and run, nor does she accept Ginger's offer to hide her. Her concern for the safety of Ginger and her family is well founded.

Reality and Denial

The fear that Roger will see right through her, as if he has the power to read her mind, will likely remain. That fear results from his brainwashing; it isn't the reality. Roger is not a mind reader. Again, tapping into the angry, determined part of her current attitude is the best way for her to overcome the fear of his power.

What an eye-opener for Hallie to see Eric's "weapons." Battered women may receive many signals that could seem like "wake up calls," but they rationalize them away before processing them. Often, a child's new behavior serves to break the mother's denial. Eric is four now and has the language skills to talk about his intentions and, as we can see, his plans. Hallie realizes that her denial and Roger's abuse have damaged Eric. If Hallie gets away from Roger, she will find her guilt over the effects on Eric difficult to deal with and work through. Eventually Hallie will see that no child should take on the role of his mother's protector. Right now, Eric needs to be free to play, fantasize, create, and feel safe as a child. It is the parents' duty to provide protection and a sense of security. The cycle of abuse takes away a part of childhood—it is a part of the damage we seldom hear much about.

Like millions of children, Eric has been deprived of a deep sense of security because Hallie and Roger were too involved in the dance of abuse to give him what he needed. In this way, both Hallie and Roger abused Eric. Hallie tried to take care of Eric and protect him, but she failed to fully understand that Eric was like a little sponge, absorbing the dynamics around him, taking in everything Hallie thought she had hidden from him. In his own way, Roger even tried to hide some of his behavior, but he is too narcissistic and paranoid to focus for any period of time on anyone other than himself.

Dangerous Waters Ahead

The chronic abuser typically uses extremely dangerous control tactics when he suspects his victim might attempt to escape the prison he has constructed. Hallie may not fool him with her cold, calculating changes, so he strikes out in attempt to rouse abject terror in Hallie. Raping her and burning her eyes with intense heat are torture tactics that he uses in order to break her spirit. How many times have we seen these same tactics depicted in television shows or movies about war victims?

Ironically, in the human rights arena, Roger's torture violates international human rights conventions and laws. In criminal courts, this kind of assault and battery could carry a heavy jail term, but in the world of domestic violence, Hallie's concerns revolve around legitimate fears that Roger could commit *her*. Even if law enforcement authorities believe her, it is unlikely that Roger would ever spend time in jail. In fact, Hallie would gladly settle for an escape plan that moves toward a situation in which Roger cannot do *further* harm to her or to Eric. We will see how Hallie carries out her plan.

12

The phone rang. Roger again. He'd called every hour on the hour since he'd left the house at 7:00 AM. Odd, Hallie thought, how energized he seemed. Apparently, torturing her renewed him in some perverse way. Hallie didn't even want to think about the previous night. Another time, she told herself, she'd cry over it another time. "I need three white shirts," Roger was saying. "Do you think you can handle ironing some clothes?"

"Of course, Roger, of course." Hallie bitterly thought about all the shirts she'd ironed for him, only to have him inspect each one before he put it on. And at least half the time, he gave it back to her and told her to iron it again.

Roger had rattled off more things she needed to do to help him get ready for his trip on Friday. Hurry, hurry, she said to herself. Just get out of here. He finally left and she'd had a few minutes to breathe deeply and focus on what she wanted to accomplish. Later, Ginger stopped by, using the back door again, and started to give her the money Nina had wired in care of Ginger and Bob. Hallie would always be grateful to Bob for agreeing to go out of his way to pick it up. On the surface, that seemed like a small thing, but it felt like one more strong shoulder to lean on. Hallie told her to keep the money until Friday morning when Roger left. She couldn't risk Roger finding it. Ginger also said that Nina would be calling Hallie around noon.

It was almost noon now and Roger had just called again and was droning on and on. Hallie so much wanted the line to be open when her mother called.

Finally, Roger said, "Remember what I said about Ginger, babe. I don't want her in my house—and it is *my house*."

"I heard you Roger. I understand. I told Ginger I was too busy to see her." The lie slid off her tongue so easily. She didn't care how many lies it took to keep his suspicions down.

"I doubt you do understand, but then you've never done your part to make this marriage work. I've accepted that now. I'm resigned to taking care of everything myself. Even dinner. I'm bringing home pizza tonight, by the way. Another easy day for you."

Roger's voice sounded hard and bitter. Hallie again was startled to realize that he believed everything he said, that his self-deception ran even deeper than her ability to deny how bad things could get. Now she understood that no matter what she did, he would never see her as a person, an individual with needs of her own, not to mention basic dignity. Over the years, Hallie had let thoughts creep into her mind about Roger's behavior as a medical professional, but she'd always pushed them away. Now she truly had to marvel at how he'd managed to build his reputation. What would his colleagues think if they saw her bruises or heard him call her names and order her to stay in the house? His ability to be those two different people had always seemed eerie, but now it just frightened her.

A minute or two after Roger finally hung up, the phone rang again and when she heard her mother's voice, Hallie burst into tears. Her mother's words soothed her, "I'm sorry, honey, so sorry it's come to this," she said. "You will be okay, though. I have faith that you will be okay."

Through her tears, Hallie managed to talk about her plan. It was Wednesday, and on Friday, Roger was scheduled to leave from his office for the airport to catch a noon flight to Denver. So, Friday represented the best window of opportunity available. She would put her plan in motion that afternoon. "Please call me, though," she said. "I don't want Roger seeing any long distance calls on our bill. Just in case…"

"You mean just in case you can't get away on Friday night?"

"Exactly. What if the trip is cancelled? I'd have to postpone the plan until he goes to work on Monday. And that would be even riskier."

Nina agreed to contact the women's shelter in her town, as well as getting in touch with a lawyer Hallie could consult with once she arrived at her mother's home. Hallie told her mother that she'd had another long talk with a counselor at the shelter and on Friday afternoon, she would drive away from the house and go directly to the shelter. The way the plan had taken form, a counselor would go with her to a magistrate to get a restraining order against Roger. Once that was issued, Hallie would leave town and, she hoped and prayed, never have the need to look back.

"Why are you so sure Roger won't come after you?" Nina asked. Her voice sounded tense, almost jittery.

"Are you worried he'll break into your apartment?" Hallie asked. "I can understand why..."

"No, no," her mother quickly said, "that's not what concerns me. What if he won't take no for an answer and tries to put you in the hospital or he files for custody of Eric."

Hallie knew she had no guarantee that Roger wouldn't attempt those very things. Any action she took carried some risk and required her willingness to gamble. But the stakes were too high to let fear take over, which is how she explained the situation to Nina.

"You know, Hallie, it's strange, but when I left your father, I knew he'd let me go without a real fight, and not just because he could no longer use you and your brother as his weapons. By the time I left, he was fresh out of threats. Even sadder in a way, I knew that in the end, the bottle would become more important than anything else, even me."

"I never thought of it that way, Mom," Hallie said, "but you're right. Dad had his cheap wine, and I think Roger's precious career—his professional reputation—may prove more important to him than coming after me, although the counselors keep warning me that he could become a master at harassment. But he could get better results if he invents a story about how I abandoned him, and then have a dozen women ready to comfort him."

"You think he still can fool people that well."

"He's smooth, very smooth, and he'd be even smarter next time. I think he'll leave me alone because his tragic story will win him what he wants. At least after an initial round of threats."

Hallie watched as Eric stretched out on the living room floor and spread puzzle pieces across the carpet. "I'm looking at Eric now," Hallie said, "and I know I have to do this. Half the time I think I'm too scared, but the rest of the time I'm driven by the belief I can do so much better for myself and Eric."

"I know you can, too. I suppose I'm just worried about your safety while you're in the process of changing so much."

"In a way, I couldn't be in any more danger than I'm in now."

For the next few minutes, Hallie and Nina went through the steps of the plan. She told her mother she'd checked and double-checked her documentation. Ginger had a set of photos and would send another second set to the lawyer Nina found. Hallie would take a set with her to the shelter. On Friday, as soon as Roger left, she would use the fax machine in Roger's office to make copies of her hospital records, her written chronology, and the letter she would leave behind.

"So far, I think I have everything covered. And thanks so much for wiring the money to Ginger. She's bringing it over on Friday. She'll help me load the car and Bob is getting the rental trailer. We can take what fits and leave the rest behind. Frankly, I don't care about any of it."

"I know just how you feel," Nina said. "I like my simple life, and my peace of mind is more precious than the house full of accumulated stuff."

For the first time, they laughed together. For some reason, the image of leaving behind houses filled with meaningless posses-sions struck them both as funny. Hallie felt almost lighthearted when she hung up the phone.

She had one last job to do that day, and it was the one she hated most. She sat on the floor next to Eric and began to talk to him about Ginger.

* * * *

For a couple of days Hallie had composed a dozen different letters in her head. As she stood at the ironing board she came up with countless ways to start. A part of her wanted to explain as a last ditch effort to get Roger to understand *why* she was leaving him. Another part of her knew it didn't matter that he understand, that it was irrelevant now; no matter what she did, he would always blame her and one way or another he'd want to extract his revenge. For that reason, everyone advised, it was better to keep her note short.

What was the purpose of even leaving a note? Hallie had to remind herself that threatening Roger was the only way that she stood a chance of escaping. She had to threaten to expose him through the pictures and the hospital records and the log of calls to the two shelters. Hallie decided to leave Sister Dorothy out of it. She didn't want to endanger her in any way. For all she knew, he could storm her office, or, knowing Roger, cause trouble for her through the church. She would put nothing past him.

Hallie spent the afternoon ironing shirts, but left the ironing board up just to give her something to be busy doing when Roger came home. He brought pizza with him and after putting it down on the table he went off to find Eric. He carried Eric into the kitchen. Did Roger even notice that Eric was pulling at his hair again and fighting back tears? Hallie could see how much he wanted Roger to put him down. Roger ignored the signs and went on with his phony baby talk and big grin.

"So, what did my big boy do today?" Roger looked at Hallie when he asked Eric the question.

"Puzzles. I did my puzzles."

Hallie smiled at Eric, knowing it was wrong to use him in this way. Not for long, she said to herself. One more day. Two more nights.

"So, did Ginger cow come over?"

Eric shook his head back and forth. "Nope."

"Are you sure Ginger wasn't here?"

"No baby today."

Hallie quickly told Roger that Ginger had stopped by alone, but like she'd said earlier, she'd told her she was too busy to visit. "I don't think Eric saw her," Hallie said. "He was in his room when she came by." Did her voice sound casual enough? Hallie so hoped Eric would continue to do exactly as she'd told him. She had instructed Eric to say that he hadn't seen Ginger or the baby all day. She'd explained that since Daddy was mean about Ginger, it was best just to pretend that she hadn't visited. Would he do that for her? If Daddy asked, would he say that he hadn't seen Ginger all day? Eric nodded, and Hallie felt sure he sensed the importance of what she'd said.

Roger put Eric down and fixed himself a plate of pizza and started walking out of the kitchen. "I can't stand to eat in here, Hallie. I'm sorry, but I'm still trying to handle what you've done. I know one thing, though, when I get back from Denver I'm making an appointment to see a priest at the church. You need to talk about those pills you took, your deception, and the sickness in your mind that would lead you to go behind my back."

"If that's what you want, Roger."

"That's all you can say these days, huh? Whatever you want, Roger, whatever you say. I don't believe a word of it. I expect your attitude to change before we see the priest."

Roger turned to leave the room. "Unlike you, I have work to do. This conference in Denver is extremely important to me. In fact, I'm meeting with someone from Florida and I expect a job offer to follow. Ed came through for me. Put me in touch with the biggest hospital in his area. Not that I expect you to care. So, you can prepare to say good-bye to the loser neighbors you like so much."

Hallie munched the pizza and thought about what she would tell the priest if she had a chance. And Ed and Kim, too, while she was at it. Something else she could hold over Roger's head. Hallie could see Roger pouring out his sad tale about the way she just packed up and left him. He'd tell them she took everything. On the other hand, he'd probably take up golf and sailing with the same focus he developed for his career. It didn't take much imagination to see Roger with a new wife and swaggering around in his new life. The sooner that happened, the sooner she would feel safe.

Roger came to bed late that night. Hallie hadn't fallen asleep because she was afraid his assault, which she fully expected, would take her by surprise. But that never happened. Around midnight, Roger slipped into bed and stayed on his side. Within minutes he was asleep.

That night, Hallie had the dream again. Just as before, she ran so fast, trying to get away from the person in the wig, the long, blond wig. She felt her body hit the wall. Thud, no place to go. And when she turned around she saw the knife first. And then the evil sneer as the person takes off the wig and it's Roger. Hallie woke up, a scream stuck at the back of her throat. She sat up quickly and pushed the hair off her face. The knife, the wig, the wall, Roger's face. It was exactly the same as the last time.

Hallie looked across the bed. Roger slept soundly. She took a few deep breaths and felt her heartbeat gradually slow down. Carefully, silently, she got out of bed and stood at the window and looked at the moon peeking out from passing clouds. Would the nightmare go away, she wondered? If she made it through one more night, would she leave the nightmare behind? She certainly hoped so. As Hallie stared out into the night, she felt the panicky tension rise from her stomach to her chest. She prayed to stay safe for one more night.

* * * *

The next night Roger came home with two bags of groceries and sandwiches and salads from the deli at the supermarket. "This food should keep you through the weekend. I'll be back on Sunday night and then we'll see if you can go out."

The bruises were healing, but much of the skin on her arms had turned an ugly yellow. Hallie was glad the magistrate would see her looking like she'd been in a big fight. She unpacked the groceries and saw that he indeed had brought enough food home to last her all weekend and into next week.

Like the previous night, Roger took his plate into his office. "I'll be through with my work at exactly 9:00," he said from the doorway, "and I want you in bed and ready for me."

Hallie nodded and tried to smile pleasantly, but Roger didn't care one way or the other. He grimaced and walked on down the hall.

The whole night felt like an assault, but Hallie knew that this time, it wasn't because Roger was forcing sex on her with his violence. In fact, he tried to be tender, even though he said nothing to her, but just began lifting her gown and spreading her legs with his hands. Hallie closed her eyes and thought that if this was as bad as it got on her last night with Roger, she could endure it. In fact, it wasn't nearly as bad as her imagination had made it.

The next morning she tried to help Roger pack, but he snatched away the clothes and did it himself. He called her a ninny, he said she was a stupid little hick, and then, just as he had done before, he pushed her down on the bed and yanked at her clothes. "A baby is going change things, Hallie. You'll see. At least you won't have so much time to waste with losers like Ginger. You're going to talk to the priest about what you've done. He'll tell you that I'm right. What you did is a sin."

Hallie didn't struggle when he forced himself into her. Somehow, though, that wasn't enough for Roger. After he dressed and shaved, he grabbed her by the arms and gave her a shake. "You're hurting me," Hallie said, "really hurting me."

"As if I cared, you whining, sniveling bitch."

Hallie struggled to get free and Roger pushed her against the wall and slapped her face. Hallie began to cry, but she also thought that it was one more thing to add to her list. He'd be sorry he left her that way.

* * * *

Roger called her twice from the office. Hallie alerted Ginger that the plan was on track, but they didn't begin packing until Roger called from the airport just before noon. "Just checking on you," he said. "Don't think about leaving the house. Do you understand?"

"Of course, I do." It was all she could do to keep from making some flip, sarcastic remark. She'd have loved to tell him she hoped to never see his face again. She wished she could tell him that her lawyer would be calling him before long. But of course, she didn't say any of those things.

In the background, Hallie heard Roger's flight called and he abruptly hung up. A few minutes later, Hallie phoned the airport and confirmed that the flight had taken off. Maybe that was over-kill, but she didn't care. It took all the rational thinking power she had to believe he was actually on that plane and not on his way back to the house. Perhaps, she thought, he had found out about her plan and the trip was a ruse, a trick. She couldn't get past the thought that he would catch her.

She called Ginger, who in turn, alerted Bob. Then she called the shelter, and finally, she went into Roger's office and started making copies of the documentation she needed. She started with the hospital records. Then she sat down and began reconstructing the history of abuse with Roger. She kept it short, to the point, and for the moment, she limited the list to the most serious incidents of the last two years.

Hallie felt efficient as she made copies on the fax machine, even feeling amused when she thought about a day Roger had called from his office and fumed with frustration because he'd for-gotten some papers he needed. It was his mistake but of course he directed his anger to her. She'd offered to fax the pages over, but he'd laughed at her as if she'd made a joke and said he didn't trust her not to break the machine. But here she was, the woman too stupid to be trusted with the fax machine, making copies of the best evidence she had against him.

Next, Hallie did something she'd never had the nerve to do before, because she knew Roger checked his file drawers in order to make sure she didn't snoop. But it was ridiculous, she thought, that she didn't know how much money Roger made, or how much money they actually had. She began to go through the files and make copies of bank statements and of investment account information. She found the records of the mortgage on the house. Hallie wasn't as surprised by what she found in the financial records as saddened by the information. She had not been allowed to buy anything for herself in many years. Roger accounted for every penny of the grocery money. Hallie had virtually no cash to spend at a coffee shop or to go out for lunch with Ginger and the kids. Having the checkbook was unheard of. She'd never used a credit card. And yet, the money had been there.

Hallie's heart began to pound when the phone rang. What if…what if… Hallie couldn't bear to complete the thought. She was relieved to hear Roger's secretary giving her instructions from Roger to be home at a certain time that evening because he'd call her then. It sounded like such a simple request. She could imagine Roger's voice when he asked the secretary to call. Probably joking about his busy wife who loved to shop or some such stupid thing. Hallie thanked her for calling. She wondered what Roger would think when he called home and she wasn't there. And then when he came home, what would he see first? Hallie guessed he would search the house and she decided to leave the letter on the kitchen table. The letter. Her next task. She'd been avoiding it, but she finally sat down with the legal pad and started writing. She started several versions before she came up with the final copy.

> Dear Roger,
>
> As you can see, I have taken Eric and left you. For years I tried to build a real marriage, but you have crossed many lines that no person should ever cross. You know exactly what I am talking about.
>
> I am taking very little with me, and as far as I am concerned all the legal issues and the property can be settled through our attorneys. My attorney will be in touch shortly. Do not consider trying to see me and do not contact me. I do not wish to talk with you.

We have lived with terrible secrets in our home, but you should know that your behavior is no longer a secret. I have photographs of the bruises you have left on my body; I have a list of dates and times of many violent acts you perpetrated on me. By the time you read this, a restraining order will be in place; in addition, my attorney and counselors at two women's shelters will have in hand the documented evidence of your abuse. If you agree to a quiet divorce, I will not use this documentation. You have my word on that. I hope you accept that my decision to move on and build a new life is final.

Hallie

* * * *

Bob carried boxes through the side door and put them in the small covered trailer he'd picked up. He'd driven Hallie's car to the lot and hitched the trailer himself. Now he and Hallie were loading it quickly. As fast as she packed the boxes, Bob hauled them out. Oh how Hallie wished she'd had a chance to get to know Bob better. Meanwhile, Ginger had the kids in the backyard and was trying to keep the boys distracted. Before the trailer arrived Hallie had told Eric they were going on a trip and by tomorrow, they'd be with Grandma.

It was all happening so fast. The documentation was complete, the cash tucked away in her handbag, the shelter called, and the lawyer alerted. Hallie made extra copies of the letter to Roger and put the original in a sealed envelope. She was tempted to add another line or two or even start over, but with so much to do, she ultimately left well enough alone.

"How are you holding up?" Ginger asked as she came through the bedroom door. She ran her hand across Hallie's shoulders.

"Not too bad," she said, "but I can't help but feel sad that I'm going so far away from you."

"I know." Ginger wiped away some tears. "I promised myself I wouldn't do this. I'm relieved for you, but I'm going to miss you."

"I hope you'll come to see me. And I know Roger will leave this town and Eric and I can come here." Hallie put some sweaters in a box and reached for the tape. "I couldn't have done this without you. You know that."

"Bob and I are glad we could help, but you're doing this, Hallie. If we hadn't been here, you would have figured out some other way to save yourself and Eric."

"I like to think so…" Hallie reached out and hugged her friend. Not long after, Hallie and Ginger did a final check of the house. With the car loaded and the trailer packed, it was time to go.

"Well, we did all this in under five hours," Bob said. "Good for you Hallie. You're a stand-up woman. You know that?"

Hallie felt hot tears run down her cheeks. "I guess it's about time. I only wish…"

"No, no. Don't say it," Bob said. "The past is over. It's what you do now that counts."

Hallie hooked Eric's seat belt and stood by the driver's side of the car. "This is it. But I can't get in the car and drive away unless you promise me you'll stay in touch."

Her friends nodded and stood at the end of the driveway and waved as she drove off. Hallie held back her tears because she still had more steps to carry out. But, she thought, the worst is over.

* * * *

It was dark when Hallie pulled into the parking lot of a motel outside of town. She had just come from the magistrate, who issued the restraining order. At one time, Hallie thought, she would have wanted to curl up in a little ball and cry with humiliation. Somehow, though, her pride didn't matter anymore. In fact, the whole issue of pride had flipped. Now she felt proud that she had the guts to be, as Bob called her, a stand-up woman. She had stood up and showed a person in a position to help her the ugly evidence of what her marriage to Roger had become.

Hallie registered under her own name and said she'd be paying cash. Once in the room, Eric lay down on one of the beds. He was asleep within minutes.

After leaving the magistrate's office, the counselor had seen her off. But before she'd driven away, she gave Hallie some pamphlets, some of which addressed the rest of Hallie's journey. "Don't be surprised if you feel sad, along with relief, and perhaps one day, some rage will appear and you'll wonder where it's been hiding."

Hallie had nodded, again fighting back the tears. But alone now at the motel, she could let them flow. She went into the bathroom and started the shower and as the hot water flowed over her shoulders and down her back, she covered her face with her hands and sobbed. For the first time in years, she thought, she *felt* safe. She couldn't say she was happy or calm. She was filled with sadness and oh so weary, but she felt safe.

When she cried herself out, she wrapped up in a nightgown and robe and sat by the phone. Using a phone card she'd picked up at a drugstore on the way out of town, she punched in the number. Nina answered on the first ring. "Mom? I'm safe. I'm in a motel. You can call Ginger and Bob and we'll see you tomorrow."

"Oh Hallie. I'm so relieved."

"I am, too, Mom. I know this is going to be hard. But I'm ready to have a life now. I'm ready to give Eric what he needs."

"A future, Hallie?"

"Yes," she said, "we're going to build a future."

When she hung up the phone, Hallie pulled back the spread and climbed into bed. She curled up in a ball and drifted off to sleep. She told herself that Roger could not break down the door. He didn't know where she was. She could let down her guard and finally get a good night's sleep. She'd face tomorrow's challenges tomorrow.

Getting to Work

What Can We Learn About the Cycle of Abuse?

In actuality, Hallie need not have feared that Roger would not have boarded his plane. Her imagination may have run wild, which is understandable, but Hallie picked a very good time to escape. We can be fairly certain that he will go on his trip, no matter how threatening he seems about everything else because:

1) He is obsessive-compulsive about his career. He is a workaholic and holds his professional reputation in higher esteem than his family. He will not do anything to jeopardize a chance to improve his image in the eyes of his colleagues.

2) He does not believe Hallie will leave him. Why should he? She has put up with all the abuse until now and he thinks she's too weak to be her own person, independent of him. That, after all, has been his goal.

3) It is part of his personality make-up to believe that he is omnipotent in most of his relationships, so why would anyone want to leave such a man as he? Of course, this is the persona he presents to himself and the world most of the time. This works for him until he becomes frightened of abandonment and then the insecure, scared "little boy" appears. He knows Hallie is pulling away from him but he has no reason to believe, at this point, that she is capable of leaving him.

Quite naturally, Hallie fears the repercussions of leaving Roger. She is wise to be vigilant and aware of her and Eric's surroundings. However, Hallie knows she has made the decision to leave after giving the marriage every possible chance. In addition, she completely understands that if she stays she is putting herself and Eric in even more danger.

Numb, but Safe

Leaving Roger in a well thought out, unemotional way is the safest thing she can do. We see that she has set up her support network with Ginger, Bob, her mother, and the women's shelter; she has a well-documented paper trail of the abuse and has given it to several people. She has made Roger aware of this documentation, and he knows she can use it at any time. Remember that a legitimate fear involved Roger using his power in his profession and by implication, the community, to paint a picture of Hallie as emotionally unstable, "crazy" in the eyes of the world. Because his ugly secret is out, his freedom to bother or harm her or Eric in any way is curtailed. Roger will be a natural suspect should anything happen to either of them.

Why Does Hallie Care What Roger Thinks?

We can see that Hallie retains a strong need to explain how and why she has decided to leave. A part of her still wants Roger's approval, and this likely will be a part of her for many years. She is attached to Roger through fear, love, and the bond of having a child together. Her life revolved around him and her dream of a happy marriage and a family. It could be years before she can let go of the attachment. Hallie hashes over what she wants to say in her letter, on some level still believing that something she says will be the magic words that he finally understands.

I've heard women say it took ten years to feel completely free of the abusive relationship. That doesn't mean Hallie wants to be with Roger, but she will not easily get over the powerful forces she experienced in the relationship. This is why some women who have been kidnapped and kept prisoner for a long period of time think they have fallen in love with their captor. This person has the ability to keep them alive, kill them, nourish them, or starve them. The captor becomes an omnipotent figure to the victim and that becomes attractive when the victim believes escaping the captor is impossible.

Sometimes, as with Patty Hearst, for example, the kidnapped person becomes brainwashed and strongly identifies with the captor. You may recall that she participated in a bank robbery with her captors and came to believe she was one of them. Later, once she was away from them, she reverted to her old values. The issue raised in her trial involved brainwashing versus personal accountability and responsibility.

Sometimes the bond between captor and victim becomes very strong because of the energy each one puts into the relationship. The opposite of love is not hate; rather, it is the lack of feeling toward someone. When we keep hate and fear alive in a relationship that still maintains energy in the relationship, and the energy of hate and fear are not far from the energy of love.

Think how many times you have felt rage and hate toward someone you love. Put simply, if you didn't feel love for the person, you couldn't experience that kind of intense anger or rage. If you don't have any feelings one way or another about a person, all that means is that you haven't put energy into the relationship. It is impossible to love a person when you have not invested energy. Hallie has invested enormous energy into Roger, so it isn't surprising she cares very much what he thinks.

Hallie's recurring nightmare is common among trauma victims. It is likely she will continue to have the nightmare until she fully resolves the memories of the torture she experienced. No doubt she will need professional help to process the events of the past and heal the damage done to her psyche and spirit. The nightmare is, in a way, part of her effort to rationalize and resolve why she stayed so long and why she finally left.

As strange as it may seem, she will miss Roger and their family life. Recall how happy Hallie was during the pleasant encounters. Even with Roger's history, she had hung on to hope. For many years, her marriage to Roger was the only existence she knew and everything about it is so familiar. We can liken her situation to that of a college freshman leaving home for the first time. She may be excited about starting college and for various reasons, she may be anxious to leave home. Still, she experiences a lonely homesickness and misses what she knew for so long. The conflicts at home may not seem so bad when she's in the midst of adjusting to a strange new setting that has its own problems.

During all the stages of Hallie's grief, sadness, loneliness, and later, when she experiences, peace, contentment, and fulfillment, she will have the satisfaction of knowing that she finally gathered the courage to break away from Roger for the one person she loved most dearly, her son. We cannot overestimate the degree of courage it took for Hallie to make her decision and carry out the plan she created. Although it was very difficult, Hallie managed to find the strength to truly become what Bob referred to as a "stand-up woman." She can feel great satisfaction over her actions.

Epilogue: Six Months Later

Roger was late with the check again, but Hallie was not too concerned. He made a habit of being late with the child support and maintenance. It was his way of trying to keep a hold on her, not to mention pay her back for what he considered her betrayal. Oh how Roger had balked at the idea of *any* of his hard-earned money going to her. He even tried to get an accounting that detailed all her expenditures for Eric—even his food! But with the family court judge, Roger had finally met his match. The judge, a no-nonsense woman who had seen all kinds of batterers over the years, didn't fall for Roger's attempts to charm her.

For months, Roger called periodically to tell Hallie that she'd destroyed his life, almost killed him. He left these pleading messages on the answering machine. When he'd first discovered that Hallie had left, he showed up at Nina's house and spoke through the unopened door in hissing, hateful tones, threatening to find a way to take Eric away. Only the reality that the police could enforce the restraining order convinced him to back off and return home.

Roger was too smart to leave his nasty messages on the answering machine, so she never could accumulate evidence of his continuing, but often subtle, harassment. Sometimes he'd call and try to talk pleasantly. Hallie always said the same thing: I do not wish to speak to you. Please call my lawyer if you wish to communicate. When he came to see Eric, she stayed in the kitchen, but at this point, Roger was not allowed to take Eric out of her house, let alone out of town. Hallie's lawyer had wisely used the paper trail and documentation of abuse to convince the judge that Roger was not to be trusted alone with Eric at this time. The judge had also interviewed Eric alone and was convinced that Eric was, indeed, afraid of his dad.

During the last weeks with Roger, Hallie had come to realize just how deep her denial had been. But she soon could see that Roger could put walls of denial around himself, too. When he had returned from Denver and found Hallie's note, he immediately called her mother's home. Nina calmly told him Hallie would be communicating through her attorney. After she hung up, her mother told her what he'd said next. "So, my best girl decided to take a little vacation. It's okay, I understand I can be a difficult guy to live with. But she knows how much I love her, so she'll be back."

It took several weeks before Roger had a lawyer respond to her lawyer's letters and it was weeks more before she received the first child support payment. Through Hal Morton, the lawyer her mother had found and who became the "keeper" of Hallie's proof of Roger's abuse, Hallie learned of Roger's insistence that he wanted to reconcile. He was certain they could make their marriage work, and he agreed to seek counseling. Of course, he denied allegations of abuse. In fact, just as Hallie had feared, his lawyer spoke of Roger's professional opinion that Hallie had always been "delicate" and prone to emotional outbursts. She also had frequent accidents, which is what the hospital report indicated. Hallie hadn't remembered saying any such thing when she'd seen the ER doctor for her broken arm. The first time she read Roger's characterization of her, she shook with rage. Sometimes, her own violent thoughts shocked her. One day, she daydreamed about pushing Roger down a flight of stairs and took pleasure imagining him with a bruised and bloodied face.

Eric's voice brought Hallie back to the present. As she pulled into her parking place at the apartment complex, Eric started talking in an excited voice about the kids in the playground. "I want to stay out and play, Mommy," he said, repeating his plea several times.

"That's fine, honey. You can stay outside for a little while."

Eric was five now, already in full day kindergarten. It was so good to see him adjust to being around other kids, although he'd had some bad experiences with an older bully in the complex. Hallie took Eric to counseling, and so far, he was doing well.

Hallie and Eric had stayed with Nina for almost two months. Hallie had experienced good days and bad days during that time. At first, her exhaustion surprised her. The morning she arrived, she'd told her mother that she would get a job immediately—by the end of the first week. How strange that she barely had the strength to get out of bed. All she managed that week were a meeting with Hal Morton and finding a storage unit for her things. She fell asleep in the afternoons and sometimes slept so long she barely had time to fix dinner before her mother came home from work.

Within weeks though, Hallie began to feel her strength return. She looked in the mirror and saw that the circles beneath her eyes were almost gone and her face looked younger than it had before. "You know, I felt a lot older than my age," she'd told her new counselor, "and I looked older, too. But I can *see* a change in myself." The counselor had agreed.

Sometimes, late at night, Hallie would feel her old fears return. One night, the dream came back and when she woke up in a cold sweat and terrified besides, she'd run to the window to look for Roger's car. Then she'd checked on Eric, who slept on his bed along the wall in her mother's dining room. For the rest of the night, she tossed and turned and her heart pounded in her chest. She hadn't been able to get past the fear.

Finally, the two lawyers hashed out a temporary separation agreement and child support and temporary maintenance payments began. Hallie felt relief, but she still didn't feel secure, nor was the money Roger sent enough to support her and Eric. Hallie circled ads for full-time nursing positions at the local hospitals, but when she drove over to pick up an application she froze and couldn't go through the doors. She ran back to the car and realized she was afraid Roger was in that hospital. Hallie was angry with herself for such irrational thoughts, but she temporarily abandoned her idea of hospital nursing. It took courage to admit that she wasn't ready to take on a challenging job, but once she faced that reality, she felt enormous relief.

Later, when she spoke to the counselor at the mental health clinic, she realized that nothing she had felt since she drove away from her home and left her life with Roger behind was unusual. "Time," the counselor said, "recovery will take time." Hallie hated that word "recovery," because she wanted a full normal life *now*. Still, she enjoyed her part-time job as an assistant in an internal medicine practice. She'd found the job through a contact of her mother's. The job description seemed so simple that she questioned the wisdom of accepting it. It didn't involve nursing, but more closely resembled receptionist work and simple tasks like settling patients in examining rooms. But after talking to her therapist, she decided to take it. She needed the money, certainly, but the job also represented a chance to adjust to working in a job without demanding responsibilities.

Hallie enjoyed the job well enough, but she felt the need to do something else. In time, she decided, she would go back to nursing. Roger's derisive attitude and sarcastic comments about her interests had not snuffed out her desire to go to graduate school. She hadn't settled on the program she would pursue, but her desire to learn and expand her horizons felt like a strong drive that would lead her when the time came. At times, the series of tasks necessary to accomplish a big goal like filling out application forms for school overwhelmed her, but her counselor had convinced her that her response was normal, and in time, she'd be up to the challenge. "Give it time, Hallie," the counselor said so often.

On a practical level, her counselor pointed out that in order to move forward with school plans or perhaps even a more demanding job, Hallie would need to tackle computer skills. Hal Morton had mentioned that, too. Roger had not allowed her to use the computer in their home, and in only a few years, much had changed. For several weeks, Hallie felt so resentful that she lacked these skills that she had imaginary conversations with Roger and screamed at him in her mind. How dare he keep her ignorant of the basic things she needed to get along in the world? But of course, that was his plan. In the end, she made a commitment to herself to go to the library and use the computer for an hour or two each week. Then, she'd take a class at the community college.

In addition to renewed interest in exploring her professional future, a desire to try new things, even small things, began to surface. Part of her wanted to have some fun, and when a woman at the new church she'd found in the neighborhood told her she was putting together a book club, she jumped at the chance to join. So did Nina. For the first time, Hallie hired a college student in the complex to watch Eric for three hours every two weeks. That felt like such a big step she even wrote to Ginger about it. It was hard to leave Eric for the first time, but she knew it was time that her little boy adjusted to seeing his mother as a separate person with an identity of her own. When Hallie went to her book group, she felt like a normal person living a normal life.

That evening, Hallie sat on the little patio outside her apartment. She wrote checks for her bills and made notations in a notebook she used to plan her budget. Things were tight, no question about it, but she managed, and Eric didn't want for anything. It wouldn't be long before the sale of the house would be final and although Roger had fought hard against it, she would receive half the profit from the sale. That money would provide a sense of security and perhaps help her start her education.

Even better, Roger was eager now to move forward quickly with their divorce. As she knew he would, Roger had told her he had met someone who really understood him and he wanted to marry her as soon as he could be free of Hallie. They would be moving to Florida very soon because he'd been offered a great position. Of course, Hallie had mixed feelings about this. Eventually, Roger might have the custody agreement changed to include visits to his new home. In time, Eric would meet his stepmother and have that adjustment to make, too. Roger had undoubtedly told his fiancée that Hallie was a terrible loser and a bad mother. One day, she might have to fight him over custody of Eric. On the other hand, it was possible that this new woman would learn the truth about Roger more quickly than Hallie had. In that case, Roger would lose some of his power.

She had resources, Hallie told herself. So far, the plan she put in place to leave Roger had served her well. She had protected herself, and in the six months that had passed, Hallie had done more than survive. Physically, she was stronger and had fewer headaches and her constant digestive complaints had gradually diminished. She woke each day with energy rather than dread. That alone was a precious change that she never wanted to lose again. Part of Hallie's new strength was her ability to realize that she had been seriously injured, emotionally as well as physically, during her years with Roger and her recovery was not yet complete. Fortunately, Hallie thought as she watched the evening sky, she had time to heal and make her dreams of a better future a reality.

Getting to Work

What Can We Learn About the Cycle of Abuse?

We have become acquainted with Hallie during some extremely difficult times in her life. Sadly, she and Roger are typical participants in the dance of domestic violence. Maybe some questions have now been answered about why she stayed and what is wrong with Roger. Naturally, most people want to know why she married him in the first place, and what is wrong with her that keeps her in the dance—and Hallie certainly tried to make this relationship work.

In some situations, it would be logical to ask why no one would help Hallie. In her situation, however, she was secretive and had been willing to hide the abuse. When she did reach out, she was given advice. In some situations, law enforcement might have been involved. Hallie and Roger's dance did not include repeated 911 calls, which is not unusual when abuse occurs in middle-class homes. For the most part, Roger's abuse didn't leave the kind of marks on Hallie that would show. At the end, when he lost control, he ordered her to stay inside. This, too, is not an unusual scenario.

What's Next?

Where will Hallie go from here and what will Roger likely do? Hallie will continue to experience a sense of relief and peace of mind for a period of time. Of course, she was terrified when he actually showed up at Nina's home. She also must face him when he sees Eric. Roger's plans to remarry do not change the fact that he is still capable of stalking her and directly harming her. In fact, she is smart to stay on guard for any attempt to change the custody agreement, which would allow him to take Eric out of state.

We also see that Hallie is strong in many ways, and she has a good support system to see her through. As her counselor tells her, she can expect her entire recovery and healing period from abuse to take a long time, even years. She will experience PTSD (Post-Traumatic Stress Disorder), some symptoms of which appeared shortly after she left Roger and may continue for years. The frightening dream occurs, for example, and Hallie experiences fear when Roger visits Eric.

At first, Hallie thought she would jump into her new life, putting the past behind her and quickly reaching forward and grabbing her future. However, we saw that once she felt safe, exhaustion took over. Hallie needed the rest, but we also saw that she regained some strength in a fairly short time. If Hallie had been unable to get busy with the tasks necessary to organize her and Eric's new life, that would be a symptom of depression.

Hallie accepts that her recovery will take time, and we see that she has had peaceful times. In many ways, Hallie is living in the present and is enjoying life on a day to day basis. She is impatient in some ways, but she has settled into a routine for the present time. Ultimately, however, Hallie must accept that she will remain hypervigilant all of her life. A part of her will always fear Roger and be "on guard" for the kind of danger he represents. This hypervigilance will get better as she gets older, but it will always be there.

More About PTSD

According to the DSM-IV (Diagnostic and Statistical Manual of Mental Disorders), Hallie's PTSD symptoms may include the following:

- recurrent and intrusive memories of the abuse she suffered from Roger, her father, and/or her brother

- recurrent nightmares about the traumas she experienced

- reliving the experiences through flashbacks

- intense emotional distress at exposure to internal or external stimuli resembling any aspect of the abuse

- physiological reactivity to stimuli resembling the abuse

- efforts to avoid thoughts, feelings, or conversations about the abuse

- inability to recall important aspects of the abuse

- diminished interest in significant activities

- feeling detached and estranged from others

- unable to have deep feelings about anyone or anything

- sense of impending doom, i.e., a short lifespan, a serious disease for herself and Eric

- difficulty sleeping

- irritability or angry outbursts

- inability to concentrate

- hypervigilance

- exaggerated startle response

It is imperative that those suffering these symptoms seek professional help. Therapy, especially EMDR (Eye Movement Desensitization and Reprocessing) is usually effective. EMDR is a state-of-the-art therapy which helps individuals desensitize and reframe traumatic experiences. A combination of therapy and medication, such as antidepressants, may be necessary. Regardless of the type of help they seek, delaying the process will only make the condition worse.

New Relationships

Hallie probably will find it hard to trust other people, especially men. At first, she may shy away from men completely, or she may jump right into another relationship, still hoping to make her dream come true. Hallie has been frightened and exhausted by her traumatic sexual experiences with Roger, and during these first six months, we do not see her pursuing relationships. She has been isolated socially and we see her just starting to venture out. Other abused women may have been less isolated. They may have held jobs because the family needed two incomes to survive, which is not an unusual situation today. Abusive situations fit every kind of description. Some women are all too eager to find tenderness and comfort in a new relationship; they may also cling to the belief that they are worth something only if a man pursues them.

If Hallie is wise, she will give herself time to heal and discover her own strengths before getting into another relationship. In general, this applies to any abused woman. In therapy, Hallie can learn why she was attracted to Roger and ignored the early "red flags." She needs this deep understanding in order not to repeat the same experience.

It is important that Hallie learn who she is and what she wants in her life, based on her needs and desires, not on what she thinks others expect of her. Group therapy with other recovering women would also be a good support system for her. Her therapist may sponsor such a group or give her leads to find one.

Moving Forward, Taking Breaks

At first, Hallie was eager to find a good job, which represented an effort to recapture what she had lost. She had longed for a nursing job, even assuming she would find a job shortly after the wedding. However, we saw a manifestation of PTSD when she became afraid to go into the hospital. The fear of Roger surfaced in a setting that represented his element, his world. The part-time job was a wise choice for Hallie. As we saw, the job was fairly easy and didn't consume her energy. This job allowed her time to assimilate all the changes in her life, and equally important, a more gradual re-entry to the workplace gives Eric time to get used to the changes in his life.

As Hallie adjusts to her new situation, she begins to think about her long-term goals, and she may find that the field she assumed she would enter may not be what she settles on when it comes time to either look for a job or apply to graduate school. Hallie may need to wait a year or two before she has sufficient mental clarity to make a decision. Meanwhile, however, her part-time job is not only financially necessary, it is helping her adjust to the world.

The Plan Worked

Hallie's escape plan was risky, but by having evidence to hold over Roger's head, he was forced to pay child support if he wanted to see his son and also maintain his professional identity and reputation. Abusive men almost always threaten to leave their families stranded without a penny—they may also threaten to take the children away, as Roger did.

We see that Roger agrees to go forward with the divorce and Hallie does indeed have some rights. The pictures she has that document his abuse help quiet some of Roger's claim that she is "delicate." Language like that is a precursor to claims that she is "emotionally disturbed." Had Hallie simply walked out one day, without a plan in place, Roger's chances of acting on his threats would have been far better. Hallie shows us how important it is for women to be smart about the way they leave an abusive situation.

The Mourning Continues

At times, Hallie may question her decision to leave. Were things really as bad as she thought? She may play out in her mind an entire fantasy of a changed Roger coming to her and "confessing" his former wrongdoing and making a string of promises about a happy future. As hard as it is to believe, some men use this tactic and some women spend months or years nurturing this fantasy.

This type of fantasy is part of the grieving process Hallie must go through, and if she experiences the process early, that is better than having it resurface much later. Interestingly enough, she may go through some intense grief when Roger tells her he is remarrying. To Hallie, this is a definitive end to this dream she carried so long. Hallie's grieving process includes several steps and usually takes about a year to move through. During this time, she likely will go in and out of the variable stages of depression, anger, denial, bargaining, rationalization, and acceptance. These are normal and actually healthy if she does not linger for destructive periods of time in each stage.

In the *depression* stage she will feel sad, less motivated, irritable, lonely, and lethargic. Hallie may need antidepressants for a period of time to improve some of the brain chemistry that may have become imbalanced during periods of prolonged stress. Her therapist can help monitor this need and refer her to a physician who can prescribe the medication.

Her *anger* will probably be directed at life in general and at herself specifically. At times, Hallie may pull away from those who try to help her and even blame them for making her leave. Feeling the anger is healthy as long as she does not use it to harm herself or others.

Denial is one way our mind tries to protect us from all the pain we don't want to feel. When Hallie is lost in a fantasy about a changed Roger, she may deny the degree of danger within her marriage. This denial may be quite strong at times. Remember that Hallie is always trying to fulfill her Lifetime Messages Blueprint, and until she understands that, she may see the denial stage as actual reality. During this stage she may actually long to be with Roger again. That does not mean she still loves him—what she wants is the dream she thought she could have with him.

Bargaining is a way of looking at "what-ifs." *What if* I had done things differently? *What if* I had asked for help sooner? Maybe I could have saved the marriage. What-ifs serve as reminders that we have choices. It's important to remember that we made the best choice possible at that time, based on what we were mentally capable of choosing. Second guessing ourselves serves no purpose at this time. We all do what we think is best at the time with all the knowledge we have and that's all that can be expected of anyone! We can hope that Hallie will learn this through her therapy.

Rationalization can be damaging if it keeps us from facing the reality of a situation. The reality is that Roger is an abusive, mentally ill person with a personality disorder. Hallie was drawn to him through unconscious messages that guided her (the LMB). She can *choose* to see the end of this relationship as a chance for healthy growth. Rationalizing that she deserved to be treated abusively, for instance, because she was not worthy of better, will only take her in the direction of another abusive relationship in order to fulfill that belief about herself.

Finally, Hallie reaches *acceptance*, a stage in which she will understand why she got into the marriage with Roger and why she chose to leave it. She will accept that the dream she had with him was not possible and she will direct her energy to making her new dreams come true.

Support Systems

It would be wise for Hallie to stay in touch with the women's shelter in her new home. These women's shelters can provide much needed support through free group sessions, free legal advice and aid, a support group for Eric, further help in any court proceeding and in obtaining another restraining order against Roger if needed. For women who escape with virtually no belongings, shelters can provide temporary clothing and shelter for women and their children. In some situations, women need a "safe house," that is a place that hides women and children for a period of time. If Roger should show up and threaten Hallie, her continued association with the shelter could prove valuable.

A man like Roger seems to have much to lose and this motivates him to hold together his public persona. But what could happen if his new wife calls the police the first time he hits her or rapes her? What if the self-important, professional Roger is exposed by someone who sees through him early on and he is embarrassed in front of his colleagues? Should that happen, Roger might focus all the blame on Hallie and renew his efforts to punish her, perhaps even using Eric as a pawn in his game. If Roger ever believes he has nothing to lose, he could become even more dangerous. Hallie must stay aware of this, and having a contact at the shelter will help her define a plan if she needs it.

Practical Matters Cause Stress

We have seen Hallie cope with Roger through the legal system. At first he refuses to acknowledge her desire for a divorce, and they haggle over custody and visitation rights. Hallie is doing all this through her lawyer and because of it, some financial agreements have been reached. Hallie's rights to half the common property have been protected.

In many situations, women have much more difficult legal battles, at least in the short-term. Men like Roger do not believe they have done anything wrong. Roger believes Hallie is acting irrationally; he thinks he is the victim because she left and "stole" his son. Roger may never believe otherwise, which points out yet again, the importance of Hallie's documentation. It is probably true that support payments began because he could not work around those all-important photos and chronology. Hallie can continue to dispute Roger's denials about his abuse through her documentation and witnesses.

For Eric's sake, as well as Hallie's, we hope the legal proceedings will go smoothly and quickly, but it is unlikely Roger will stand back and let other people dictate the terms. Sooner or later, Roger will turn on his charm and attempt to influence the outcome, most likely in areas involving his visitation rights. Roger is charismatic, intelligent, and manipulative; he has fooled many people, and Hallie leaving him in the manner she did will not force him to see reality.

In some ways, Hallie is relieved Roger is remarrying because he will not fight the divorce. It is true that she may get better terms than she would if he were focused–obsessed–with getting her back or punishing her. However, unless he shows his true colors to his new wife early on, he may have found an ally to fight for custody of Eric, for example, or at least take him for long periods of time. Roger's new wife might see him as the victim of a cold woman who treated "poor" Roger so unfairly. Hallie must be willing to fight Roger in the courts, perhaps for the rest of Eric's childhood.

Setbacks and Bad Times

Eventually Hallie will realize that all the changes in her life are not positive. Even with some forced support from Roger (who, we notice, is always late with the payments), she is on a tight budget and her housing choices may be quite limited. Her socioeconomic status has changed, no question about it. It is a sad fact that most divorced women and their children have less money and must cope with reduced resources, while divorced men actually end up with greater resources. Although Hallie does not fit into this category, many of the poorest women in our society are poor because they have run away from abusive husbands or live-in partners.

Even as the years pass, Hallie may never feel completely free of Roger's influence, especially while Eric is still a minor. Furthermore, she may never be free of the fear that Roger might come after her at any time. However, just as she endured the last horrific and fear-filled days with Roger, she can't let ongoing fear of him stop her. She can learn ways to deal with the fears through therapy and support systems, just as she can learn ways to work effectively within the legal system.

More than anything else, Hallie needs to focus her attention on her new life and the path she wants to follow. Her strength and belief in herself will serve to deter Roger from continuing his attempts to control her. That may happen over time, and each time she resists his behavior, she gains a little more strength. Hallie also would benefit from training in assertiveness and effective communication. Over the long run, this will help her in her professional life, but also in future relationships with other men.

For now, she needs to experience accomplishments of all kinds and "sizes." For example, agreeing to participate in a book group is important in itself, but Hallie will also gain confidence in her ability to make friends and join in the give and take of social conversations. Her friendship with Ginger provided some social experience, but it was quite limited. Hallie's job; interactions with neighbors; conversations with the lawyer, Eric's teacher, and the babysitter; and her work in therapy, all will lead to increased self-confidence and self-esteem. Eventually, Roger will sense these changes in Hallie and he may think twice before trying to undermine her.

What About Eric?

Eric is still young but he has taken in many confusing messages about himself and about life in general. We've already discussed the fact that he has been deprived of a healthy childhood. Hallie has seen to it that he has counseling with a therapist who specializes in working with children. Eric needs a safe place to express his feelings and fears. Hallie can expect him to fluctuate between obvious relief, happiness, sadness, and alternating between missing his dad and not wanting to see him at all. He will likely show anger at both his dad and Hallie, and he may engage in acting out behavior such as hitting other children and striking out at Hallie. For example, he may balk at going to bed and then hit Hallie when she takes his arm and leads him into his room.

Roger Will Not Disappear

What about Roger? As previously discussed, Roger is likely to find another willing victim. He may grieve for a while, but his grief will focus on *his* losses, rather than on what he did to his family. He will rationalize everything he did, and go through life believing that Hallie "did him wrong." In his eyes, he always will be her victim, and it is doubtful he will ever change. Sadly, a new woman in his life may be as vulnerable to his perceived charm and power as Hallie was, and she will, at least for a time, view Hallie as the "bad person" who victimized poor Roger—she'll see herself as comforting and rescuing him.

Statistics show that Roger will mellow in later years, but he will always be personality disordered. He will continue with his life, with emphasis on his career and his attempts to look perfect in others' eyes. He *may* go to counseling for a while to find support for his grief but, sadly, it is doubtful he will ever admit wrongdoing or take responsibility for his abusive behaviors. Most likely, he will never discuss his behavior with Hallie, nor will he ever apologize to her or to Eric. As Eric grows up he may keep a shallow relationship with his dad, and Roger will probably blame Hallie for influencing Eric to turn away from him, still refusing to take responsibility for his abusive behavior to Eric.

The Important Continuum

A final word about domestic violence in general. First, it does not have to become so horrific in all cases. Research shows that abusive personalities can be viewed on a continuum. Some abusers are much *less* dangerous than Roger and are more likely to be candidates for rehabilitation; others are even worse than Roger and are abusive to everyone they encounter, not just their families. In the reference section that follows I have listed a few resources that expertly detail this continuum. I have also listed warning signs of abuse and a map, so to speak, of guidelines to follow if you find yourself in an abusive relationship.

According to resources mentioned, Roger is not capable of rehabilitation. His personality disorder is a combination of extreme narcissism, paranoia, and obsessive-compulsive traits. We can only hope that he will not fatally hurt someone and that he will mellow in his older years to the point that he is just an unbearable pessimist.

Turning on the Light of Hope

Carl Jung, a famous Swiss psychiatrist, talked about "the shadow," the parts of ourselves we don't want others to see. We tend to hide these parts, hence keeping the darkness in place. Jung taught that these shadow sides influence us in ways we are not always consciously aware of. He believed that if we try to totally suffocate and ignore the shadow sides, they tend to demand more of our attention and eventually will dominate us.

The shadow sides contain both positive and negative traits and tendencies, depending on how they're applied. It's important that we decide how much of the shadow we expose in order to be a healthy, integrated whole person, because when we expose the shadow sides, we take away some of their power to dominate us.

Domestic violence can be viewed as one of society's shadow sides, and as such, exposing the abuse in our homes is the best thing we can do to eliminate it on both a personal and a group level. It is the healthiest step we can take for the victims and the abuser. If done in a smart way, we can find help and prevent disastrous events from continuing. First, however, we must believe that we have a right to live free of fear and abusive control.

Shining the light on anything allows it to be seen, which may be an unpleasant experience. Sure, when we shine the light on domestic violence, it is like seeing the accumulated dust and cobwebs in the corner of the room. We can see all the work we must do to clean the dirt out of the room. But shining the light on domestic violence also diminishes its power and hold on us.

As a society, we must provide safe places for the many

women like Hallie. If we expect them to cry out for help before it is too late, we must believe what they tell us. We can all begin breaking the cycle of abuse by crying out for help as soon as we experience it, whether it happens to us or to someone else.

Finally, a personal note: If this book helps just one woman and prevents further suffering, or even death, resulting from abuse, it has been well worth the agony it took to hear these stories and put them to paper.

LIFETIME MESSAGES BLUEPRINT

Using the Lifetime Messages Blueprint (LMB)

At birth, and perhaps even in utero, we begin to take in messages about ourselves and the world around us, beginning with significant individuals in our immediate environment such as Mom, Dad, siblings, and our extended family. As we develop, this world expands to include teachers, friends, and acquaintances in our community and the world at large. We use these messages, especially those early messages, to develop what I have called the Lifetime Messages Blueprint (LMB).

This blueprint serves as a "map" that demonstrates how we will conduct our lives as we grow up. We can think of it as a powerful set of "rules" that tells us what to do and what not to do, based on what others have told us we should think, feel, and do. For example, if our family of origin did not allow us to show anger, then we will adapt to that dictate and find a way to suppress anger. Often, the anger isn't hidden so much as it is disguised as another more acceptable feeling such as fear, inadequacy, and so forth.

The brain stores information we need to operate automatically, and this includes the early messages that condition behavior. This is a normal conditioning process and much of human behavior can be described in terms of stimulus-response. Hunger is a stimulus and seeking food is a response—this is an obvious example. More subtle messages condition behavioral responses we may not understand. A present day stimulus may bring these messages into our conscious minds, making us aware of a reaction we are having to a particular event or circumstance. For example, some adults are afraid of the dark and must sleep with the lights on. An underlying message in their LMB says this is a perfectly normal response because an old introjected event (one they have unconsciously incorporated into their value system and ego structure) left–conditioned–a message of fear. However, once that old message is uncovered, adults can begin to see that the fear response is not rational today. In this way, adults can change behavior that is based on old patterns and messages.

Most of the time, these introjected messages are deeply buried in the unconscious and we are not aware of their existence. We may be consciously aware of feelings and thoughts we have in our present life when a certain stimulus elicits them, but we may not be aware of their origins. We can spend considerable time working on conscious feelings and thought patterns and we will probably achieve some success in changing our behavior. But we may not make permanent change until we get in touch with the deep unconscious messages driving our present feelings, thoughts, and behaviors.

I believe most battered women do not readily leave an abusive relationship partly because they struggle with deep unconscious messages and feel compelled to live up to them; put another way, the responses to certain stimuli are experienced as *necessary* responses and they feel normal. Thus, the Lifetime Messages Blueprint drives behavior that to an outside person may look irrational at best and quite destructive at worst.

As we will see in Hallie's LMB, she introjected messages from events in her childhood that told her she was a burden and not worthy of respect. Therefore, she was drawn to a man who would help her live that message; consequently, she found it very hard to leave him, even though she eventually knew on a conscious level that her life and probably the life of their son were in jeopardy much of the time.

Our dictates to live up to this blueprint are so compelling that we will use any excuse to keep us in a situation as long as we are fulfilling them. We can see from Hallie's story that it took her a long time to absorb the reality of her situation. We also see her thought processes about her behavior. She literally began to see herself as the stimulus that triggered Roger's violent response. When women do that, they work to change themselves and their behavior in a vain attempt to become what the batterer wants them to be.

Working with the LMB

I believe it is extremely important for a therapist to facilitate the uncovering of a client's early LMB, along with the process of bringing these messages to the conscious mind. Most people need help determining which messages are not working today and help with choosing to change the behavior.

As a self-report tool, the LMBI (Lifetime Messages Blueprint Inventory) is simple and easy to understand and takes only 15 to 20 minutes to complete. (To avoid confusion, I have defined the LMBI as the basic tool and the LMB as the individual client's result.) It proves useful in giving the client a way to understand her responses, even when they are not always the ones she wants. So many times I've had clients say, "I have no idea why I feel this way, but I just don't know any other way to feel about it!" This represents the perfect time to pull out the LMBI because the answers are found there, "hidden in plain view."

It is not necessary for the client to have numerous childhood memories to complete the LMBI because the tool looks at recent memories of feelings, thoughts, and behavior in order to form a pattern or "blueprint" of possible messages originating in the past. Using current life situations creates a sense of control and the client does not feel threatened by her fear of memories from the past that may "pop up" and scare her.

Who Can Use the LMBI?

Therapists, physicians, allied medical staff, and anyone in the helping fields can use the LMBI with a person whom they suspect is being abused and is not choosing to either leave the situation or seek help. It is frustrating to treat clients/patients who will not help themselves, even when they realize they are in danger. However, by using the LMBI, we can bypass the behavior that blocks progress. I have found that it produces healthy change quickly because it empowers a woman to engage in self-exploration and choose behaviors based on what she has learned about herself.

The LMBI also teaches clients to separate feelings from thoughts. Most people understand that behavior is different from either feelings or thoughts, but many do not understand the difference *between* feelings and thoughts. For example, I may ask a client how she "feels" about a certain experience, only to have her tell me what she thinks about it. Thoughts contain evaluations, judgments, and analysis, so the language a client chooses often indicates whether she is falling into "thinking" expressions or is using the words we associate with "feeling" language.

The LMBI has the added advantage of being an inexpensive tool for a therapist to use in the office. It requires only a few sheets of paper and a pen and because it is subjective the therapist's opinion cannot get in the way. The client can do her own work at her own pace in a safe environment, with the therapist facilitating but not interfering.

Hallie's LMB

This book revealed Hallie's path, from the time she met Roger until she left him. In the epilogue we also saw glimpses of her life after she left Roger and went about the hard work of changing her life, not just on the outside, but on the inside. It may be instructive to look at what Hallie's LMB might look like. The information provided helps us see the areas that contributed to Hallie's thought and behavior patterns; just as important, we can determine the areas Hallie needs to explore in order to be sure that she will not repeat the destructive behavior in the future. Sadly, women who have been in abusive relationships are at risk of living with or marrying another abusive man. As difficult as Hallie's life has been, she could get "fooled" again if she lacks an understanding of the childhood messages that set her up for the early infatuation with an abusive man. The LMB can serve as one tool among many that can prepare Hallie for a better future.

PART ONE (LMBI)

Directions: Please answer the following questions with the first answer that comes to you.

1) Name a time you were proud of yourself:

<u>*My son was born*</u>

   A) What did you feel then?

<u>*Happy and proud*</u>

   B) What did you think about yourself then?

<u>*I can do something worthwhile*</u>

2) Name a time you were ashamed of yourself

<u>*when I disappointed Roger*</u>

   A) What did you feel then?

<u>*inadequate and stupid*</u>

   B) What did you think about yourself then?

<u>*I'm always fouling things up*</u>

3) Name a time you were the most content?

<u>*alone, on the beach*</u>

   A) What did you feel then?

<u>*peaceful*</u>

   B) What did you think about yourself then?

<u>*I'm okay being alone*</u>

4) Name a time you were the least content?

<u>*When Roger is mad at me*</u>

   A) What did you feel then?

<u>*anxious*</u>

   B) What did you think about yourself then?

<u>*I'll never learn*</u>

5) Name a time you were the most productive?

in nursing school

A) What did you feel then?

proud

B) What did you think about yourself then?

I'm smart

6) Name a time you were the least productive?

after my marriage

A) What did you feel then?

helpless

B) What did you think about yourself then?

I'm worthless

7) What is the most positive thing you ever heard your parents (or the person/s who raised you) say about you?

A) Your father (or father figure)

I'm sweet and kind

B) Your mother (or mother figure)

I can accomplish anything I want

8) What is the most negative thing you heard your parents (or the person/s who raised you) say about you?

A) Your father (or father figure)

I'm a burden

B) Your mother (or mother figure)

I'm in the way

9) Overall, what is the message about yourself that you got from your mother (or mother figure)?

I should find a better life for myself

10) Overall, what is the message about yourself that you got from your father (of father figure)?

I'm a burden I'm not worth his love and attention

PART TWO (LMBI)

Directions: Complete these sentences by transferring your answers from part one. For example, transfer only the answers in question 1 A to the corresponding blank of 1 A on this page. Then transfer 1 B of part one to I B of this page, etc.

1) When my life is right for me, I feel

    A) *happy and proud*

and I know that

    B) *I can do something worthwhile*

2) When my life is not going right for me, I feel

    A) *inadequate and stupid*

and I know that

    B) *I always foul up*

3) I often struggle to find

    A) *peace*

and to believe that

    B) *I'm okay alone*

4) Instead, I easily slip into feeling

    A) *anxious*

and believing that

    B) *I'll never learn*

5) I wish I could always feel

    A) *proud*

and believe that

    B) *I'm smart*

6) But, I often choose to feel

    A) *helpless*

and believe that

    B) *I'm worthless*

7) I want others to see me as

    A) _sweet and kind_

and believe that

    B) _I can accomplish anything I want_

8) But I often think they see me as

    A) _a burden_

and they believe that

    B) _I'm in the way_

9) The best way for me to survive and to feel secure is to (**answer from part one, #9 & #10)

    find a better life, be a burden, and don't be worthy of love and attention

PART THREE (LMBI)

Directions: Transfer answers from part two to correspond with answers on this page. For example: 1-A in part two goes in the blank after 1-A on this page, and 1-B in part two goes in the blank after 1-B on this page, etc.

When I feel: **I may be living the message of:**

1-A) *happy and proud* 1-B) *I can do something worthwhile*

2-A) *inadequate and stupid* 2-B) *I always foul up*

3-A) *peace* 3-B) *I'm okay alone*

4-A) *anxious* 4-B) *I'll never learn*

5-A) *proud* 5-B) *I'm smart*

6-A) *helpless* 6-B) *I'm worthless*

7-A) *sweet and kind* 7-B) *I can accomplish*

8-A) *like a burden* 8-B) *I'm in the way*

Most of the time I may be living my life as if *I'm finding a better life* (part 2 #9) and I may choose people in my life who will facilitate my belief that *I'm a burden and I'm not worthy of love and attention.* (part 2 #9)

Instances in relationships which have facilitated my thinking and feeling these messages are: (List the incident/s and what you thought and felt.)

Proud to marry Roger—I thought I was finding a better life; I often feel like a burden to Roger and I feel unworthy of his love.

Do these messages hinder or help me? *hinder*

Do I want to keep these messages? *no*

If not, what messages will I choose instead?

I am capable of making my own life healthy; I am not a burden; I can be autonomous and I am worthy of a peaceful healthy life and relationship.

Hallie's Lifetime Messages Blueprint: What Does it Tell Us?

Based on Hallie's LMB, we see evidence of her negative beliefs about her intelligence, her worth to others, and her abilities. Look at the words she uses: stupid, inadequate, anxious, helpless, a burden, in the way. It is no exaggeration to say that from the day she was born she heard these negative messages, although the message may not have been delivered through the spoken word. Oral language is less than twenty percent of communication. Body language, facial expressions, and a look in the eyes provide profound information about another person's reactions to us. Think of the times you heard someone say something, but you didn't believe the person because of the way he was folding his arms, or the way she used her hands. The tilt of the head or posture can communicate approval or disapproval, agreement or disagreement. A look in the eyes can give us clues about the truth of what the other person is saying.

We also react to energy fields, that is, the atmosphere around another person's body and the space he or she occupies. We may not realize we're reacting to such covert signs, but these more subdued messages come across stronger than verbal messages. We often do not know what has caused us to jump to a certain conclusion. We just know that it "felt right" or "seemed right." Conversely, something may just feel wrong.

Roger only needed to look a certain way to instill fear in Hallie, and as a young child, Eric began reacting to Roger's energy field and body language even before he could understand his words. Eventually, Hallie had physical symptoms that triggered her fear. Her heart pounded and her head began to ache. Over time, these fear responses became part of normal life for Hallie. In addition to his powerful body language, Roger's degrading remarks to Hallie matched the message that she is worthless, stupid, and inadequate.

Why would Hallie want to fulfill such a message? The blueprint we set up from birth (and perhaps pre-birth) is much like a map to guide us through our lives. We feel lost and insecure without our map, just as a traveler in a foreign country or a new city feels disoriented or lost without her maps. We rely on these unconscious messages to keep us going in a familiar direction, regardless of the quality of that direction.

We like to think we are rational beings who make logical decisions, but being in familiar territory always feels more predictable and controllable than being in unfamiliar and, therefore, unpredictable surroundings. We don't know what will happen next and that could mean we would lose control of our life. Even if the familiar is abusive and unhealthy, it is still predictable; therefore, we think it is more manageable than trying something different. This type of belief system keeps Hallie from seeing Roger's inability to change. She desperately wants him to change so that she can continue with her blueprint, which as you can see, also gives her positive messages.

Seeking the Good

The positive messages we see in Hallie's blueprint show her belief that she is smart, proud, sweet, kind, and can find peace. If she lets them, these messages can be just as powerful as the negative ones. However, most of the time I find that my clients more easily believe the negative ones than the positive ones. Ideally, therapy includes working with the positive messages in order to override those that bring such negative influence.

It may not be obvious, but Roger also helps Hallie live her positive messages. For example, she feels worthwhile, proud, and smart whenever she pleases him. Unfortunately, this is one of the hooks that keeps her in such abusive, unpredictable circumstances. When Roger cycles into his loving, gentle, boyish phases, Hallie is hooked all over again because she feels the positive messages. Two major problems appear: his positive cycles convince her that he can and will change, and in addition, Hallie doesn't realize that it is her responsibility to maintain the knowledge that she is capable of living the positive messages no matter what Roger does.

With both positive and negative messages, trying to fulfill the blueprint traps Hallie and the messages are self-fulfilling prophesies. On the one hand, she must be sure she's in a situation that coincides with her beliefs that she is stupid, anxious, helpless, a burden, and in the way. Roger provides the opportunity to feel all of those things; therefore, unconsciously, a part of her knows she is in the right place. At the same time the messages of being sweet, kind, proud, and happy tell her she must stay in her place with Roger.

Unconscious Drives

Remember that none of this is really in Hallie's conscious thinking. She isn't likely to figure this out without some type of professional help. First, she is too busy surviving the relationship and taking care of Eric and second, her mother and father did not teach her that her feelings or opinions count. Again she was too busy surviving an alcoholic father and a submissive mother. Hallie learned to survive, but she did not learn to think independently and be autonomous. This does not mean that Hallie is incapable, lacks intelligence, or is mentally ill. It only means that she is unaware of the content of her Lifetime Messages Blueprint.

One of Hallie's "mixed" beliefs is that she should find a better life, but one that proves she is a burden and not worthy of love and attention. It is easy to see that marrying Roger would appear to be a better life than the one she had with an alcoholic father. Because of this, she ignores the early "red flags" in their relationship; after all, Roger controlled her from the moment they met. She felt a strong attraction and a "push" toward him from her introjected messages. At the same time she unconsciously realizes that she can feel like a burden and unworthy of love and attention from him. She ignores those early "red flags," too. What a perfect match!

Breaking the Pattern

Hallie's LMB conditioned her to accept the situation Roger offered and even led her to comply with his rules and take his extreme abuse. Hallie's compliance does not mean she has to stay there the rest of her life. Once she realizes that she is capable of making healthy decisions and carrying them through, she will begin to change her lifetime messages blueprint to believe that she can be healthy. She will eventually believe she is not a burden and she will also believe in her ability to be autonomous and worthy of a peaceful, healthy life and relationship.

Sometimes a tragedy will catapult the battered woman into changing her blueprint. On an individual level, as well as what is advantageous for society, it is best if a woman can see the blueprint before tragedy hits. Once she understands her blueprint and realizes that it is not working for her, she is more open to consciously change it and live a new blueprint. She also learns to trust and take care of herself, as well as avoid traps that force her to fall back into the old blueprint. As her self-esteem and self-confidence rise, she can look back and wonder whatever possessed her to marry this person. The danger in not knowing the blueprint messages lies in the risk that she continues to choose the same types of surroundings and relationships over and over again. That's why so many women continue to marry abusive men.

Working on the LMB Messages

The LMB may sound complicated but just use it to become more aware of your reactions, thoughts, feelings and note how they play off each other. Once you are aware of the messages, you can notice those times that you turn your power over to other people by making decisions based on what you think they want you to do rather than following your own gut feeling. Hallie did this again and again. But, as we saw, little by little, she questioned the inevitability of her life with Roger. She began to see possibilities rather than remaining resigned to living a painful, terribly constricted life.

As an exercise, use events as a starting point to make lists of your thoughts, feelings, and behaviors. When you do this, you will see patterns, and from these patterns, you will become more acquainted with the one person you can rely on the most–yourself.

Lifetime Messages Blueprint Inventory (LMBI) Part One

Directions: Please answer the following questions with the first answer that comes to you.

1) Name a time you were proud of yourself

____

    A) What did you feel then?

____

    B) What did you think about yourself then?

____

2) Name a time you were ashamed of yourself

____

    A) What did you feel then?

____

    B) What did you think about yourself then?

____

3) Name a time you were the most content?

____

    A) What did you feel then?

____

    B) What did you think about yourself then?

____

4) Name a time you were the least content?

____

    A) What did you feel then?

____

    B) What did you think about yourself then?

____

5) Name a time you were the most productive?

____

A) What did you feel then?

____

B) What did you think about yourself then?

____

6) Name a time you were the least productive?

____

A) What did you feel then?

____

B) What did you think about yourself then?

____

7) What is the most positive thing you ever heard your parents (or the person/s who raised you) say about you?
A) Your father (or father figure)

____

B) Your mother (or mother figure)

____

8) What is the most negative thing you ever heard your parents (or the person/s who raised you) say about you?
A) Your father (or father figure)

____

B) Your mother (or mother figure)

____

9) Overall, what is the message about yourself that you got from your mother (or mother figure)?

____

10) Overall, what is the message about yourself that you got from your father (or father figure)?

____

Part Two (LMBI)

Directions: Complete these sentences by transferring your answers from part one. For example transfer only the answers in question 1A to the corresponding blank of 1A on this page. Then transfer 1B of part one to 1B of this page, etc.

1) When my life is right for me, I feel

    A) _______________________________________

and I know that

    B) _______________________________________

2) When my life is not going right for me, I feel

    A) _______________________________________

and I know that

    B) _______________________________________

3) I often struggle to find

    A) _______________________________________

and to believe that

    B) _______________________________________

4) Instead, I easily slip into feeling

    A) _______________________________________

and believing that

    B) _______________________________________

5) I wish I could always feel

    A) _______________________________________

and believe that

    B) _______________________________________

6) But, I often choose to feel

    A) _______________________________________

and believe that

    B) _______________________________________

7) I want others to see me as

    A) ____

and believe that

    B) ____

8) But I often think they see me as

    A) ____

and they believe that

    B) ____

9) The best way for me to survive and to feel secure is to (**answer from part one, #9 & #10):

____

____

Part Three(LMBI)

Directions: Transfer answers from part two to correspond with answers on this page. For example: 1-A in part two goes in the blank after 1-A on this page, etc.

When I feel: I may be living the message of:

1-A)_________________________   1-B)_________________________

2-A)_________________________   2-B)_________________________

3-A)_________________________   3-B)_________________________

4-A)_________________________   4-B)_________________________

5-A)_________________________   5-B)_________________________

6-A)_________________________   6-B)_________________________

7-A)_________________________   7-B)_________________________

8-A)_________________________   8-B)_________________________

Most of the time I may be living my life as if

(part 2 #9)____

and I may choose people in my life who will facilitate my belief that

(part 2 #9)____

Instances in these relationships which have facilitated my thinking
    and feeling these messages are:

(List the incidents and what you thought and felt.)

____

____

____

Do these messages hinder or help me?_____________________

Do I want to keep these messages? _____________________

If not, what messages will I choose instead?

____

____

A Fact Sheet on Domestic Violence

Obtained from

The North Carolina Coalition Against Domestic Violence

www.nccadv.org

(Used by Permission)

Approximately 95% of the victims of domestic violence are women. (National Clearinghouse for the Defense of Battered Women, Ruth Peachey, M.D. 1988)

Domestic violence is the leading cause of injury to women between the ages of 15 and 44 in the United States; more than car accidents, muggings and rapes combined. ("Violence Against Women, A Majority Staff Report," Committee on the Judiciary United States Senate, 102nd Congress, October 1992, p.3)

About 1 out of 4 women is likcly to be abused by a partner in her lifetime. (Sara Glazer, "Violence Against Women" CO Researcher, Congressional Quarterly Inc., Volume 3, Number 8, February 1993, p. 171)

One woman is beaten by her husband or partner every 15 seconds in the United States. (Uniform Crime Reports, Federal Bureau of Investigation, 1991)

One out of 4 women who attempt suicide are battered. ("Battered Families ... Shattered Lives," Georgia Department of Human Resources. Family Violence Teleconference Resource Manual, January 1992)

Three to four million women in the United States are beaten in their homes each year by their husbands, ex-husbands or male lovers. ("Women and Violence," Hearings bcfore the U.S. Senate Judiciary Committee, August 29 and December 11,1990, Senate Hearing 101-939, pt.1, p.12)

Domestic violence ranks as one of the nation's most expensive health problems. (*American Medical News*, American Medical Association. 1992)

According to one study, family violence alone may cost the country as much as $5 to $10 billion every year in health care and associated costs. ("The Response to Rape: Detours on the Road to Equal Justice." Committee on the Judiciary United States Senate. May 1993)

Women of all cultures, races, occupations, income levels and ages are battered by husbands, boyfriends, lovers and partners. (For Shelter and Beyond, Massachusetts Coalition of Battered Women Service Groups, Boston, MA 1990)

Police report that between 40% and 60% of the calls they receive, especially on the night shift, are domestic disputes. (Cartillo, Roxanna "Violence Against Women: An Obstacle to Development," Human Development Report, 1990)

Fifty percent of all homeless women and children in this country are fleeing domestic violence. (Joseph Biden, U.S. Senate Committee 011 the Judiciary, Violence Against Women Victims of the System, 1991)

A recent survey of corporate security directors revealed that more than 90% of those surveyed had seen at least three cases of men stalking women employees. Domestic violence was rated as a high security problem. (Family Violence Prevention Fund, Fall/Winter 1994)

Forty percent of assaults on women by their male partners begin during the first pregnancy, pregnant women are at twice the risk of battery than non-pregnant women. Fifteen to 25% of pregnant women are battered. As a result, these women are 4 times more likely to bear infants of low birth weight and have an increased risk of miscarriage or injury to the child. (Martin, S.R, Holsapfels,

S. and Baker, P. (1992). Wife Abuse: Are We Detecting It? Journal of Women's Health 1(1).77-80 Evan Stark and Anne Flitcraft, 1992 U.S. Senate, Committee on the Judiciary (August 29 and December 11, 1990) Hearings on Women and Violence. "Ten Facts about Violence Against Women" p. 78)

Domestic violence is not only physical and sexual violence but also psychological. Psychological violence means intense and repetitive degradation, creating isolation, and controlling the actions or behaviors of the spouse through intimidation or manipulation to the detriment of the individual. ("Five year State Master Plan for the Prevention of and Service for Domestic Violence." Utah State Department of Human Services. January 1994.)

Domestic violence is both a national and worldwide crisis. According to a 2000 UNICEF study, up to half the female population of the world become victims of domestic violence. ("Domestic Violence Against Women and Girls," UNICEF, June 1, 2000)

In 1998, 1,320 women, more than three women per day, were murdered by their husbands or boyfriends. (U.S. Department of Justice, Violence by Intimates: Analysis of Data on Crimes by Current or Former Spouses, Boyfriends, and Girlfriends, March 1998.)

Over 30% of Americans are acquainted with a woman who has suffered violence from her male partner. (Family Violence Prevention Fund and the Advertising Council, 1998.)

Most evidence suggests that incidents of domestic violence often go unreported, meaning that in reality, these numbers could all be much higher. (The American Medical Association, 1998.)

Statistics of Domestic Violence

Obtained from the U.S. Department of Justice

Bureau of Justice Statistics

www.ojp.usdoj.gov

Nearly one-third of American women (31 percent) report being physically or sexually abused by a husband or boyfriend at some point in their lives. (The Commonwealth Fund 1998 Survey of Women's Health, May 1999.)

It is estimated that 503,485 women are stalked by an intimate partner each year in the United States. (National Institute of Justice, July 2000.)

Estimates range from 960,000 incidents of violence against a current or former spouse, boyfriend, or girlfriend each year to 4 million women who are physically abused by their husbands or live-in partners each year. (Violence by Intimates: Analysis of Data on Crimes by Current or Former Spouses, Boyfriends, and Girlfriends, U.S. Department of Justice, March, 1998.)

Child abuse occurs in 30-60% of family violence cases that involve families with children. ("The overlap between child maltreatment and woman battering," J.L. Edleson, Violence Against Women, February, 1999.)

Women are 5 to 8 times more likely than men to be victimized by an intimate partner (and women are less likely than men to be victims of violent crimes overall.) (Violence by Intimates: Analysis of Data on Crimes by Current or Former Spouses, Boyfriends, and Girlfriends, U.S. Department of Justice, March, 1998.)

Violence by an intimate partner accounts for about 21% of violent crime experienced by women and about 2% of the violence experienced by men (Violence by Intimates: Analysis of Data on Crimes by Current or Former Spouses,

Boyfriends, and Girlfriends, U.S. Department of Justice, March, 1998.)

In 92% of all domestic violence incidents, crimes are committed by men against women. (Violence Against Women, Bureau of Justice Statistics, U.S. Department of Justice, January, 1994.)

Of women who reported being raped and/or physically assaulted since the age of 18, three quarters (76%) were victimized by a current or former husband, cohabitating partner, date or boyfriend. (Prevalence Incidence, and Consequences of Violence Against women: Findings from the National Violence Against Women Survey, U.S. Department of Justice, November, 1998.)

Women separated from their spouses have a victimization rate 1-1/2 times higher than separated men, divorced men, or divorced women. (Sex Differences in Violent Victimization, 1994, U.S. Department of Justice, September, 1997.)

Among all female murder victims in the US, 30% were slain by their husbands or boyfriends. (Uniform Crime Reports of the US 1996, Federal Bureau of Investigation, 1996.)

31,260 women were murdered by an intimate from 1976-1996. (Violence by Intimates; Analysis of Data on Crimes by Current or Former Spouses, Boyfriends, and Girlfriends, US Department of Justice, March, 1998.)

A child's exposure to the father abusing the mother is the strongest risk factor for transmitting violent behavior from one generation to the next. (Report of the American Psychological Association Presidential Task Force on Violence and the Family, APA, 1996.)

Forty percent of teenage girls age 14 to 17 report knowing someone their age who has been hit or beaten by a boyfriend. (Children Now/Kaiser Permanente poll, December, 1995.)

Females accounted for 39% of the hospital emergency department visits for violence-related injuries in 1994, but 84% of the persons treated for injuries inflicted by intimates. (Violence by Intimates: analysis of Data on Crimes by Current or Former Spouses, Boyfriends and Girlfriends, U.S. Department of Justice, March, 1998.)

Family violence costs the nation from $5 to $10 billion annually in medical expenses, police and court costs, shelters and foster care, sick leave, absenteeism and non-productivity. (Medical News, American Medical Association, January, 1992.)

Husbands and boyfriends commit 13,000 acts of violence against women in the workplace every year. (Violence and Theft in the Workplace, US Department of Justice, July, 1994.)

One in five female high school students reports being physically or sexually abused by a dating partner. (Massachusetts Youth Risk Behavior Survey, August 2001.)

Women age 35-49 were the most vulnerable to intimate murder, while females age 16 to 24 were the most vulnerable to nonfatal violence. (Intimate Partner Violence and Age of Victim, 1993-99.)

POSSIBLE SIGNS OF A CONTROLLING AND ABUSIVE PERSONALITY

Most women would not knowingly choose to become involved with a controlling and abusive person. They are often surprised when the abusive characteristics appear and may think that the person has changed. However, it is more likely that the controlling and abusive signs were there all along, but they were not so dominant at first. When we are caught up in the "romance" of a new relationship, the last thing we want to see are reasons to leave.

Listed below are some possible warning signs that may let you know that trouble is just around the corner. Remember that the abuser will reframe these behaviors as part of his intense love for you.

- Hypersensitivity—overreaction to events of everyday life; seeing life as "black or white"—for him or against him.
- Gives others control of how he feels—often uses the phrase, "You make me happy/sad/angry, etc." or "I can't help how I feel."
- Wants others to feel guilty for his feelings and situations-"You control how I feel."
- Jealousy—needs to know where you have been, whom you saw and talked to, why you were late, whom you are thinking about, etc.
- Possessiveness—tells you what to wear, how much make-up to use, how to wear your hair, how to act with others, and becomes angry when you don't follow his advice.
- Intense, quick involvement—believes in love at first sight; comes on strong and pushes you for total commitment to the relationship.
- Isolation—tries to keep you from your friends, family and acquaintances; expects you to meet all of his needs and believes that you can "learn" how to meet all of them.
- Public Persona—he's a fun person to be around and can appear caring and sensitive; however, he finds it difficult to show these traits in personal relationships.
- Moodiness—he has a Dr. Jekyl/Mr. Hyde personality; his charismatic persona can quickly change to moodiness and explosiveness.
- Intense emotions—his anger and disappointment are out of proportion to the precipitating events; he expresses love and passion very strongly.
- Low self-esteem—he is insecure about his abilities and appearance; however, he may not outwardly show it. He may present an over-confident, even arrogant, persona to cover his insecurities.

- Cruelty– he may not like animals and children. He may brutally harm animals and expect children to behave at all times. He may tease children until they cry for help and then laugh at them.
- Emotional and Psychological Abuse–he verbally abuses others by degrading them; trying to make them feel guilty; cruelly teasing them; belittling their work, screaming at them, etc.
- Physical Abuse–includes any physical act with intent to harm, such as, shoving, pushing, hitting, biting, burning, holding down, tickling, and many more.
- Threats of violence–actual spoken threats, such as, "I'll kill you," "I'll throw you out," "I'll break your arm," etc.; destroying prized possessions; striking/ breaking objects in front of you. This gives the message that he can do the same to you.
- Past violence in relationships–he may admit to being abusive in the past but he will blame the woman for making him do it or he will claim to have gotten help for that behavior and to feel bad about it now.
- Sex–he may be rough during sex; force you to try new experiences or to have sex when you do not want to; he may use forced sex (rape) to punish you; he may have an insatiable appetite for sex and get angry when you do not go along with him.
- Love-hate relationships–he may claim to like/respect women one minute and hate them the next; he may have this love-hate relationship with his mother; mostly, he is contemptuous of women and believes that they are the weaker sex.
- Family history–he may come from a family of abuse; either he was abused as a child or his father abused his mother.
- Teaching you a lesson–he may be obsessed with "teaching you a lesson" so that he does not have to "punish you again."
- Weapons–he may have an irrational attachment to weapons and an obsessive need to keep them in the house.
- Substance abuse–he may use drugs, including alcohol; however, don't be fooled into thinking a "teetotaler" cannot be abusive.

- Inability to empathize–he is unable to see someone else's opinion if it goes directly against his; he is unable to understand other's feelings; he really doesn't care how someone else feels.
- Inability to apologize–he rarely apologizes or claims responsibility for his abusive behavior.
- Tells lies–he finds it easy to lie to others, especially if it means making himself look better.
- Authority–he may like positions of power and control in his community and/or work; he definitely wants to be "head of the household."
- Obsessive/Compulsive–he is obsessively competitive in his work and play; he expects the home to be run according to his rules and needs; he obsesses about others' opinions of him, but claims not to care. In his public life, he obsessively adheres to his own value system, such as religious beliefs, but often exhibits the opposite behavior in his private life.
- Narcissistic–his world revolves around his wants and needs.
- Psychopathic–he derives pleasure in manipulating others and inflicting harm.

A Safety Plan:

Tips for Survival

These suggestions are commonly provided to women; however, not all of them may be safe in every case. Pick the ones that are safe for your situation.

1) Be aware of your body's signals and "red flags" and listen to the warning signs.

2) Talk about your situation to a trusted friend, family member, or professional.

3) Call your local women's shelter for information, support and free advice.

4) Begin keeping a journal of your partner's behavior and moods and log any incidents of abuse.

5) Hide anything that could be used as a weapon.

6) Get information on a restraining order (your local women's shelter can guide you in doing this).

7) Develop an escape plan and teach your children how to use it.

8) Have extra car keys hidden in a convenient place.

9) Keep extra changes of clothes hidden with a friend or some other safe place.

10) Make copies of all important papers, i.e. marriage certificate, birth certificates, social security cards for yourself and your children, paycheck stubs for income verification, savings plans, IRAs (yours and his), etc. and acquire a safe deposit box, in your name only, in which to keep them in.

11) Keep prescription medicine in a safe, convenient location. Keep a record of prescription numbers for you and your children so the medicine can be refilled.

12) Keep change, i.e. quarters, dimes and nickels hidden for telephone calls.

13) Save up money that your partner does not know about and keep it with your hidden clothes and car keys.

14) Open a checking account in your name only.

15) Open a postal mail box in your name only and in a safe area away from your neighborhood to have your checking account information sent to.

16) Have pictures taken of any marks on you from abuse and lock these in the safe deposit box along with any related medical records, police reports, court affidavits, diary, letter, tapes, and virtually anything related to your claims of abusive behavior.

17) Acquire credit cards in your name, if possible, and keep them hidden.

18) Post emergency phone numbers next to the phone.

19) Call police whenever you are attacked, even if it's the first time, to establish a possible pattern.

20) Read books and literature about domestic violence. Be well informed!

21) Ask your local women's shelter to recommend a lawyer who specializes in domestic violence cases.

22) Teach your children what to do if you are being physically attacked. Teach them how to contact the emergency numbers.

23) Begin secretly looking for a job.

24) Secretly, if possible, take a self-defense class.

25) Get professional help from a therapist or call your local women's shelter if you cannot afford a private therapist.

26) Gradually and discreetly remove items you and your family will need in a way that will not make your batterer suspicious.

27) Prior to your departure, collect your batterer's guns and other weapons and turn them into the police department.

28) Don't be fooled and pulled in by the "Honeymoon Phase" of the cycle of violence. This is when your abuser tempts you to forgive and forget by showering love and attention on you and your children. He may also act very remorseful during this phase.

29) Have a pre-established safe place to run to and, if necessary, someone to help you get there.

Resources and References

National Domestic Violence Hotline: PO Box 161810; Austin, TX. 78716 1-800-799-7233 (SAFE); 1-800-787-3224 (TTY); FAX: (512) 453-8541. website: **www.ndvh.org**

American Psychiatric Association: *Diagnostic and Statistical Manual of Mental Disorders*, Fourth Edition. (1994). Washington, D.C., American Psychiatric Association.

Betancourt, M. (1997). *What to do when love turns violent: a practical resource for Women in abusive relationships*. New York: Harperperennial.

Brinegar, J.L. (1992). Breaking free from domestic violence. Center City, MN: Hazelden.

Browne, A. *(1987). When battered women kill. New* York: The Free Press.

Browne, A., & Bassuk, S. S. *(1997).* Intimate violence in the lives of homeless and poor housed women: Prevalence and patterns in an ethnically diverse sample. *American Journal of Orthopsychiatry, 6, 261-278.*

Browne, A., Miller, B., & Maguin, E. (1999). Prevalence and severity of lifetime physical and sexual victimization among incarcerated women. *International Journal of Law and Psychiatry, 22, 3-4, 301-322.*

Dutton, D.G. (1988). *The domestic assault of women: Psychological and criminal justice perspectives.* Boston, MA: Allyn and Bacon.

Groetsch, M. (1996). *The battering syndrome.* Brookfield, WI: CPI Publishing.

Groetsch, M. (1997). *He promised he'd stop.* Brookfield, WI: CPI Publishing.

Hayes, C., Anderson, D., & Blau, *M. (1993). Our turn: the good news about women and Divorce.* New York: Pocket Books.

Helpmate, Inc., 56 College Street, Suite 201, Asheville, NC 28801

Herman, J.L. (1992). *Trauma and recovery.* New York: Basic Books.

Jones, A. (2000). *Next time, she'll be dead: battering & how to stop it.* New York: Beacon Press.

Kubler-ross, E. (1997). *On Death and Dying.* Simon & Schuster/ Scribner.

Laszlo, V.S. (ed.) (1959). *The basic writings of C. G. Jung.* New York: Modern Library.

National Coalition Against Domestic Violence. website: **www.webmerchants.com/ncadv**

Neidig, P.H. & Friedman, D.H. (1984). *Spouse Abuse: a treatment program for couples.* Champaign, IL: Research Press Co.

North Carolina Coalition Against Domestic Violence, 115 Market Street, Suite 400, Durham, NC 27701. website: **www.nccadv.org**

Weiss, E. (2000). *Surviving domestic violence: Voices of women who broke free.* Agreka Books.

About the Author

Linda DeWeese is a psychotherapist in private practice in Asheville, NC. She is a Licensed Professional Counselor, a National Certified Counselor, and holds a BA degree in psychology and a MA.Ed. degree in counseling. She is a member of the American Counseling Association (ACA) and the Eye Movement Desensitization and Reprocessing International Association (EMDRIA). For the past sixteen years she has specialized in working with victims of past and present trauma, many of whom have been victims of domestic violence. In addition, Linda presents workshops and seminars to educators, businesses, and professionals within the judicial system on stress management, self-enhancement, assertiveness training, and effective parenting and stepparenting.